Skills for Successful 21st Century School Leaders

STANDARDS FOR PEAK PERFORMERS

John R. Hoyle

Fenwick W. English

Betty E. Steffy

Academic Director
Area I

American Association of School Administrators

ACKNOWLEDGMENTS

The authors wish to thank Ginger O'Neil for her encouragement and skilled editing of the manuscript. She made the task of a major rewrite of this text less stressful and kept us on deadline. Thanks also to Bill Ashworth Jr. for his dedicated and creative assistance. Bill is a valuable member of the Department of Educational Administration at Texas A&M University.

We also wish to recognize Jim McGinnis of Mac Designs for the terrific design of this text. Jim's expertise and outlook made it possible for us to get this book off press on an extremely tight deadline.

And a special thanks from John to his spouse, Carolyn Hoyle, for editing John's chapters — often after a long day of teaching and advising a Blinn College where she is an English instructor.

American Association of School Administrators
1801 N. Moore St.
Arlington, VA 22209
(703) 528-0800
http://www.aasa.org

Executive Director, Paul D. Houston
Deputy Executive Director, E. Joseph Schneider
Editor, Ginger R. O'Neil, *GRO Communications*
Designer, Jim McGinnis, *Mac Designs*

Printed in the United States of America.

AASA Stock Number: 236-002
ISBN: 0-87652-234-7
Library of Congress Card Catalog Number: 97-78468

To order additional copies, call AASA's Order Fulfillment Department at 1-888-782-2272 (PUB-AASA) or, in Maryland, call 1-301-617-7802.

Skills for Successful 21st Century School Leaders
STANDARDS FOR PEAK PERFORMERS

Introduction

Skills for Successful 21st Century School Leaders attempts what might seem the impossible: To provide a clear recitation and description of the standards and related skills school leaders must master and apply to make the most of their important positions. Repeated use of this book's predecessor, *Skills for Successful School Leaders*, indicates the need for such a publication. Certainly, just as no single theory of leadership accounts adequately for all the leadership dimensions of successful performance, no single set of administrative standards and related skills and dispositions will solve every problem facing school leaders today. However, *Skills for Successful 21st Century School Leaders* provides a good starting point by synthesizing the prevalent research into a set of useful standards and skills and presenting a thoughtful discussion of each along with supporting research references for further investigation.

The material in *Skills for Successful 21st Century School Leaders* can be used and useful in many ways. It provides a comprehensive survey of the areas today's practicing school leaders must understand and be skilled in to lead successfully. It also presents the most comprehensive set of skills and program components available to help improve campus- and field-based preparation programs for principals, superintendents, and central-office personnel. Two recent initiatives — the American Association of School Administrators' (AASA's) Leadership Institute for School Administrators and the Interstate School Leaders Licensure Consortium — make this text particularly timely.

Leadership Institute for School Administrators

AASA is embarking on a bold new venture by creating the Leadership Institute for School Administrators (LISA), which is based on the standards in this text. LISA will provide the "best and brightest" superintendents in America an avenue to be recognized for their expertise. LISA participants will engage in advanced professional development in several strategic areas and undergo a performance assessment by a national board of examiners, leading to the awarding of advanced certification. The LISA program will collaborate with several leading research universities and state administrator associations, and will benefit from corporate support provided by MetLife Insurance Co. The outcome will be an exciting opportunity for superintendents to earn the highest level of professional certification.

The Interstate School Leaders Licensure Consortium

The Interstate School Leaders Licensure Consortium (ISLLC), a program of the Council of Chief State School Officers (CCSSO), has created standards for school principals and an examination for the state licensure for elementary and secondary principals. The six standards present a common core of knowledge, dispositions, and performances very similar to the 1993 AASA *Professional Standards for the Superintendency* and the National Council for the Accreditation of Colleges of Education's (NCATE's) *Curriculum Guidelines for School Administrators*. Approximately 25 states require the exam to gain the principal's credential.

• • •

Skills for Successful 21st Century School Leaders, like the ISLLC Standards, draws from the *AASA Guidelines for the Preparation of School Administrators,* the first widely distributed set of preparation guidelines/standards for administrators, which was published in 1983, and AASA's *Professional Standards for the Superintendency,* as well as NCATE's *Curriculum Guidelines,* which are used to judge the quality of university preparation. Other documents that have influenced the standards and skills covered in this book are *Performance-Based Preparation of Principals*, published by the National Association of Secondary School Principals (NASSP) in 1985; *Principals for the Twenty-First Century*, published in 1990 by the National Association of Elementary School Principals (NAESP); *School Leadership: A Preface to Action*, created by The American Association of Colleges for Teacher Education (AACTE) in 1988; and *Principals for Our Changing Schools*, an outline of 21 knowledge and skill domains published by the National Policy Board for Educational Administration (NPBEA) in 1993. Each of these publications drew from the knowledge base first outlined by AASA and subsequently by other associations. Therefore, we have been able to synthesize the standard base and present it in one useable text.

Every school leader needs a well-defined educational philosophy or ideology to make the deeply personal decisions that may not be handled by the knowledge base and skills alone. This publication reaffirms and builds on the philosophical, performance, and ethical dimensions of school leadership to assist those charged with preparation and development programs and those who undergo them.

Chapter 1 challenges administrators to provide Visionary Leadership. This standard includes the skills and dispositions needed to lead others to peak performance, driven by a clear and compelling vision centered on the success of all children and youth.

Chapter 2 presents the political skills and dispositions upon which leadership in Policy and Governance are based. This standard looks at school governance in a democracy and the formulation of policy derived from collaborative efforts to build the best schools for students and the community.

Chapter 3 details Skills in Communication and Community Relations. The clear and ethical articulation of the district or school vision, mission, and priorities to the community and mass media are among the key skills school leaders must master to build consensus and support for public schools.

Chapter 4 builds on the growing knowledge about systemic change and the skills required to make data-driven decisions that show good stewardship of resources as part of Organizational Management.

Curriculum Planning and Development is detailed in Chapter 5. This standard and its related skills center on school leaders' abilities to develop a curriculum design and delivery system for diverse school communities based on high standards and what we know about students' developmental needs.

Closely tied to curriculum development skills are those skills related to Instructional Management, which is covered in Chapter 6. This standard involves the development of a data-based student achievement monitoring and reporting system, and the skillful analysis and assignment of available instructional resources to enhance student learning.

Chapters 7 and 8 focus on Staff Evaluation and Staff Development, respectively. Chapter 7 details the skills and dispositions required to develop a staff evaluation system based on the latest research and best practice; Chapter 8 follows with a discussion of the need for targeted staff development to improve the performance of individuals, schools, and school systems.

Chapter 9 takes a look at the knowledge school leaders need to make the most of Educational Research, Evaluation, and Planning. This standard involves skills in conducting research and using research methods to improve program evaluation and short- and long-term planning. This chapter provides a review of survey research, basic research design, and statistics.

Chapter 10, which is entirely new to this edition, covers skills related to the Values and Ethics of school leadership. The skills and dispositions in this chapter focus on understanding and modeling appropriate value systems, ethics, and moral leadership for our democratic, multicultural society and schools.

Appendices A and B provide "how to" information. Appendix A presents an overview of the major advances in recent years in standard setting and suggestions about teaching the standards, skills, and dispositions covered in this text. The appendix details the "Ideal Leadership Preparation Model," which includes the latest research ideas of the Professional Studies Model, and presents a sample step-by-step method for teaching the standards. Appendix B overviews some of the Future Trends school leaders must heed as they plan for success in the 21st century. The trends are selected from U.S. Department of Education statistics and other sources, including the World Future Society.

Readers will find that the unifying themes of leadership, planning, empowerment, ethics, diversity, and equity are integral within each standard and the related skills and dispositions. No leadership standard has an exclusive set of skills because our knowledge base is a combination of years of research, tacit knowledge, and best practice in the broad field of educational administration.

The standards and related skills and knowledge areas in this book have and continue to serve as a content bridge for communication between practitioners, professors, and agency personnel about the values and meaning of modern school leadership. Too many times in the past, these groups talked past each other, which resulted quite often in research with little or no practical value, and practitioners repeating past mistakes because of lack of adequate preparation or self-renewal.

Informed leadership in America's schools is even more important today than when the first edition of this book was published. We and AASA hope professors and students in university graduate programs, practicing administrators, participants in school district and state training institutes, chief state school officers, and other professionals involved in administrator training and licensure will use these standards and related skills and dispositions to stimulate thinking about the preparation and licensure of school leaders for the 21st century to ensure that our school administrators are successful leaders of high-performing schools for all students.

Because this book represents a distillation of practitioners' and professors' beliefs about the essentials of modern school leadership for principals and superintendents, it can be used:

By practicing school leaders to establish:
• A baseline for assessing job performance.
• A basis for designing staff development and needs assessment instruments.
• A focus on the recruiting, training, and performance of school administrators at the national level.
• A basis for preparing for the examination for the Leadership Institute for School Administrators (LISA).

By aspiring school leaders as:
• A starting point for graduate study research projects.
• A tool for preparing for Master's and Doctoral degree orals and comprehensive exams.
• A study guide for licensure exams.

By educational administration professors to establish:
• Criteria to examine the content of preparation courses and programs.
• Criteria for preparing students for state and national exams based on ISLLC and other standards.
• Criteria for recruiting faculty members to prepare school leaders.
• A basis for required research.
• A basis for building collaborative graduate degree programs with school districts.

chapter 1 | *Skills in Visionary Leadership*

The "vision thing" may be time worn or overused, but its impact cannot be ignored. Visionaries and their visions have inspired the creation of magnificent monuments that have withstood the ravages of time — the Greek temples, the Egyptian pyramids, the Roman coliseum, Salisbury Cathedral, and Epcot Center all had their genesis in someone's vision. "Quality is Job One" has helped propel Ford Motor Company to the top in total sales in America. Similarly, "All Students Producing High-Quality Work and Becoming Successful Lifelong Learners" energizes Principal Lowell Strike and his faculty and students at the Stephen F. Austin 9th grade campus in Bryan, Texas, to seek higher performance in leadership, teaching, and achievement.

Kouzes and Posner (1995, p. 95) define vision as ". . . an ideal and unique image of the future." Futurist Joel Barker (1992) indicates the value of vision by stating that "A dream consists of ideas about the future; a vision is a dream in action." When individuals are encouraged by leaders to share their mental models, personal and professional goals, and dreams and visions, great learning organizations emerge (Senge 1990). A vision that energizes others to share in the task of creating exemplary learning communities is the driving force for school change with a purpose.

For these reasons, school leaders must communicate a worthy vision clearly and often to all stakeholders. Once a vision is clear and shared by others, school leaders must initiate the development of a strategic plan for the district or school. Then, after a vision and strategic plan have been developed and put in place, school leaders must continuously conduct school and district climate evaluations, and assess and analyze demographic and student achievement data to determine whether the goals of the strategic plan are being worked toward and met. Such data collection and analysis are integral in monitoring and aligning financial, human, and material resources to ensure continuous progress toward high-quality education for all children and youth in a multicultural context.

This chapter details the skills successful 21st century school leaders must possess to:

- Create and communicate a district or school vision;
- Establish priorities in the context of the community culture and student and staff needs;
- Conduct district and school climate assessments;
- Assess student achievement data;
- Develop a strategic plan for the district or school;
- Empower others to reach high levels of performance; and
- Align financial, human, and material resources with the vision, mission, and goals.

Creating and Communicating a Vision

The Importance of Vision

Successful individuals in all lines of endeavor are guided by a vision of top performance. According to Robert Carlson (1996, p. 141), "New visions challenge our willingness to trust in the capacity of ourselves and others. . . ." According to Paula Short and John Greer (1997, p. 39), the underlying values and beliefs of a school district and a school must be "embedded in a school's vision . . . . Often such values remain unspoken and unexamined unless a skillful group facilitator helps the group to explore the subtleties of a particular set of values."

For a vision to be effective, it must be centered on the enduring beliefs and values that motivate individuals to strive for the highest ideals and performance. Once skillful school leaders carefully study the district and school culture to determine the underlying values, beliefs, history, traditions, and heroes and heroines, they must begin shaping a vision that can capture the imagination and energy of others. The old saying, "You can't light a fire with a wet match," means more than ever to leaders in education. "Empowerment," "shared visions" and "teamwork" may be the action words of the day, but unless an energetic visionary ignites the fire in others, very few visions will be shared or realized.

Working to get district and school staff and community members to accept a vision usually produces some frustrating moments for busy, driven school leaders, but if a vision statement has been carefully considered, written, and widely shared, its chances of surviving, at least in part, are good. Impatient superintendents and principals sometimes fail to take the time and energy to carefully state and restate their initial vision to people — all people. This is a mistake.

Visionary principals and superintendents can create team loyalty, ideas, goals, and shared dreams (Hoyle 1995). Conger (1989) found that subordinates of visionaries tend to like their jobs, work longer hours without complaint, trust their colleagues and their leaders, and have higher performance ratings than the followers of non-visionary leaders. Visionary leaders who strive for excellence develop team loyalty around ideas and shared values; non-visionary administrators "run" the school, but make few bold and challenging things happen.

Creating a vision certainly involves risk, as does launching any new idea or product, but risk-taking creates "competitive intelligence" (Kahaner 1996), which enables an organization to go into uncharted territory to discover new products or ideas that lead an industry. The central focus of any vision for education must spark an unwavering commitment to children and youth to find better programs and ideas to challenge and prepare them to thrive as well-adjusted, adaptable citizens in the years ahead. The vision must inspire the school and the entire community.

Vision Statements and Mission Statements

Some confusion exists among educators and others about the differences between a vision statement, a mission statement, and goal statements. The three together define a district or school's reason for existing and ultimate aspirations. The vision statement is the "why," the mission statement is the "what," and the goal statements are the "how." As Figure 1.1 on page 3 shows, the vision statement

directs and inspires the staff to work toward a vision of success for all students; the mission statement clarifies what the district or school staff will do for the students to make the vision happen; and the goal statements guide the staff in how to carry out and measure the success of the mission. While many school districts and schools combine the vision and mission statements, the two have different purposes and each is vital in creating the strategic plan for the school district or the school.

Vision statements. A written vision statement is designed to inspire the future efforts of individuals within the organization. Quality management literature describes a vision statement as a brief, compelling statement that motivates the internal customer (the employees) to produce the highest quality product using the most efficient processes. Thus, in school districts, the vision statement is for the individuals who provide the teaching and learning activities and the products and processes that support those activities. The statement should be brief (preferably 25 or fewer words; never more than 50), simple, and, above all else, inspiring. The following are three sample vision statements:

- Conroe ISD is a learning community united in its commitment to ensuring all students graduate with confidence and competence.
- The Mountain Top School District believes that all students are valued and challenged to be top performers and community leaders.
- The Department of Educational Administration at Texas A&M University is committed to developing and modeling educational leadership for inclusive, moral communities that contribute to a just and moral society.

Mission statements. A mission statement is developed to explain to the external customer (primarily the student and the parent) what the school does and how it carries out its role and the tasks of educating each child. Mission statements are more detailed than vision statements because they include the multiple missions in the education of every student whether gifted, at risk, or with special needs. Covey (1990, p. 166) asserts that, "To be most effective, your mission statement should deal

The only kind of leadership worth following is based on vision.

— Max DePree 1989, p. 133

with all four basic human needs: economic, or money need; social, or relationship need; psychological, or growth need; and spiritual, or contribution need." The following is a sample mission statement:

> The mission of the Mountain Top School District is to create a learning atmosphere where all students will gain academic, social, and lifelong knowledge and skills through excellent teaching, mentoring, and modeling by the faculty and staff. The students will be encouraged to develop their integrity and talents to become productive contributors to our democracy and to the world community.

Goal statements. Goals are general statements of intent or purpose that guide students and school staff in carrying out the mission. The following is a sample goal statement:

> All Mountain Top School District students will acquire the basic skills necessary to be socially and economically competent. Example indicators to determine if this goal is reached are as follows:
> • Students will read, comprehend, and assimilate written materials. Students will acquire necessary computational skills through the use of computers.
> • Students will make the necessary arithmetical, geometrical, and other mathematical calculations essential to their jobs and to daily living (Texas Education Agency 1990).

Communicating the Vision

For a vision and its accompanying vision statement to be enduring and embraced by most people, it must be presented to and discussed in small groups in a variety of settings. All districtwide and local school site-based teams must work to "hammer out" and embrace a vision statement that will inspire the best efforts of administrators, teachers, students, parents, businesses, and other community stakeholders.

Richard Wallace (1995) challenges school leaders to communicate their vision to all segments of the community. He believes that principals and superintendents must envision strong schools and clearly communicate those strengths to energize professionals and the community to bring about the

Figure 1.1 **Vision, Mission, and Goals**

Vision Statement
(The "Why" for staff)

•
25 words or less
•
Shared within the organization
•
Inspires future efforts

Mission Statement
(The "What" and "How" for clients)

•
25–50 words
•
Shared with external clients
•
Contains multiple missions

Goal Statements
(Benchmarks for productivity)

•
10–20 words
•
Measureable statements for organization and clients to accomplish

conditions that will ensure high-quality education. Short and Greer (1997) encourage school leaders and other staff to create small discussion groups composed of community members and educators to communicate visions for better schools. They say that "in such settings, the beliefs and values of the vision [can] be easily explored. From such meetings, a consensus supporting the new vision [can] emerge. At the very least, the members of the school staff [will] become aware of the community's fears or objections to the course of action representing the new vision" (p. 41).

Small-group discussions work equally well for shaping the districtwide vision statement and the statements for each school in the district. With care-

One proven strategy to help groups focus on a vision and the visioning process is to show a visual of a "Generic Kid" (a smiley face with big eyes and a sprig of hair). The notion of the generic kid can be used to lead a discussion about vision by helping everyone engage in discussing the meaning behind each word in the vision statement. The "Generic Kid" image reminds discussion participants about why they must make the best decision for all children and youth.

ful attention to community norms, culture, and special interest groups — even the most radical and vocal — these group sessions can promote successful communication and good will toward the school staff and lead to strong parent/community support for school programming.

When Conroe, Texas, ISD used small-group meetings as part of its visioning process, the following groups were invited to participate: all schools, the area's 10 largest employers, all school-based PTA/PTO organizations, the Parent Advisory Council, chambers of commerce, government representatives, and the district Strategic Planning Task Force.

Once the vision statement is shared and supported, it should appear in clear view in each school, on stationary, and as part of all communications to parents and other stakeholders. A positive, shared vision that focuses on efforts to ensure that every child succeeds in life can energize others and secure higher standards for the schools and the community. (See Chapter 3 for more information about vision, mission, and goals.)

Establishing Priorities in the Context of the Community Culture and Student and Staff Needs

The visioning process that leads to the mission and goals statements must be centered on the cultural context of the community, the diversity of the students, and the needs and capabilities of the professional staff. The district's and each individual school's culture must be carefully analyzed to determine the enduring qualities and values that should not be overlooked during decision making. When school leaders overlook the cultural history and the

"things that count" to the community, they risk upsetting community members whose support the schools need to serve all students well. "Organizational culture helps us explain the idiosyncratic nature of individual schools that exist in a common milieu. We often puzzle at how two schools in the same community with the same conditions and resources will vary so greatly from one another" (Carlson 1996, p. 46.). Cultural and organizational culture often hold the answers.

School leaders must read the cultural road signs that give directions about the district and school culture, that is, its history, values, visions, storytellers, rituals, traditions, beliefs, heroes, and heroines. This cultural knowledge not only helps in the shaping of the district and school vision, but also in determining the curriculum design and instructional strategies that best fit students' learning patterns and interests.

Superintendents, principals, and other school

A Trophy Case in Point

Displaying an insensitivity to local history and a school's cultural roots led to the firing of an otherwise very talented young principal. A first-year principal in a Missouri school district decided to clean up her school by discarding most of the antiquated equipment and "stuff" that had been stored away for years. At the back of the old trophy case in the entrance hall she found a small scratched track trophy inscribed: "Second Place in the County, April 3, 1931." The principal tossed it in the trash because it was no longer displayed in the front of the trophy case and, she reasoned, the winner was probably long dead or moved away.

The following week, during an open house, an elderly gentleman asked the principal if she knew where he could find his trophy. He said, "Somebody put my little track trophy in the back of the case where nobody, especially my grandkids, could see it. I am paying to have the school trophy case enlarged so that my 1931 trophy can be seen. My second place finish trophy will be the centerpiece of the new trophy space." The principal then had to tell the gentleman that his trophy was discarded during a house cleaning. The former track man left the school and led the charge to get the principal fired at the end of the year. She and the trophy were history.

leaders must realize they are usually perceived by the community as "outsiders" or "cosmopolitans" (Gouldner 1954). Unless school administrators spend their entire professional careers in a community and become embedded in the community life, they rarely shake the "outsider" label. The advantage of this "outsider" label is that it allows school leaders the opportunity to create positive change in the district and school. Energetic, visionary leaders take advantage of the "honeymoon" period to help bring in new ideas, proven curriculum, and staff development programs and to increase the involvement of parent, business, and community groups in school programming.

To get a better handle on the district and school culture, school leaders must cultivate the culture, captivate the culture, and celebrate the culture.

Cultivating the Culture

Because all students are multicultural and have differing learning, family, and religious orientations and varied interests, the school superintendent or principal needs to understand the variety of differences among the school and greater community and prepare the school community for inclusion of all children and youth. People from different cultures or with different languages are often uncomfortable around others who seem secure in their own language and surroundings. For the seeds of multicultural understanding and inclusivity to grow, the ground must be cultivated.

School leaders can gain a much needed picture of the community by creating a community/school culture committee to help provide information about the diversity of the community's ethnic populations and their history, rituals, celebrations, and traditions. A thorough, systematic study of the community provides foundation knowledge to help guide key program decisions over the long haul. This careful cultivation can remove the weeds of resentment, ridicule, and racism and bring about student-centered learning that excludes the three b's of boredom, bigotry, and bias.

Captivating the Culture

When the seeds of enlightened school and community programs grow into visible forms of cooperation and understanding, school leaders need to capture the moment by drawing on the rich cultural collage of personalities in the community. Local artists, musicians, poets, sports personalities, craftspersons, business and industry leaders, and medical specialists should become regular visitors and role models for students. These community figures and other interesting people can inspire students to develop a positive image of their own future. Students who have positive visions about their future careers and lives make better grades, attend school more regularly, and have fewer behavior problems in school. A focus on the future encourages students to more carefully select courses and seek information when making important life decisions. Challenging students to write futures scenarios about their careers and adult lives is motivational and often encourages reluctant writers to spin interesting stories. School leaders should capture the district culture by using the rich cultural resources available to inspire students to build their dreams.

Celebrating the Culture

When the seeds of positive role modeling and mentoring have grown to help students dream about and plan their lives, it is time to celebrate small and big victories in the district and school. When a student, teacher, or staff member succeeds, someone should notice and celebrate the accomplishment. The old pattern of looking for people's mistakes must be abandoned. Catching people succeeding, telling others, and celebrating the success is the new pattern for successful school leaders.

Sensitive school leaders focus the spotlight on the achievements of teachers, other staff members, advisory council members, and students in many ways. It is possible to select a hero or heroine of the week, semester, and year in several categories and arrange for these success stories to appear in the local newspaper and district newsletter, as well as on television and radio, or to throw school parties for these stars. A family atmosphere where praise and recognition are plentiful and targeted produces motivated contributors and is a morale booster for everyone.

The written vision statement and goals should be created to encourage and look for the best in every person and celebrations of little and big successes should become a habit. In time, this habit of looking for and celebrating successes will produce small and large miracles in student and staff performance. William Cunningham (1991) of Old Dominion University writes about the power of celebrating a person's accomplishments. "Encouragement, like empowerment, is the process whereby you focus on the assets and strengths of a person to build their self-confidence and self-esteem. You try to help people to believe in themselves and their natural abilities" (p. 55). Celebrate a person's accomplishments enough and the person will not only become more productive, but will recognize the successes of others and give them encouragement. School leaders need to lead the celebration parade by modeling what is positive, productive, and sincere.

Conducting District and School Climate Assessments

School climate may be one of the most important ingredients of a successful instructional program in a district or school. A broad term, "climate" refers to the environment of the school as perceived by its students, staff, and patrons. It is the school's "personality." Without a harmonious, safe, and well-functioning school climate, a high degree of academic achievement is difficult, if not downright impossible, to obtain. However, designing a positive, successful climate within a school, much less an entire district, is no easy task. School leaders cannot do it alone. At best they can set the tone for their staffs who must ultimately create such an environment. Erickson (1981, p.46) said it best, ". . . the most effective schools are distinguished not by elaborate facilities, extensively trained teachers, small classes, or high levels of financial support, but by outstanding social climates."

School climate researchers generally support the assertion made by Rowan, Bossart, and Dwyer (1983, p.24) that a winning school climate is one that, ". . . is conducive to learning – one that is free from disciplinary problems and that embodies high expectations for student achievement." To successfully support such a climate, school leaders need a good grounding in motivation and climate theory and an understanding of the relationship between climate and student achievement.

Motivation and Climate Theory

The writings of prominent motivational theorists Abraham Maslow, Douglas McGregor, Frederick Herzberg, Victor Vroom, and others have strongly influenced educational practices and research (Owens 1994, Silver 1983, and Hoy and Miskel 1996). Notable experts in organizational dynamics, led by Kurt Lewin (1935), Amitai Etzioni (1975) and more recently Stephen Covey (1990), have strengthened the foundation for additional educational research and practice. These theorists have developed compelling explanations of human behavior driven by individual needs.

Maslow and Herzberg. Maslow (1954) describes the force that drives people to goals in terms of a "hierarchy of needs." His theory states that people have a series of sequential needs, which, once basic needs are fulfilled, actuate them to strive to fulfill the next higher need in the sequence (see Figure 1.2).

Figure 1.2 **Maslow's Hierarchy of Needs**

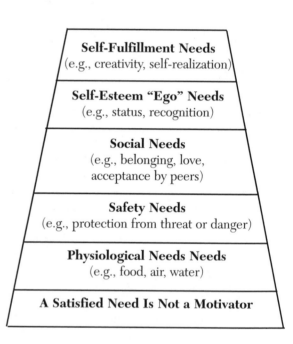

Self-Fulfillment Needs
(e.g., creativity, self-realization)

Self-Esteem "Ego" Needs
(e.g., status, recognition)

Social Needs
(e.g., belonging, love, acceptance by peers)

Safety Needs
(e.g., protection from threat or danger)

Physiological Needs Needs
(e.g., food, air, water)

A Satisfied Need Is Not a Motivator

Maslow's theory has been extended to examine the hygienic (maintenance) and psychological (motivational) factors that motivate workers in research by Herzberg (1968) of Case Western University. Herzberg has found work achievement and responsibility to be among the leading factors that motivate workers (see Figure 1.3 on p.7).

McGregor's Theories X and Y and Deming's TQM. Douglas McGregor's (1960) Theory X and Theory Y explain two sides of human nature. Theory X takes the position that people dislike work, are lazy, and must be pushed and directed to work. Theory Y embraces the notion that people enjoy work as much as play and are creative, autonomous goal seekers. These two views of human nature influenced the work of

Figure 1.3 Maslow's Needs and Herzberg's Motivators

Maslow's Hierarchy of Human Needs	Herzberg's Motivators and Non-Motivators	
Self-Fulfillment Needs	Work Itself, Achievement	Motivators
Self-Esteem Needs	Advancement, Status, Recognition	
Social Needs	Supervision, Company Policies	Non-Motivators
Safety Needs	Job Security, Working Conditions	
Physiological Needs	Salary and Benefits	

Herzberg (1968), and the revolutionary Total Quality Management (TQM) ideas of W. Edwards Deming (l983, 1986, and 1993).

Deming posited that a worker's motivation level can be changed by improving the quality of the work system, including its inputs, processes and outputs, and the working environment. He believed that people must be trusted and provided support to improve their own performance and the product they produce. Deming stressed that a "constancy of purpose" and the use of statistics and good data for quality control would produce higher morale and a higher quality product. Deming's well-known 14 principals have been translated to fit schools by several writers. Perhaps the most useful translation was created by Jay Bonstingl (1992, p. 17-82). The following is an adaptation of Bonstingl's translation. It restates Deming's 14 principles into a set of principles for school leaders.

According to Deming's TQM theory, school leaders must:

(1) **Create a constancy of purpose.** Establish a process for always trying to improve on the quality of teaching and educational programming

(2) **Adopt the new philosophy.** Commit to making the school a great place to teach and learn by welcoming change, team efforts, and a sense of empowerment for everyone in the learning community

(3) **Cease dependence on mass inspection.** Initiate a process to ensure that true teaching and learning are taking place rather than continue the constant pressure to teach to the test. School leaders must remember that ratings (scores, averages, etc.) do not improve performance; only the dedication of everyone to quality teaching and learning produces lasting results.

(4) **End the practice of doing business by price tag alone.** New or novel ideas for teaching and learning should not be regulated by the cost factor alone. If cost becomes the bottom line in all decisions, the quality of teaching and learning will diminish. Cost-saving measures are important, but should not be allowed to reduce the quality of education.

(5) **Constantly improve every system in the organization.** Because the school system is a human organization, it is important that administrators, teachers, parents, and school board members work in harmony to help their primary customers – the students. Subsystems of schools within the district, departments within schools, content and subject specialists, suppliers, and other internal and external groups need a grasp of the big picture and should constantly try to synchronize with other subsystems to improve the overall operation for the students.

(6) **Institute training on the job.** New and seasoned teachers, counselors, and administrators need constant training to "sharpen their professional saws." Even the best university preparation programs cannot cover all the skills and knowledge needed to keep pace with new developments in brain research, curriculum, and learning technologies. Training and renewal are essential to keep improving the system for everyone.

(7) **Institute effective leadership.** School leaders must change the concept of leadership from "boss" management to "servant" leadership by becoming "keepers of the dream" for all people in the district or school, modeling shared teamwork, and building an open culture that encourages ideas and constant improvement. This move from top-down power game playing to bottom-up power sharing does not imply that the superintendent or

Figure 1.4 McGregor's Theories X and Y and Deming's TQM

Theory X	Theory Y	TQM
People dislike work and will avoid it.	Work is as natural as play.	Workers take pride in doing things properly.
People must be forced to work.	People are self-directed and will strive to accomplish objectives.	Workers will produce quality in a quality system.
People want to be directed and will avoid responsibility.	People will learn to accept and seek responsibility.	Workers will look for defects and check for quality.

principal is merely one of the crowd, but productive change (improvement) only happens in an open climate where ideas are tested. Effective leaders for tomorrow's school must be a blend of initiators, persuaders, facilitators, and servants to keep schools and their clients competitive in the 21st century.

(8) **Drive out fear.** If administrators, teachers, and students are reprimanded for making honest mistakes, they will seek the shadows and try nothing new. Principals who fear the superintendent's criticism for trying a new instructional program or new class schedule will keep the status quo. Teachers who try new methods and are criticized by the principal before the new methods can produce positive results will never again try to be different (and better). Without trust and mutual support, efforts to improve will be stagnated. .

(9) **Break down barriers between departments.** A system cannot improve if the free exchange of ideas is blocked by artificial barriers between and among departments and people. When departments and individuals guard their precious turf and refuse to share ideas to help others succeed, systems quality is thwarted.

(10) **Eliminate meaningless slogans, exhortations, and targets.** Slogans like "All Children Learn Here," or "Great Teachers Have Pride" can be very motivational if the system really believes in the children and the teachers. However, slogans or targets created without teacher or staff input are empty words and can be insulting to professional staff members.

(11) **Eliminate letter grades and management by numbers.** Numerical quotas are fine for a football team, but not for schools. Standards or quotas are merely caps for some type of academic performance. Mutually developed goals can be motivational, but arbitrary standards or quotas do not cre-

ate high-quality teaching and learning in schools. Such standards and attempts to reach them can create fear, lack of trust, and superficial efforts.

(12) **Remove barriers that reduce pride of workmanship.** The use of staff appraisal and its hammer, merit pay, is a barrier to free exchange of ideas and open communication. Attempts to create career ladders based on the best evaluation strategies have not improved student performance. Current performance appraisal systems tend to destroy collegiality and teamwork because of the competitive environment they create. No threatening and divisive attempt to measure and reward teaching and administrative performance will create pride in workmanship in the science and art of teaching.

(13) **Institute a program of education and self-development.** (This principle is closely related to principle number six.) The success of any school is based on staff development for self-improvement. Most people want to improve their job skills and will take advantage of relevant training programs. Therefore, school leaders should encourage and support staff development that truly leads to self-improvement.

(14) **Ask everyone to participate in continuous improvement of the organization.** If quality schools are to become a reality, every person in the district or school must become linked to continuous improvement efforts. The administration will never be able to insert continuous improvement without the support of those who do the actual day-to-day teaching and working with students. All of the previous 13 principles must be carefully explained and implemented into every "nook and cranny" of the system to make continuous improvement a habit for all employees. Unless this careful planning is shared by those who must make it work, the goals of con-

tinuous improvement will become just another fad and will be ignored by important constituencies in the district and in each school.

Motivation and Action

McLelland. Motivation is not behavior; it is an internal set of needs, desires, drives, and wants that causes an individual to act. Great writers, poets, athletes, and school administrators have a greater need to achieve than others. David McClelland (1985) calls this the n-achievement theory. Some individuals have a burning desire to succeed and take the necessary and calculated risks to reach their goals. Others are satisfied with less achievement and are not driven to seek higher goals. McClelland believes that a person with a high n-achievement need is very competitive and likes to work alone or with other highly competent people. These driven individuals need constant feedback about their performance and can have difficulty working with others on team projects.

Vroom. Victor Vroom (1964) based his motivation theory on expectancy theories and models; asserting that individuals will strive for high performance if their efforts are rewarded. Vroom's expectancy model has three key components: valence, instrumentality, and expectancy. Valence is based on the value one places on the vision, mission, and goals of an organization and how these factors affect them personally; it is a person's inner desire to put forth the effort to reap the benefits for that effort. Instrumentality refers to the old ideal of "a hard day's work for a good day's pay;" that is, if individuals know that their efforts will produce nice rewards they are likely to keep striving and improving their performance. For example, principals who see that leadership in teacher staff development produces higher student performance and receive recognition for that improvement will have high instrumentality. Expectancy is similar to valence. It posits that individuals who believe their effort will pay good dividends have high expectancy levels. If athletes believe their team can win the next basketball game if they shoot 500 extra free throws in practice, they have a high expectancy for their extra effort.

Weiner and Demoulin. Bernard Weiner (1986) calls this link between hard work and success "attribution theory." He believes that people link past efforts to success or failure and seek new ways to alter the outcomes to attain a certain level of performance. Others call this internal need to succeed "self-efficacy." Donald Demoulin (1993) found that people who believe they have the capacity and skills to accomplish their goals have high efficacy. Teachers who have a strong belief that they can help students perform at high levels, for example, have high self-efficacy.

Rotter. Internal-external locus of control theory (Rotter 1966) is also worthy of mention in this motivation review. J.B. Rotter believes that some people feel they have little or no control over what happens to them in life. Individuals who believe that politics, the "good ol' boy" system, or some other external factor will prevent them from becoming a school principal have an external locus of control. Others who believe that talent, perseverance, and active pursuit of a principalship can result in their attaining their goal have an internal locus of control.

Not surprisingly, educational researchers have tried to link motivation theory to the workplace and job satisfaction. Thompson, McNamara, and Hoyle (1997) report that findings on job satisfaction from 474 articles published in the first 26 volumes of *Educational Administration Quarterly* are mixed. Their review supports earlier findings that as role ambiguity and role conflict increase, overall job satisfaction decreases. There also seems to be a weak but positive relationship between overall job satisfaction and school level; "that is, teachers in elementary schools reported higher levels of job satisfaction than those in secondary schools" (p. 24). Thompson, McNamara, and Hoyle (1997) recommend that future research on job satisfaction pay more attention to the construct definitions, research designs, statistical treatments, unit of analysis, and practical significance of the findings published in research journals.

Despite the mixed findings of current motivation research, certain job factors clearly do motivate workers. These factors include the nature of the work itself, recognition for good performance, achievement and responsibility, promotion, and attainment of new job skills. School leaders need to monitor and support these factors at the school and district level. The use of carefully designed portfolio assessment along with traditional evaluation methods hold considerable promise for improving staff members' skills and job satisfaction and, in turn, the overall school climate. (See chapter 7 for a more extensive review of staff evaluation.)

Climate Assessment Methods and Skills

No two learning climates are exactly alike.

9

Even within the same district, schools have organizational personalities, which include unique organizational styles and human dynamics. One of the most definitive works on the relationship between environment and student achievement is *Educational Environments and Effects: Evaluation Policy and Productivity*, edited by Herbert Walberg (1979), which is a series of investigations that deal with environments outside the school as well as with various aspects of the classroom environment.

Several standardized climate instruments have been developed and tested over the past several decades. These include teacher self-reports, student self-reports, principal interpersonal sensitivity instruments, and leadership behavior instruments.

Teacher self-reports. Andrew Halpin and Don Croft (1963), pioneers in the measurement of school climate, developed the Organizational Climate Description Questionnaire (OCDQ). They reasoned that each school had its own personality or "feel," which could be measured, analyzed, and acted on. The initial OCDQ instrument was developed from hundreds of items about the quality of the relationships and interactions among the teaching staff and between the teaching staff and the building principal.

When teachers work well together and the principal carefully guides, mentors, coaches, and uses good interpersonal skills, the OCDQ climate measures indicate an open school climate. Conversely, if the teachers are disengaged, aloof, and critical of each other, and the principal is viewed as a rule maker, enforcer, and dictator with poor interpersonal skills, the school climate registers as closed.

Several revisions have been conducted to improve the accuracy of the original OCDQ in measuring a wider variety of schools, including large urban and secondary schools. The revised OCDQ-RE is a 42-item instrument with 6 subtests for assessing the climate as perceived by elementary teachers and principals (Hoy and Clover 1986; Hoy, Tarter, and Kottkamp 1991). The six dimensions of the OCDQ-RE are Supportive Behavior, Directive Behavior, Restrictive Behavior, Collegial Behavior, Intimate Behavior, and Disengaged Behavior. Other revisions of the OCDQ have made it appropriate to measure the climates of middle schools and high schools (Kottkamp, Mulhern, and Hoy 1987; Hoy, Tarter, and Kottkamp 1991; Hoy et al. 1994; Hoffman et al. 1994). These revisions are leading to a more accurate climate picture in all kinds of schools in various communities.

Another helpful teacher self-report instrument is the Learning Climate Inventory (LCI) (Hoyle 1972) (see Exhibit 1 at the end of this chapter). The LCI assesses the learning climate in schools by gathering teacher perceptions about their administrators, peers, and teaching situation. The reliability coefficients for each of the five factors assessed by the LCI range from 0.50 to 0.75; test-retest reliabilities range from 0.75 to 0.92. The five factors assessed are:

- **Leadership.** Teachers' perceptions of administrators' leadership behaviors.
- **Freedom.** The extent to which teachers feel free to experiment (take risks) and to determine their own teaching and instructional activities in their classrooms.
- **Evaluation.** The extent to which teachers and students feel involved in teacher and administrator evaluation.
- **Compliance.** The extent to which teachers feel the pressure to conform to the rules of the system.
- **Cooperation.** The extent to which teachers feel supported in their efforts to team teach and to use a variety of resource people to enhance classroom learning.

Selected studies using the LCI have found strong and positive relationships between an open climate and the principal's leadership influence (Dudney 1986). Ibanez (1991) found a positive relationship between the open learning climate and achievement scores of secondary students and Resendiz (1994) found that Chapter 1 schools were more open than non-chapter 1 schools.

Student self-reports. Student self-reports are also helpful in climate assessment. The Pupil Control Ideology (PCI) is a 20-item instrument that measures pupil control orientation along a continuum from custodial to humanistic. It differs from the OCDQ and the LCI in that it focuses solely on teacher-student relations. A strong relationship is evident between humanism in the pupil-control orientation of schools and the openness of the school's organizational climate (Hoy and Miskel 1996).

The Secondary School Attitude Inventory (SSAI) is another teacher-student relations instrument designed to asses students' perceptions of (1) classroom climate and (2) futures-oriented, higher-order thinking and problem-solving skills (See Exhibit 2 at the end of this chapter.). The research base for the SSAI is derived from the work of Steele

(1969), who developed the Classroom Activities Questionnaire, and Anderson (1979), who developed the Learning Environment Inventory (LEI). The results of the SSAI, which can be used in grades 7-12, can be very helpful to teachers concerned about students' perceptions of the cognition levels of instruction and how conducive their classroom climate is to higher levels of learning. Teachers can also respond to the SSAI to see if their perceptions on the two dimensions are similar or different from those held by students.

Principal interpersonal sensitivity instruments. A recent set of instruments to measure principals' interpersonal sensitivity have proven helpful in gathering the perceptions of staff, community members, and administrators during school climate assessment. The Principal's Interpersonal Sensitivity for Students Inventory; the Staff Sensitivity Scale; the Parent, Business, and Community Agency Sensitivity Scale; and the Principal's Sensitivity Scale Toward the Central Office are easy to use and can provide helpful data to principals and teachers trying to create a more sensitive and effective working climate (Hoyle and Crenshaw 1997). A recent study in Texas revealed that teachers in a large school district believed their building principals were generally sensitive, but signs of insensitivity were present in the areas of teacher career development and individual teacher-principal communication patterns.

Leadership behaviors instruments. The best known and most widely used leadership questionnaire is the Leadership Behavior Description Questionnaire (LBDQ). Hemphill and Coons (1957) created the instrument to gather staff perceptions of a leader's behavior. Two distinct leadership dimensions — Initiating Structure and Consideration — have emerged from the LBDQ, which consists of a series of short, descriptive statements concerning a leader's behavior. *Initiating Structure* refers to a leader's ability to effectively delineate the relationship between himself or herself and members of the workgroup. This dimension also involves how well a leader defines channels of communication and procedures. *Consideration* refers to behavior indicative of friendship, mutual trust, respect, and warmth in the relationship between a leader and staff members. Most effective leaders score high on both Initiating Structure and Consideration (Halpin 1966). Outstanding leaders are those who can instruct and support others in accomplishing tasks while modeling trust and warm human relationships in all dimensions of the organization.

The LBDQ, like other climate assessment instruments, remains no more than a tool to gather an observer's perception. All studies, no matter how carefully done, have weaknesses, and all findings must be carefully interpreted. The LBDQ, however, should be in the arsenal of every researcher and

Over 70 climate assessment instruments that assess everything from student attitudes about math to community perceptions of school effectiveness have been compiled by the Northwest Regional Educational Laboratory. Copies are available from The Test Center NREL, 101 SW Main Street, Suite 500, Portland, OR 97204-3297 (phone 503-275-9582).

Other helpful instruments for checking the climate of schools, along with their sources, are:

- **School Profile: Climate** — Jim Sweeney, Iowa State University, College of Education, Des Moines, IA 50011.

- **School Effectiveness Questionnaire (SEQ)** — Harcourt Brace Educational Measurement, Order Service Center, P.O. Box 839954, San Antonio, TX 78283.

- **Dimensions of Excellence Scales: Survey for School Improvement** — RBS Publications, Research for Better Schools, 444 N. Third St., Philadelphia, PA 19123.

- **Teacher Opinion Inventory, Parent Opinion Inventory, Student Opinion Inventory, and Community Opinion Survey** — National Study of School Evaluation, 5201 Leesburg Pike, Falls Church, VA 22041

- **Secondary School Attitude Survey** – John Hoyle, Climate Research Associates, 8409 Whiterose Court, College Station, TX 77845.

- **School Climate Survey (form A)** – National Association of Secondary School Principals, 1904 Association Drive, Reston, VA 22091.

- **School Climate Observation Checklist** — Exhibit 3 at the end of this chapter.

administrator who wants to analyze a school or district climate.

Designing Your Own Questionnaire

A strong case can be made for nonstandardized, "homemade" school climate questionnaires, particularly those constructed to assess attitudes or opinions on a set of specific issues. An excellent example is the opinionnaire designed by the Lewisville, Texas, school district to gather perceptions about the curriculum needs of the students for the next five years (see Montgomery 1996). Mike Killian, Lewisville's deputy superintendent, found that the questionnaire tailored for the Lewisville community provided valuable data for curriculum planning. The items for the Lewisville instrument were written by teachers, curriculum specialists, parents, and community leaders in business and industry. The items relate directly to the philosophical, instructional, and human variables that affect school climate and student achievement. Thirty-nine percent of the 12-page questionnaires sent out in 1995 were returned — an astounding number compared to similar community opinion assessment efforts. The key to the high returns was total community ownership in the design of the opinionnaire and open communication links to all patrons.

The climate and leadership assessment questionnaires listed in this section can provide valuable information to help improve interpersonal relationships and team building, necessary elements of a high-performing school and district.

Assessing Student Achievement Data

Increasing calls from parents, business leaders, community members, state departments of education, and others to raise student test scores require that school leaders have a strong handle on student test data and interpretation. No longer can a superintendent or principal go before a school board or community group and simply claim that students are doing a great job. School leaders must be able to explain how well the students compare to other schools and districts and how much the scores and achievement differ from one year to the next in all content areas. Mike Schmoker (1996, p. 1) declares, "All school efforts should be focused on results. . . . [A]ll schools can improve if they gear up to get better results by examining and refining the processes that most clearly contribute to designated results. Attention to increased standards and appro-

priate measures of their attainment are key factors in the remedy of poor performance."

Effective schools have a well-developed system to determine how well students are progressing in all academic and social areas. The system of detailed evaluation identifies students who are lagging behind and those who are leading the pack. School district and individual school effectiveness is reliant on both standardized and criterion-referenced tests and their interpretation, as well as informal observation, performance, and other authentic assessment measures, which add another dimension to the database for each school, classroom, and student. (See Chapter 9 for information about specific research methods and data analysis related to student achievement.)

Developing a Strategic Plan for the District or School

Erlandson, Stark, and Ward (1996) assert that strategic planning and long-range planning are one and the same. Given that no roadmap to the future exists, it is imperative that everyone in a school or school district be involved in the strategic planning process. If computer literacy, mathematics, science, social studies, language arts, logical thinking, and interpersonal team skills are needed for success in the new millennium, then any strategic plan should include strategies to teach and measure those skills. Most schools and districts have some form of strategic plan in place, but fall short of having a solid method of evaluating the success or failure of the plan in place. Hoy and Tarter (1995) observe that many school administrators fail to really consider the consequences of their strategic decisions and merely "muddle through" without a system of benchmarking their activities and goal accomplishments.

A Constructivist View

Constructivism and other postmodern approaches to planning encourage people to engage in exploration and risk taking to maintain a position of "red alert" so organizations can meet dynamic changes in society and technology. Margaret Wheatley (1992), author of *Leadership and the New Science,* acknowledges that the old ways of believing that everything is in its place and predictable are over. Wheatley affirms the postmodern belief that leadership is changing from power brokers in charge to individuals in relationships, and from old top-down bureaucracies to bottom-up empowerment models. Thus, human relationships that encourage creativity, risk-taking, and personal support are leading to more inclusive organizations where people are free to make necessary adjustments as they go. Planners must remember that strategic planning is a "people-intensive" process and must develop alternative strategies and goals that allow people to adjust to inevitable change.

The Mixed Scanning Model

Amitai Etzioni (1967, 1986, and 1989) believes most standard strategic planning unwisely results in inflexible sets of policies, goals, and assessments. He believes in alternative strategies called "mixed scanning," or "humble decision making." The concept of mixed scanning for purposes of planning and decision making is similar to the methods

A Strategic Plan Model

Developing a strategic plan involves three stages: the context stage, the resource stage, and the monitoring stage

The Context Stage
Even though plans often fail to hit the center of the target, the planning process is indispensable. Solid plans, after all, are designed to be adaptable to necessary change. The context, or needs assessment, stage of strategic planning looks at the current status of the systems' programs in operations, staffing, technology, curriculum, instructional strategies, evaluation, and so on versus the vision, mission, and goal statements about where the district or school wishes to be in the next 5, 10 or 15 years. The context stage is the most important part of determining the priorities for the years ahead.

The Resource Stage
The resource stage of planning must include an examination of the feasibility of supporting the vision, mission, and goals with the necessary funding, personnel, and time given the various alternatives outlined in the context stage. Defining clear goals, objectives, and contingencies in the resource stage reduces the problem of running out of money or not having the right people or adequate time to accomplish set goals.

The Monitoring Stage
This stage is perhaps the least developed and understood in most strategic planning efforts. The weakness of standardized test scores to assess the accomplishments of students and teachers, the flaws in teacher and administrator evaluation, and the complexities of assessing organizational effectiveness and financial efficiency make the monitoring stage the most suspect and confusing. However, in spite of these weaknesses, the success of a strategic plan depends on sound economic and evaluation principles. Thus, in the instructional programs, a wide array of assessment methods, including testing, portfolios, and other authentic performance measures, must be used during decision making. With precise, accessible information, school leaders can make informed decisions about staff, operations, and other key areas. Through comparing the data with the established benchmarks for accounting and assessment, adjustments can be made when necessary.

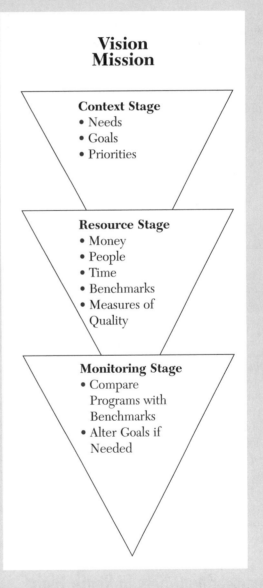

Vision
Mission

Context Stage
• Needs
• Goals
• Priorities

Resource Stage
• Money
• People
• Time
• Benchmarks
• Measures of Quality

Monitoring Stage
• Compare Programs with Benchmarks
• Alter Goals if Needed

medical doctors use to conduct a general diagnosis of a patient to determine the exact source of an illness. The doctor diagnoses or "scans" the general health of the patient to locate the specific spot or area of the pain or problem before making a diagnosis. If the treatment fails, the doctor scans and tries another one. Thus, arriving and the right diagnosis, like strategic planning, becomes an incremental search for the answers to problems (Etzioni 1989).

Because no tried and true, perfect information exists for use during educational assessment and planning, school leaders must guide others in taking the broad "futures" view of where society and the schools are heading. This "broad brush" view helps curriculum planners, facility designers, and policymakers consider the context of how schools and learning will be configured in the 21st century.

All sound strategic planning must involve the following questions:

- Where are we now?
- Where do we wish to go?
- How do we get there?
- How are we doing along the way?
- What has been successful and what must be changed?
- How much will it cost in terms of human and financial resources?
- Who is responsible for carrying out the plan?

A strategic plan can be a highly detailed, complex, and confusing document that is ignored, or a usable, flexible guide that helps school leaders monitor progress on multiple educational fronts. Because change is constant, plans must be adaptable and based on constant assessment from a wide variety of sources. When stakeholders are kept informed and engaged in the planning process, and when the best possible assessment data are monitored and applied, stakeholders remain advocates for the plan and those in charge of the planning. (More information about the strategic planning process is included in Chapter 9.)

Empowering Others To Reach High Levels of Performance

The secrets of training great leaders elude the best university and academy training programs. Some researchers focus on the "situational" nature of leadership while others study the personal or physical traits of leaders. More than 40 years ago, writers argued that leaders who wish to empower others should be good listeners, that they need to understand the social structure of the organization, and that, above all else, they must understand workers' sentiments. Hoyle (1995) believes that the three most critical attributes of visionary leaders are:

- **Their belief in a cause greater than themselves.** School leaders who are viewed as true servants for children and youth lead their communities to establish exemplary schools. Albert Schweitzer gave up a prominent and lucrative medical practice to spend his life healing the sick in the jungles of Africa. Mother Teresa, a symbol of love for destitute people in India, could have chosen a less demanding and more comfortable life. Those who have chosen to educate others may not spend their lives among the sick and helpless, but the challenge to become servant leaders is equally important. Great school leaders must have a cause that is larger than any personal agenda or desire for self-enhancement.
- **The ability to communicate a clear message in simple, persuasive words.** John F. Kennedy, Winston Churchill, Barbara Jordan, and Martin Luther King Jr. were great communicators who could persuade others to join their causes. This attribute is a gift that great leaders acquire. Without the ability to sell an idea, individuals fall short of greatness in leadership. School leaders must develop the skill to choose the right words to help rally teachers, parents, and community members in establishing goals and procedures to support schools, teaching, mentoring, and learning for all students. (See Chapter 3 for information about effective communication.)
- **The commitment to persist under the most difficult circumstances.** A poignant example of true grit was displayed in the 1968 Olympic games by John Steven Agrearri, who finished last in the marathon, the last event of the games. He entered the dark, empty stadium and crossed the finish line wearing a heavy bandage on his leg, which was injured in a bad fall during the race. A lone sportswriter asked him why he hadn't quit hours before. Agrearri responded, "My country didn't send me 5,000 miles to start the race; my country sent me 5,000

miles to finish the race" (Braden 1996). When school leaders face school board politics, state and federal mandates, and people who want to "return to the good old days," persistence is often the best weapon. When a superintendent or principal takes the high ground for children and youth with the determination not to surrender, positive change can occur.

These three attributes — three of the many found in the available lists of leadership skills — are the foundation for leaders who desire to empower and inspire others to "pick up the torch" and work for higher achievement for all students.

Multicultural and Ethnic Understanding

School leaders must ensure that the schools value and provide multicultural and multiethnic information in curriculum and staff development. Skills in shared decision making and in creating a supportive school and district climate that accommodates racial and ethnic differences are critical to community building, just as they are vital to a democratic form of government (Baptise 1988, Lachman and Taylor 1995). Administrators must possess the skills to be effective in providing education for the many ethnic groups in our nation. This involves:

- Finding data sources in the community to monitor demographics;
- Understanding and celebrating the cultural backgrounds of the members of the school community;
- Developing networks with church leaders and social service agencies to reach all sections of the community;
- Seeking curriculum materials and textbooks relevant to other cultures and languages;
- Hiring and keeping faculty and staff who mirror the racial, ethnic, and cultural composition of the community; and
- Avoiding materials and language that treat any segment of society in inferior or demeaning ways.

Working with Others

The search is endless for the secret to motivating people to work toward the accomplishment of school goals. People in leadership positions claim to value and believe in their staffs but sometimes turn around and psychologically "drop kick" them to get things done. They talk about applying the humanizing elements of Theory Y and Deming's "trust in the worker" philosophy but apply the dictator tactics of Theory X or the political schemes of Machiavelli. They assert that they trust people, but suspiciously watch them.

Assumptions leaders make about others' backgrounds, abilities, and motives often determine how well they work with others. School leaders who are cynical about the motives of other administrators, teachers, parents, students, and board members fail to lead them in accomplishing school goals. On the other hand, school leaders who like themselves, flaws and all, and believe in their own abilities' like other people, believe in their abilities, and support them in getting the job done. School leaders must remember that their interpersonal communication sends out clear signals about how much they trust and believe in others, and can create the kind of teamwork that accomplishes miracles. Leaders must be mentors and team learners if organizations are to live their vision and reach their goals (Bell 1996). A high level of faith in others is a must for making schools good places to work and learn.

Aligning Financial, Human, and Material Resources with the Vision, Mission, and Goals

This set of skills is closely related to strategic planning. Obviously, if financial, human, and material resources are not carefully aligned with the overall planning process, disaster will result. A district's or schools' resources, namely time, materials, people, and money, all need to be considered in effective program budgeting and planning. A school leader need not be a financial wizard to understand the allocation of resources, but must have a sound grounding in school finance, accounting, cash flow, and investments.

School leaders must be knowledgeable about securing and allocating human and material resources; developing and managing a district or school budget, and maintaining accurate fiscal records. Careful planning will help ensure that the financial, human, and material resources will be correctly supportive of the district's or school's vision, mission, and goals. (A more thorough treatment of these skills is provided in Chapter 4.)

15

Conclusion

This chapter has stressed the importance of visionary leadership and skills to help school leaders better understand the culture and assess the climate of the district and school. It has also provided a review of motivation and leadership theory and best practice to remind school leaders and potential school leaders of the human dimension of school improvement. These vital skills are prerequisites for creating a strategic plan based on the priorities established for the children and youth in the community.

A vision to inspire, a mission to guide, and a flexible, dynamic plan to monitor progress help ensure that the dimensions of diversity, empower-

ment, and higher student and staff performance are embedded and encouraged in every school district and building. When the vision is focused on all students and the system and school allocate their resources, energy, and passion for excellence to that end, schools become places where all children and adults find success. The simple truth is that only school administrators who believe in a "cause greater than themselves" and can inspire others to share a vision through their words and deeds and persist through difficult times deserve to be called school leaders.

Use the Skill Accomplishment Checklist on page 19 to assess your skill level on each of the important topics discussed in this chapter.

EXHIBIT 1 Learning Climate Inventory

Directions:
1. Read each statement carefully.
2. Draw a circle around the scale number that best indicates your opinion on each statement.
3. Do not place your name on the form. No attempt will be made to identify the person completing this inventory.

never	seldom	occasionally	often	always			
1	2	3	4	5	6	7	1. You are free to experiment with teaching methods and techniques in your classroom.
1	2	3	4	5	6	7	2. You are free to bring supplementary materials (e.g., paperbacks, magazines, newspapers, films, slides, videos, computers, etc.) into your classroom.
1	2	3	4	5	6	7	3. You are "encouraged" to "teach the test" to improve student achievement.
1	2	3	4	5	6	7	4. You feel free to discuss students' learning difficulties with your principal.
1	2	3	4	5	6	7	5. You participate in the administrative decisions affecting your classroom teaching.
1	2	3	4	5	6	7	6. You are free to discuss controversial issues in your classroom.
1	2	3	4	5	6	7	7. Your are free to invite resource people to assist you in your classroom.
1	2	3	4	5	6	7	8. You are supported in your efforts to employ team teaching or other mentoring/cooperative teaching plans.
1	2	3	4	5	6	7	9. You are free to use your own judgment in evaluating and grading each student.
1	2	3	4	5	6	7	10. You are discouraged from teaching higher level, critical thinking skills to your students.
1	2	3	4	5	6	7	11. Your teaching is evaluated by a mutually agreed upon set of objectives.
1	2	3	4	5	6	7	12. You possess high expectations for yourself and model this behavior for your students.
1	2	3	4	5	6	7	13. Your principal keeps the teaching staff working together as a team to improve the learning climate.
1	2	3	4	5	6	7	14. You feel free to discuss students' learning difficulties with other teachers.
1	2	3	4	5	6	7	15. Building inservice programs are planned to help you improve the teaching/learning process in your classroom.
1	2	3	4	5	6	7	16. Your creative teaching techniques are highlighted (praised) by your principal.
1	2	3	4	5	6	7	17. Your are invited to evaluate the performance of your principal.
1	2	3	4	5	6	7	18. You invite students to evaluate your teaching.
1	2	3	4	5	6	7	19. You invite your colleagues to evaluate your teaching.
1	2	3	4	5	6	7	20. You are satisfied with your teaching.

EXHIBIT 2 Secondary School Attitude Inventory for Grades 7–12 (Student Self-Report)

For each sentence below, circle the letters that show the extent to which you **Agree** or **Disagree**

Circle **SA** if you **strongly agree** with the sentence.
Circle **A** if you **agree** moderately with the sentence.
Circle **D** if you **disagree** moderately with the sentence.
Circle **SD** if you **strongly disagree** with the sentence.

1.	The students usually enjoy their class assignments. (CI)	SA	A	D	SD
2.	Most students feel free to take part in discussions. (CI)	SA	A	D	SD
3.	The teacher talks during all class time. (CL)	SA	A	D	SD
4.	The teacher stresses memorization too much. (CL)	SA	A	D	SD
5.	Every member of the class is treated fairly by the teacher. (CI)	SA	A	D	SD
6.	Students are expected to explore new ideas. (CL)	SA	A	D	SD
7.	The teacher encourages us to solve problems and to think creatively. (CL)	SA	A	D	SD
8.	The teacher disciplines troublemakers. (CI)	SA	A	D	SD
9.	Only the smart students get special treatment. (CI)	SA	A	D	SD
10.	Students are allowed to make some class decisions. (CI)	SA	A	D	SD
11.	The teacher expects all students to learn. (CL)	SA	A	D	SD
12.	Students cooperate with each other. (CI)	SA	A	D	SD
13.	The teacher believes that all students can learn the classwork well. (CL)	SA	A	D	SD
14.	The students believe that they can learn the classwork well. (CL)	SA	A	D	SD
15.	The teacher motivates all students to learn. (CL)	SA	A	D	SD
16.	Students are encouraged to consider more than one solution to problems. (CL)	SA	A	D	SD
17.	Students are encouraged to use step-by-step logic to solve problems. (CL)	SA	A	D	SD
18.	The teacher discourages student discussion about classwork. (CL)	SA	A	D	SD
19.	Students are under too much pressure to make good grades. (CI)	SA	A	D	SD
20.	Students feel they can have fun and laugh in class. (CI)	SA	A	D	SD
21.	Classmates are friendly to each other. (CI)	SA	A	D	SD
22.	Students feel threatened in the class. (CI)	SA	A	D	SD
23.	The teacher is patient in helping all students. (CI)	SA	A	D	SD
24.	Certain students try to push others around. (CI)	SA	A	D	SD
25.	The class makes students feel good about their future. (CI)	SA	A	D	SD
26.	Students are often confused about what the teacher is trying to teach. (CL)	SA	A	D	SD
27.	The teacher enjoys teaching the class. (CI)	SA	A	D	SD
28.	Students look forward to this class. (CI)	SA	A	D	SD
29.	The classwork usually relates to the real world. (CL)	SA	A	D	SD
30.	The teacher cares about all students. (CI)	SA	A	D	SD

Scoring: For each item, assign a score of 4 to SA, 3 to A, 2 to D, and 1 to SD. Determine the mean scores for each item.

Climate items (CI) 1, 2, 5, 8, 10, 12, 20, 21, 23, 25, 27, 28, and 30 should have mean scores of 3 or better.
Climate items (CI) 9, 19, 22, and 24 should have mean scores of 2 or 1.
Cognitive level items (CL) 6, 7, 11, 13, 14, 15, 16, 17, and 29 should have mean scores of 3 or better.
Cognitive level items (CL) 3, 4, 18, and 26 should have mean scores or 2 or 1.

Source: John R. Hoyle, Texas A&M University.

EXHIBIT 3 School Climate Observations Checklist

(Note: Information can be gathered through observations and interviews.)

Directions: Check each item appropriately as it applies to your school. Scoring directions are at the end.

1. **Amount of Open Space for Instruction in the Building**
   ____ 100%
   ____ 50%
   ____ 10%
   ____ 0%

2. **Instructional Group Size** (Note: Indicate the percentage of time students spend in each.)
   ____ Large group, more than 30 students
   ____ Medium group, 16-29 students
   ____ Small groups, 2-15 students
   ____ Individual

3. **Staff Organization**
   ____ Extensive use of team teaching
   ____ Moderate use to team teaching
   ____ Limited use of team teaching
   ____ No team teaching

4. **Grouping**
   ____ Determined by continuous assessment of student achievement
   ____ Determined by occasional assessment of student achievement
   ____ Determined by limited assessment of student achievement
   ____ Determined by normed tests at beginning of school year

5. **Noise in Classrooms**
   ____ Noise level is comfortable
   ____ Noise level is disorderly
   ____ Noise level is distracting
   ____ Noise level is silent

6. **Seating in Classrooms**
   Students are:
   ____ Seated on floor
   ____ Seated on "homey" furniture
   ____ Seated in movable desks or tables
   ____ Seated at fixed stations

7. **Instructional Materials**
   ____ Wide variety of teaching material
   ____ Multiple texts
   ____ Extensive use of A-V equipment, including computers
   ____ Instruction is confined to a single text

8. **Teaching Strategies**
   ____ Wide variety of teaching strategies in all classrooms
   ____ Moderate variety of teaching strategies in all classrooms
   ____ Limited variety of teaching strategies in all classrooms
   ____ No variety of teaching strategies in all classrooms

9. **Student Movement**
   ____ Students are free to move about as they wish
   ____ Students may move freely with teacher's permission
   ____ Students have limited movement with teacher's permission
   ____ Students have little opportunity to move about

10. **Teacher Work Areas**
    ____ Used by more than 20 teachers
    ____ Used by 11-19 teachers
    ____ Used by 5-10 teachers
    ____ Used by fewer than 5 teachers

11. **Instructional Time to Promote Mastery by Students**
    ____ Extensive use of flexible instructional time
    ____ Moderate use of flexible instructional time
    ____ Limited use of flexible instructional time
    ____ No flexible instructional time

12. **Use of Media or Resource Center**
    ____ Heavily used by students all day long
    ____ Heavily used by students during portions of school day
    ____ Limited use by students
    ____ Rarely used

13. **Teaching and Learning Time**
    ____ No classroom time is taken from instruction by outside influences
    ____ Little classroom time is taken from instruction by outside influences
    ____ Considerable time is taken from instruction by outside influences
    ____ Too much time is taken from instruction by outside influences

14. **Instructional Goals**
    ____ Instructional goals are clear and understood by all students
    ____ Instructional goals are clear and understood by most students
    ____ Instructional goals are not clear and understood by only a few students
    ____ Instructional goals are not clear and students are confused

15. **Community Resources**
    ____ Resource people are used extensively
    ____ Resource people are used occasionally
    ____ Resource people are used rarely
    ____ Resource people are never used

16. **Inservice Education for Staff**
    ____ Extensive use of inservice for morale building and cooperative problem solving
    ____ Moderate use of inservice for morale building and cooperative problem solving
    ____ Occasional use of inservice for morale building and cooperative problem solving
    ____ Morale building and cooperative problem solving are never stressed

Scoring

1. Items 4, 5, 8, 11, 13, 14, 15, and 16 are scored by giving four (4) points if the first choice is checked and one (1) point if the last choice is checked. The higher total score indicates a more open and businesslike climate.

2. Items 1, 2, 3, 6, 7, 9, 10, and 12 checked but given no weight. The evaluator uses the information as background or context for the scored items.

Skill Accomplish Checklist for Chapter 1

Skills	Readings and Activities for Skill Mastery
Create and effectively communicate a district or school vision statement	**Readings:** Conger (1989), Hoyle (1995), Kouzes and Posner (1995), Short and Greer (1997), Uchida et al. (1996) **Activities:** 1. Write a vision statement for your district or school and share it with the executive team in the central office or the site-based team in the school. 2. Rewrite the vision statement and distribute it to a wide audience for open discussion. 3. Conduct a visioning workshop on the future of the district or school using exercises found in Hoyle (1995).
Establish priorities in the context of community culture and student and staff needs.	**Readings:** Cusick (1987), Deal and Kennedy (1982), Hoyle and Crenshaw (1997) **Activities:** 1. Create a multicultural task force to identify all the cultures and ethnic groups represented in your community. 2. Create a written community and school plan that include activities that cultivate, captivate, and celebrate the diversity and customs of the people in your community.
Conduct district and school climate assessments.	**Readings:** Hoy and Miskel (1996), Sweeney (1987), Walberg (1979) **Activities:** 1. Design a workable climate improvement plan for your school or district. 2. Visit local corporations to discuss their climate improvement plans. 3. Administer the OCDQ, LCI, and SSAI. 4. Design and administer a "homemade" teacher self-report instrument.
Assess student achievement data.	**Readings:** Borg and Gaul (1989), Isaac and Michael (1987), Schmoker (1996) **Activities:** 1. Analyze a set of disaggregated test scores in math or science for the district or a school. 2. Prepare a report for the board of education, the faculty, or the PTA on test results for the past year.
Develop a strategic plan for a district or school.	**Readings:** Carlson and Awkerman (1991, Erlandson et al. (1996), Etzioni (1989), Kauffman et al. (1996) **Activities:** 1. Review the district strategic plan; pay close attention to its vision, mission, and goals. 2. Compare your school or district strategic plan with another school or district plan.
Empower others to reach high levels of performance.	**Readings:** Covey (1990), Greenleaf (1991), Hoyle (1995), Short and Greer (1997) **Activities:** 1. Design a staff recognition and motivation plan for the school or district 2. Help teachers frame a definition and plan for teacher empowerment (See Chap. 8, Short and Greer 1997.) 3. Conduct trust-building exercises with a central office team or school faculty.
Align financial, human, and material resources with the vision, mission, and goals of a district or school.	**Readings:** Kauffman et al. (1996), Vornberg (1996). **Activities:** 1. Review the district strategic plan to link programming with financial, human, and material resources. 2. Work with a site-based team to analyze the relationship between programming and budget allocations.

19

Resources

Anderson, G. A. (1979). "The Assessment of Learning Environments." In H. *Educational Environments and Effects*, edited by H. Walberg. Beverly Hills, Calif.: McCuthan.

Baptise, P. H. (1988). "Multicultural Education." In *Encyclopedia of School Administration and Supervision*, edited by R. Gorton, G. Schneider, and J. Fisher. Phoenix, Ariz.: Oryx Press.

Barker, J. (1992). *Future Edge*. New York: William Marrow Publisher.

Bell, C. (1996). *Managers as Mentors: Building Partnerships for Learning*. San Francisco, Calif.: Berrett-Koehler Press.

Bolman, L., and T. Deal. (1992). *The Path to School Leadership*. Newbury Park, Calif.: Corwin Press.

Borg, W., and M. Gaul. (1989). *Educational Research: An Introduction*. 5th ed. New York: Longman Publishers.

Bonstingl, J.J. (1992). *Schools for Quality*. Alexandria, Va.: Association for Supervision and Curriculum Development.

Braden, B. (July 17, 1996). "Letter to the Editor." *The Bryan-College Station Eagle*. A 11.

Burchart, T. (1995). *Successful Planning*. Thousand Oaks, Calif.: Corwin Press.

Carlson, R. (1996). *Reframing & Reform: Perspectives in Organizational Leadership and School Change*. White Plains, N.Y.: Longman Publishers.

Carlson, R., and G. Awkerman. (1991). *Educational Planning*. New York: Longman Publishers.

Conger, J. (1989). *The Charismatic Leader*. San Francisco: Jossey-Bass.

Covey, S. (1990). *Principle-Centered Leadership*. New York: Simon & Schuster.

Cunningham, W. (1991). *Empowerment: Vitalizing Personal Energy*. Atlanta: Humanic New Age Press.

Cusick, P.A. (1987). "Organizational Culture and Schools." *Educational Administration Quarterly* 29, 3: 110-117.

Deal, T., and A. Kennedy. (1982). *Corporate Cultures: The Rites and Rituals of Corporate Life*. Reading, Mass.: Addison-Wesley.

Deming, W.E. (1993). *The New Economics for Economics, Government, and Education*. Cambridge: Massachusetts Institute of Technology, Center for Advanced Engineering.

Deming, W.E. (1986). *Out of Crisis*. Cambridge: Massachusetts Institute of Technology, Center for Advanced Engineering.

Deming, W.E. (1983). *Quality, Productivity, and Competitive Advantage*. Cambridge: Massachusetts Institute of Technology, Center for Advanced Engineering.

Demoulin, D. (1993). "Efficacy and Educational Effectiveness." In *In a New Voice*, edited by J. Hoyle and D. Estes. (First Yearbook of the National Council of Professors of Educational Administration.) Lancaster, Pa.: Technomic Pub. Co. Inc.

DePree, M. (1989). *Leadership Is an Art*. New York: Dell.

Dudney, W. (1986). "The Principal's Influence upon the Educational Climate of a School as Perceived by Teachers in San Antonio North Side School District." Unpublished dissertation. Texas A&M University.

Erickson, D. (December 1981). "A New Strategy for School Improvement." *Momentum* 46.

Erlandson, D., P. Stark, and S. Ward. (1996). *Organizational Oversight: Planning and Scheduling for Effectiveness*. Larchmont, N.Y.: Eye on Education.

Etzioni, A. (1989). "Humble Decision Making." *Harvard Business Review* 67,4: 122-126.

Etzioni, A. (1986). "Mixed Scanning Revisited." *Public Administration Review* 27:46: 8-14.

Etzioni, A. (1975). *A Comparative Analysis of Complex Organizations*. New York: Free Press.

Etzioni, A. (1967). "Mixed Scanning: A Third Approach to Decision Making." *Public Administration Review* 27: 385-392.

Gouldner, A. (1954). *Patterns of Industrial Bureaucracy*. New York: Free Press.

Greenleaf, R. K. (1991). *Servant Leadership: A Journey into the Nature of Legitimate Power and Greatness*. Mohwah, N.J.: Paulist.

Halpin, A. (1966). "How Leaders Behave." In *Theory and Research in Administration*, edited by A. Halpin. Chicago: Midwest Administration Center of the University of Chicago.

Halpin, A., and D. Croft. (1963). *The Organizational Climate of Schools*. Chicago: Midwest Administration Center of the University of Chicago.

Hemphill, J., and A. Coons. (1957). "Development of the LBDQ." In *Leadership Behavior: Its Description and Measurement*, edited by R. Stogdill and A. Coons. Columbus, Ohio: The Ohio State University Press.

Herzberg, F. (1968). "One More Time, How Do You Motivate Employees?" *Harvard Business Review* 46, 1: 55-62.

Hoffman, J. D., D. Sabo, J. Bliss, and W. Hoy. (1994). "Building a Culture of Trust." *Journal of School Leadership* 4, 5: 484-502.

Hoy, W., and S.I. Clover. (1986). "Elementary School Climate: A Revision of the OCDQ." *Educational Administration* 22: 93-110.

Hoy, W., J. Hoffman, D. Sabo, and J. Bliss. (1994). "The Organizational Climate of Middle Schools: The Development and Test of the OCDQ-RM." *Journal of Educational Administration* 34, 1: 41-58.

Hoy, W., and C. Miskel. (1996). *Educational Administration. Theory, Research and Practice*. 5th Ed. New York: McGraw-Hill.

Hoy, W., and C.J. Tartar. (1995) *Administrators Solving the Problems of Practice*. Boston: Allyn and Bacon.

Hoy, W., C.J. Tarter, and R. Kottkamp. (1991). *Open Schools/Healthy Schools: Measuring Organizational Climate*. Beverly Hills, Calif.: Sage.

Hoyle, J. (1995). *Leadership and Futuring: Making Visions Happen*. Thousand Oaks, Calif.: Corwin Press.

Hoyle, J. (1972). "The Learning Climate Inventory". Oxford, Ohio: Miami University School Climate Research Project.

Hoyle, J., and H. Crenshaw. (1997). *Interpersonal Sensitivity*. Larchmont, N.Y.: Eye on Education.

Hoyle, J., and A. Oates. (1997). "Principals' Interpersonal Sensitivity Toward Staff, Central Office Staff Personnel, Parents, Business, and Community Members." Paper Delivered at the National Conference of Professors of Educational Administration, Vail Colorado, August 1997.

Ibanez, D. (1991). "The Relationship Between Organizational Climate and Achievement Scores of Secondary Students in the Northside School District Middle Schools." Unpublished dissertation. Texas A&M University.

Isaac, S., and W.B. Michael. (1987). *Handbook in Research and Evaluation*. (2nd Ed.) San Diego: Edits Publishers.

Kahaner, L. (1996). *Competitive Intelligence*. New York: Simon & Schuster.

Kauffman, R., J. Herman, and K. Watters. (1996). *Educational Planning: Strategic, Tactical, and Operational*. Lancaster, Pa.: Technomic Pub. Co. Inc.

Kottkamp, R., J. Mulhern, and W. Hoy. (1987). "Secondary School Climate: A Revision of the OCDQ." *Educational Administration Quarterly* 23: 31-48.

Kouzes, J., and B. Posner. (1995). *The Leadership Challenge*. San Francisco: Jossey-Bass.

Lachman, L., and L. Taylor. (1995). *Schools for All*. Albany, N.Y.: Delmer Publishers.

Lewin, K. (1935). *A Dynamic Theory of Personality*. New York: McGraw-Hill.

Manatt, R. (March 1997). "Feedback from 360 Degrees: Client-Driven Evaluation of School Personnel." *The School Administrator* 3, 54: 8-13.

Maslow, A.H. (1954). *Motivation and Personality*. New York: Harper & Row.

McClelland, D. (1985). *Human Motivation*. Glenview, Ill.: Scott Foresman.

McGregor, D. (1960). *The Human Side of Enterprise*. New York: McGraw-Hill.

Miskel, C. (1982). "Motivation in Educational Organizations." *Educational Administration Quarterly* 18,3: 65-88.

Montgomery, R. (1996). "Collaborative Planning for the 21st Century: A Suburban School District Envisions the Educated Child." Unpublished dissertation. Texas A&M University.

Owens, B. (1994). *Organizational Behavior in Education* (5th Ed.). Englewood Cliffs, N.J.: Merrill.

Resendiz, B. (1994). "Comparison of School Learning Climate in Selected Chapter 1 and Non-Chapter 1 Schools in the Northside Independent School District." Unpublished dissertation. Texas A&M University.

Rotter, J. B. (1966). "Generalized Expectancies for Internal Versus External Control of Reinforcement." *Psychological Monographs* 80(1 whole No. 609).

Rowan, B., S.T. Bossart, and D.C. Dwyer. (1983). "Research on Effective Schools: A Cautionary Note." *Educational Researcher* 12: 24-30.

Santeusanio, R. (1997). "Using Multi-Raters in Superintendent's Evaluation." *The School Administrator* 3,54: 12.

Schmoker, M. (1996). "Results: The Key to Continuous School Improvement." In *The Association for Supervision and Curriculum Development Yearbook*. Alexandria, Va.: ASCD.

Senge, P. (1990). *The Fifth Discipline*. New York: Doubleday.

Short, P., and J. Greer. (1997). *Leadership in Empowered Schools*. Columbus, Ohio: Merrill, Prentice Hall.

Silver, P. (1983). *Educational Administration: Theoretical Perspectives on Practice and Research*. New York: Harper Row.

Steele, J. M. (1969). *C.A.Q.: Instrument for Assessing Instructional Climate Through Low-Inference Student Judgments*. Dekalb, Ill.: Northern Illinois University.

Sweeney, J. (1987). *Tips for Improving School Climate*. Arlington, Va.: American Association of School Administrators.

Texas Education Agency. (1990). *Goals for Instructional Improvement*. Austin, Texas: author.

Thompson, D., J. McNamara, and J. Hoyle. (1997). "Job Satisfaction in Educational Organizations." *Educational Administration Quarterly* 33,1: 7-37.

Uchida, D., M. Cetron, and F. McKenzie.(1996). *Preparing Students for the 21st Century*. Arlington, Va.: American Association of School Administrators.

Vance, M., and D. Deacon. (1995). *Thinking Out of the Box*. Franklin Lakes, N.J.: Career Press.

Vornberg, J. (1996). "Educational Accountability and Systems in Texas." In *Texas Public School Organization and Administration*, edited by J. Vornberg. Dubuque, Iowa: Kendall/Hunt.

Vroom, V. (1964). *Work and Motivation*. New York: Wiley.

Walberg, H. (Ed.) (1979). *Educational Environments and Effects*. Berkeley, Calif.: McCutchan.

Wallace, R. (1995). *From Vision to Practice*. Thousand Oaks, Calif.: Corwin Press.

Weiner, B. (1986). *An Attribution Theory of Motivation & Emotion*. New York: Springer-Verlag.

Wheatley, M. (1992). *Leadership and the New Science*. San Francisco: Berrett-Koehler.

chapter 2 | *Skills in Policy and Governance*

Policy and governance are inextricably linked to influence, and school leaders are engaged in influencing internal and external audiences all the time. The process of influence is dynamic, relational, and situational. And though approachable perhaps with a scientific mind set, it remains an art that requires sophisticated use of formal and informal means of communication. (For more about communication, see Chapter 3.)

The issues with which school leaders deal are not trivial; they involve the justification of the larger social order (Getzels 1958). And because the most contentious issues of any social order are ethical and moral, school leaders become representatives of that moral order, and advocates of its majoritarian values. Therefore, for a school leader to engage in policy and governance issues requires "an insight into, if not a vision of, the nature of reality and into the ultimate purpose of the individual life," (Greenfield 1993, p. 222) a purpose thoroughly imbued with larger socio-cultural values, which makes the art of influence culturally specific and significant.

This chapter details the skills successful 21st century school leaders must possess to:

- Understand the system of public school governance in our democracy;
- Implement procedures for effective superintendent/school board and principal/site-based team relations;
- Formulate and shape policy;
- Demonstrate conflict-resolution and interpersonal sensitivity skills in working with groups whose values and opinions may conflict; and
- Establish collaborative, school-linked services.

The issues with which school leaders deal are not trivial; they involve the justification of the larger social order.

The Socio-Cultural Base for Exercising Skills in Policy and Governance

Governance is a formalized set of relations between individuals or groups. Building coalitions, developing policies, and working through problems of governance require consummate skills on the part of school leaders who work within the complex fabric of cultural, political, social, economic, and legal frameworks. Undergirding the school leader's work as a mediator of moral and ethical questions are critical understandings in the five domains of contract and truth, affiliation, life, property and law, and legal justice (Gibbs, Basinger, and Fuller 1992).

Contract and Truth

Contracts are forms of promise keeping. For example, school leaders engage in informal promise keeping when they offer to support teachers in maintaining classroom decisions about discipline or say that if innovative programs are developed the necessary resources to support them will be made available. Formal promise keeping involves legal documents such as those that govern conditions of employment, conference attendance, and budgetary support for classroom equipment acquisition. Promise keeping is necessary to support any system of school governance because it provides for organizational trust between participants in schools.

At the core of promise keeping is the faith that the exchanges between individuals and parties are based on truth. Truth, however, does not connote agreement. It simply means that explanations must be genuine. Disagreement is very much a part of building political consensus. Expression of disagreement is vital to developing workable coalitions, which depend on promise keeping and truth telling.

Affiliation

Affiliation refers to interpersonal relationships and friendships and includes perceptions of work obligations and duties. Affiliation deals with the exchanges between leaders and followers and how those exchanges occur, whether as quid pro quo agreements or altruistic understandings. At the core of affiliation is the expectation that directives or suggestions will be obeyed or heeded.

Mature affiliation in human relationships involves empathic role-taking and generalized caring (Gibbs et al. 1992). As Beck (1994, p. 20) indicates, the purposes of caring are to promote human development and to respond to human needs. A commitment between people who care "shifts from being a conditional act dependent on merit or whim, and moves . . . toward being an unconditional act marked by acceptance, nurturance, and grace." Affiliation is the hallmark of the interdependent network of relationships necessary to form a learning community.

Life

Because life is precious, it is everyone's duty to help others reach their potential. Education, therefore, is one of the most important duties because it enriches life; it is central to character development and the construction of conscience. Children must be wisely taught in order to use the gifts they have been given. The purpose of school policy and governance is to maximize the value of time spent teaching children.

Property and Law

Schools are directly concerned with teaching justifications for the laws that enable a stable social system to persist. School values concerning order and control are foundational to preventing social lawlessness. The creation of laws make life (in and out of schools) more enjoyable and harmonious. Laws exist, after all, for the common good and can be changed within the system through proper channels as warranted.

Legal Justice

The idea of deterrence, that is, actions taken against policy breakers, is central to school administration. School leaders may have to mete out punishments for rules or policy infractions that range from reprimand to severing employment for staff and reprimand to expulsion for students. Dealing with law and policy breakers prevents the social structure from dissolving into chaos. If everyone's rights are to be protected, those who abuse others' rights must be confronted and stopped. A school governance structure codifies the duties involved with legal justice through policies that describe expected behavior and how school leaders are to act to ensure that such policies are followed.

Understanding the System of Public School Governance in Our Democracy

Former New York Commissioner of Education Edward B. Nyquist once remarked that local control in American education was a minor branch of theology (Murphy 1980). His comment aptly captures American sentiments about the sanctity of elementary and secondary education staying close to the citizenry. The founding of American education in the New World was decidedly connected to events in the Old, notably the Protestant revolution. Many settlers in America were persecuted Protestants. Of these groups, the Calvinistic Puritans contributed the most to the educational system of America.

By 1640, nearly 20,000 Puritans had migrated to New England (Cubberley 1948). Their form of government was the town meeting, and from this unit came the town grammar school. In fact, the roots of the modern-day board of education can be traced back to the time when a few select men of the town committee tended to education (Flinchbaugh 1993).

It was in the New England states that the local school district was created. Rural areas were called "districts," and when attempts to transfer teachers to these units failed, the legislature simply delegated to these units the power to hire teachers and establish a curriculum. During Western expansion, Americans took the local school district concept with them. That organizational pattern fit the circumstances perfectly at a time when the "population was sparse, travel was difficult, the obligations of state government were small, and educational aspirations were low" (Butts and Cremin 1953, p. 104).

The State's Role

The state's role in education was advanced in 1647 in New England with the Old Deluder Satan Act. The act prescribed that towns of 50 or more households had to employ a teacher of reading and writing, and towns with 100 or more households had to provide a grammar school that would prepare students to attend the university (Cubberley 1948). The establishment of schools by state statute 130 years before the U.S. Constitution explains why that founding document was silent on the subject of education.

The Old Deluder Satan Act was precedent-setting in that it was premised on the assumption that:

- Universal education of the young was related to the well-being of the state;
- While the obligation of education of the young was a parental responsibility, the state had the right to enforce that obligation;
- The state could fix a standard for education and its proper content and determine a minimum amount of education to be offered;
- Public money could be raised through a general tax to support education; and
- Schooling beyond the rudiments could also be supplied by the state to prepare some youngsters to attend the university.
 (G. Martin as cited in Cubberley 1948)

Since the Puritans, the local school district, functioning within the apparatus of state control, has been the dominant form of educational operations in American schools, despite the fact that the number of local school districts has been steadily shrinking due to consolidation. In 1932, there were 127,422 school districts, of which over 40 percent were contained in the 12-state North Central region (Greider, Pierce, and Rosenstengel 1961). In 1945, this number had been reduced to 103,000; by 1957, the number of local school districts had decreased to 53,000 (AASA 1958). By the 1990s, the number had dropped to below 16,000. All the while, the number of schools has risen.

As the number of school districts has decreased, the power and authority of the state agency in public education has increased. Since the 1960s, a relentless wave of successive laws has brought forth greater state control of curriculum, increased testing and public reporting of test results, expanded mandates to serve special education populations, and minimum competency standards for teachers and students. Between 1983 and 1985 alone, "state legislatures enacted more than 700 statutes stipulating what should be taught, when it should be taught, and by whom it should be taught" (Futrell 1989).

Roberts and Murray (1995) summarize the states' statutory initiatives between 1987 and 1992 as follows:

Number of Statutes	Percentage	Statute Area of Emphasis
50	15	curriculum changes
48	14	teacher certification
45	13	community involvement
45	13	accountability
33	10	restructuring
31	9	personnel roles
30	9	schools of choice
29	8.5	merit pay/career ladders
29	8.5	school-based management
340	100.00	**TOTAL**

Educational change fostered by the states is rampant with tensions between powerful groups of superintendents and the agendas developed by agencies (Madsen 1994), and many reforms run amuck because of the lack of understanding of the differences between local and state cultures and priorities (Fitzpatrick 1996).

The Federal Role

The federal role in U.S. education has shifted over time as well. A federal department of education was established during the Grant administration in 1867. It had a staff of three clerks and a budget of $18,600 (Lunenburg and Ornstein 1991). Over the subsequent decades, the federal education function was pigeon-holed in the Department of Interior, the Federal Security Agency, and the Department of Health, Education and Welfare. The National Institute of Education (NIE), a research arm of the federal government, was established during the Nixon administration. The NIE was the initial administrative structure behind the federal labs and research centers (Bell 1988).

In 1976, President Jimmy Carter pushed for and got a cabinet-level Department of Education as a payback to the National Education Association for its support in his successful election bid (Kirst 1984). By 1989, the Department of Education employed more than 4,525 persons administering over 200 separate programs requiring budgetary expenditures of nearly $25 billion (Department of Education 1989).

The federal education policy strategy consists of two prongs. The first rests on coercion (i.e., the use of legal sanctions against the states and local boards to meet the requirements of education law). The second centers on capacity building through technical assistance. Federal assistance to promote capacity building is contingent upon constructing successful means to implement proven or promising research-based practices in the schools (Elmore and McLaughlin 1982).

The Protestant world view on which our system is rooted, however, is deeply suspicious of centralized forms of political control. Antipathy toward centralized forms of education, especially federal education, is still virulent and alive (see Manatt 1995). The most recent fracas occurred over national tests proposed by the Clinton administration. One of the key issues was dislodging the oversight of the tests from the Department of Education to an independent governing board because of fears of politicization (Kronholz 1997, Finn 1997, Lawton 1997).

Local school boards. In contrast to European and Asian nations, the United States continues to rely on local school boards, despite calls for change. Nearly 40 years ago, Conant (1964) identified this reliance and the lack of a national educational policy as a major deficiency in American education. That the problem has not been resolved and is hindering American school achievement continues to be underscored by educational theorists and researchers (McAdams 1993).

Archbald (1993) found in a study of a sample of proposals submitted by local educators to President George Bush's national call for "Next Century Schools" sponsored by the private sector that local school districts and schools applying for funds primarily proposed "add-ons" to the existing organizational structure, rarely challenging the efficacy of existing arrangements. Archbald (1993, p.393) summarized his research by noting:

> Clearly, a daunting challenge confronts reformers envisioning sweeping structural changes in our schools. The vast majority of schools experience no pressure to embark on big changes and get no extra resources — and bold and visionary change is far from the minds of two and a half million teachers and principals showing up for work each morning.

Conant (1964, p. 110) summed up his view about the problems of reliance upon local school boards by saying that "without a drastic Constitutional amendment, nobody is in a position to establish an educational policy in the United States." And Finn (1992) flatly declares that local school boards are not only superfluous, but dysfunctional.

Shannon (1992, p. 31), on the other hand, claims local school governance performs the following indispensable functions:

- Translation of federal and state laws into local action efforts;
- Mediation of educational testing against the context of community characteristics;
- Evaluation of the entire educational program on behalf of the community;
- Monitoring of the work of the superintendent and teaching staff; and
- Service as the final appellate body short of court action on appeals of citizens and employees regarding administrative decisions.

These functions are so critical, according to Shannon, that if local school boards did not exist, they would have to be invented.

Implementing Procedures for Effective Superintendent/School Board and Principal/Site-Based Team Relations

Like the state and federal roles in education, the role played by school administrators has also evolved over time. The first shift came when the principal–teacher role turned into a full-time principalship in large schools. The second change came with the creation of the chief financial officer on school boards — a position designed so that one board member could devote full time to fiduciary responsibilities. This change and the next, the hiring of superintendents, created the problem of "dual control" as two chief executive officers were then reporting to the board, thus violating the principle of a single line of authority (Cubberley 1929). Vestiges of this problem remain today in public school systems.

Superintendent/School Board Relations

The superintendent/school board relationship is the most problematic in local school district governance today, and has been called a "fulcrum of conflict" (English 1992). Part of the problem stems from the fact that school boards ran things for a long time before school administrators ever appeared on the educational scene (Institute for Educational Leadership 1986). As the U.S. population mushroomed in the cities, school boards became larger and larger. Eventually, the size of boards became unwieldy, sometimes including dozens of citizens. Graft became common on some city school boards as teacher positions were sold to the highest bidder. Even Boss Tweed of New York's Tammany Hall became a board member and systematically plundered the city's schools (Ravitch 1974).

Part of the call for a change in school governance as a general thrust of municipal reform came from the newly minted university professors-turned-efficiency-experts (Callahan 1962). These experts argued for the hiring of a full-time school administrator who would report to the board of education (Spring 1986). Also as part of general reform, school boards were reduced to the 5-12 member range most common today (Nasaw 1979; Button and Provenzo 1989).

The superintendent's duties were carved from the board's overall responsibilities for the oversight of the schools. A theoretical dividing line was drawn that gave boards the power to determine policy and superintendents responsibility for executing policy. While conceptually clean, the line has proven elusive or non-existent in the day-to-day realities of governing schools (Institute for Educational Leadership 1986, Streshly and Frase 1993, Nichols 1996). Part of the problem is that the board's first responsibility — to develop policy — is actually one of most board's greatest weaknesses (White 1962). At the same time, the power of the superintendency to engage in management was "derived ... much more from common consent than from state law or resolution of the board of education (Department of Superintendence of the NEA 1923, as cited in Cunningham and Hentges 1982, p.23).

This unclear division of duties and lack of skill has resulted in a great deal of superintendent/board conflict, which was noticed by the public as early as 1895 (Callahan 1966). In a 1971 AASA study of the American superintendency, the "low caliber of board members" ranked third among the six most pressing matters confronted by respondents. Administrator/board relations ranked sixth of 20 challenges to the superintendency in the 1982 AASA study and remained sixth in the 1992 study (see Glass 1992). Also in the 1992 study, "conflict with board members" ranked second of 11 reasons why superintendents actually left their jobs.

The need for policies. One of the most effective ways to reduce superintendent/board conflict is to have a solid set of district policies. Up-to-date, written policies (White 1962, p. 63):

• Foster improved superintendent/board relationships by clarifying each party's sphere of influence;
• Reduce the pressures of special interest groups;
• Foster continuity, stability, and consistency of board actions;
• Save time and effort by eliminating the necessity of having to make a decision each time a recurring situation develops;
• Facilitate the orderly review of board practices;
• Help in the orientation of new board members;
• Enable staff members to understand the nature of their work better and how it relates to the overall activities of the school system;
• Facilitate the improvement of staff morale by providing uniform and fair treatment;
• Keep the public and school staff informed of board actions; and
• Provide citizens with a better understanding of ways they can work with school administrators to build a good school system.

Superintendents who want to develop sound working relationships with their boards of education should heed the fact that boards were there first in the business of school governance. Therefore, it is the board "sharing" their work, and not the superintendent sharing his or hers (Konnert and Augenstein 1990). When the board meets, it's the "board's meeting" not "the superintendent's meeting to which the board is invited."

A seasoned superintendent understands that it is critical for the board to make independent judgments, and that those judgments depend upon a clear recommendation from their executive officer. Superintendents must work to enable their boards to make good decisions by providing them with full information in a timely manner. In the 1992 AASA superintendent study, 93.9 percent of board members surveyed indicated that the superintendent was a "very great" source of information. A superintendent who complains that a board made a bad decision but who did not provide board members with all of the data and reasonable time upon which to formulate a judgment has only himself/herself to blame for the quality of that decision.

School board members, on the other hand, must remember that the superintendent is not there to tell them what they want to hear, but what they must hear. The board cannot afford to "kill the messenger" if the superintendent shares a problem or points out troubles in the school district. Boards cannot play "gotcha" with their superintendent and expect honesty and a full account of the strengths and weaknesses of school operations.

Board members who strike secret deals with their constituencies and fail to keep the superintendent informed play a deadly game with their superintendent's tenure. The average tenure of the American school superintendent in 1992 was 6.47 years (Glass 1992), and urban superintendents are even more mobile. In a survey conducted by Ornstein (1990) of the 86 largest school districts in the nation, fully 48 percent of the districts' superintendents had been in their positions for less than five years.

Principal/Site-Based Teams

One visible trend in school governance is a move toward site-based management (SBM). SBM is based on the notion that small is better because change occurs in individual schools much more quickly than in larger ones. Supporters of SBM assert that because parents and students identify with schools and not the more impersonal school district, it is much easier to involve teachers, students, and parents in change through the local school unit (Levine and Eubanks 1992, Murphy and Beck 1995). Most of the research on SBM, however, reveals that, while popular, it is "primarily a symbolic response" rather than a deep reform (Malen, Ogawa, and Kranz 1991, p. 327). A review by Reitzug and Capper (1996) reached the same conclusions, but sketched out hope that ultimately SBM could become a substantive reform.

One focus of SBM is the idea of empowerment, particularly teacher empowerment (Blase and Blase 1994), but some SBM research paints a different picture. Radnofsky (1994) found in a study of 30 teachers in Chicago that few opted for empowerment. Teachers, noted Radnofsky, "chose instead their traditional realms of power — their classrooms — over reform-mandated 'empowerment.' Principals still held the key to how much involvement teachers really had in schools."

Levine and Eubanks (1992) identify the following as problems with school site councils and empowerment:

- Inadequate time, training, and technical assistance;

- Difficulties in stimulating consideration and acceptance of inconvenient changes;
- Unresolved issues involving administrative leadership and enhanced power among participants;
- Constraints on teacher participation in decision making;
- Reluctance of administrators at all levels to give up traditional prerogatives; and
- Restrictions imposed by school board, state, and federal regulations and by contracts with teacher organizations.

The "'Lone Ranger-take-charge' [administrator] is doomed to failure in the context of SBM" because an administrator's expertise in working with small groups is key to making SBM work — expertise that must be accompanied by "the ability to forge a shared vision, to promote local autonomy, and to develop consensus amid diversity" (Wardzala and Murphy 1995, p. 9). Herman, Herman, and Oliver (1995) studied the impact of the implementation of SBM in 12 Southern states and concluded that primary barriers to SBM include principal reluctance to share power and teacher aversion to participating and using power. Their study concluded that "the educational leaders who are to implement school-based management must be recruited with a careful eye toward the skills, knowledge, and attitudes required for successful implementation" (p.465). In too many cases, principals still rule SBM councils because of inadequate preparation in group dynamics.

Formulating and Shaping Policy To Provide Quality Education for Children and Youth

School policy is "the official choice of a school board or local school to achieve a purpose systematically and consistently" (Gallagher 1992, p. 3). The common elements of policy are that it is a formal act based on consensus as agreed-upon intent; it receives the official sanction or approval of an institutional body or authority; and it provides a consistent standard for assessing actions and outcomes. The 1982 AASA study of superintendents found that, "Regardless of district enrollment, superintendents view themselves as in control of policy development" (Hentges 1982, p. 71). In the 1992 AASA study, 67 percent of superintendent respondents indicated that they were the initiators of new policies in their school systems.

Superintendents base policy formulation on six kinds of policy arguments (Dunn 1981). These policy arguments are:

- Authoritative — justifying a policy advocated by an expert or a higher power. Example: developing a policy based on research or one recommended by state school boards association.
- Intuitive — justifying a policy based on inner mental states or judgments. Example: creating a policy based on an idea of "fairness" or "equity."
- Analycentric — justifying a policy using rules or common procedures. Example: using basic steps of the scientific method to lay out steps for problem solving.
- Explanatory — justifying a policy based on causes and effects or laws. Example: developing lab safety procedures based on known properties of chemicals.
- Pragmatic — justifying a policy using similarities among cases. Example: defining school-related services for known groups of similar students (e.g., students with learning disabilities).
- Value-critical — justifying policy based on ethical or moral principles. Example: postulating that tougher academic standards are essential to basic civil rights.

The essential steps of developing policy are: (1) defining the problem; (2) developing criteria for making choices; (3) developing alternatives, models, and decisions; (4) determining political feasibility; (5) engaging in policy choice; and (6) repeating the cycle (MacRae and Wilde 1979). Problem definition is perhaps the most crucial of the steps in creating effective policies.

Policies, however, rarely innovate school practices. Most are politically conservative and aimed at reinforcing the status quo, and they often reflect prevailing political arrangements and orthodoxies (Bowman and Haggerson 1992). For example, Spring (1989) has shown how federal mandates have moved toward creating improved efficiency in the workforce by using the schools as social sorting machines. And, according to Weinberg (1967), before racial integration, when establishing neighborhood schools, the proximity of a child's home to a school became one standard in assigning schools, but such a benchmark was reserved for white children. African-American children had to walk to assigned schools, which were often not in their neighborhoods, in order to maintain practices of school segregation.

Successful school leaders must work to develop and implement policies that ensure a high-quality education for all students, not maintenance of the status quo.

Demonstrating Conflict-Resolution and Interpersonal Sensitivity Skills When Working with Groups Whose Values and Opinions May Conflict

In the 1992 AASA superintendent survey (Glass 1992), respondents identified the board of education, ineffective staff members, inadequate

Areas of Conflict and Associated Coping Strategies

Area of Conflict	Coping Strategies		
	Avoidance	Collective Bargaining (win-lose)	Collective Gaining (win-win)
-Access to power	Refuse to discuss	Power plays	Power sharing
-Access to resources	Distribute by formula	Win more by leveraging	Consensus
-Access to rewards	Distribute by category	Increase by leveraging	Sharing

financing, racial and ethnic problems, state reform mandates, and collective bargaining issues as areas of conflict that impinged on their effectiveness. The following table summarizes the three major areas of conflict for both organizational (internal) and extra-organizational (external) issues. These areas pertain to access to power, resources, and rewards.

At any given time, some groups within and outside school systems desire changes in the system's allocation of resources and the dispersal of rewards, while others work to maintain the status quo. The most common false arguments used by change resisters include(Odiorne 1981, pp. 76-77):

- We have already tried that.
- The boss won't approve that.
- That is against our policy.
- Somebody else tried that and it failed.
- That would cost too much.

The first ploy used by change resisters to maintain the status quo is to refuse to discuss change, particularly related to access to resources and rewards.

Collective Bargaining and Collective Gaining

In collective bargaining, which views power as attainable and finite, conflict is produced as parties engage in a struggle for more power and threaten each other through withholding services, boycotts, and lock-outs. Power must be "won" according to the collective bargaining outlook. Conflict over resources and rewards can be avoided somewhat by depersonalizing the allocation using formulae and rules, categories, and schedules. When unions and organized groups press for changes in rules, categories, or schedules by employing forceful confrontations involving blocking or shutting down services or operations through demonstrations, picket lines, sit-ins, boycotts, or strikes, the perspective supporting their tactics is collective bargaining — a "win-lose" mentality.

The collective gaining perspective is based on the belief that shared power means more power for everyone. This perspective views power as expandable and infinite (Herman and Megiveron 1993). Collective gaining depends on arriving at consensus about resources and rewards based on power sharing. It relies upon consensus building, which requires a great deal of honest communication between all parties. Because school leaders usually enter into these discussions with more authority than other participants, it is important that they do so with an open mind and that they view power sharing as positive for all parties.

Functional Conflict

Conflict itself is neither positive nor negative. In fact, conflict is functional when "it moves the organization from stagnation to generation; it stimulates and energizes. Ideas and issues are often clarified. Productivity increases and creative problem solving is exhibited" (Johnson and Evans 1997, p.42). Dysfunctional conflict results in organizational chaos and reduced capacity to engage in problem solving or other creative activities. At the school building level, nearly 75 percent of a principal's time is consumed with interpersonal contact (Martin and Willower 1981). The principal is the key agent in constructing a collaborative culture that sees conflict as healthy and recognizes and uses it to improve communication, trust, and consensus building (Leithwood, Begley, and Cousins 1992).

As school sites become more decentralized and collaborative in nature, new types of conflicts may emerge. For example, Parkay, Shindler, and Oaks (1997) found that as teacher-leaders assumed greater responsibility for school improvement in a high school moving toward collaborative decision making and restructuring, previously dormant hostilities emerged among the faculty along gender and departmental lines and due to differing value orientations. As collaboration increased, conflict did also. The collective gaining perspective and skills in consensus building are the key to success during such power reallocations.

Cultural Diversity and Conflict

Given the increasing heterogeneity of American society, schools must move beyond seeing cultural diversity as something to be tolerated to seeing it as an opportunity to move forward through functional conflict. School leaders can begin by replacing the monoculturalism that has been the hallmark of curriculum and instructional practices (Nieto 1992). Administrators must move beyond merely showing sensitivity to differences through actions such as adding on "Black History Week," to creating schools that incorporate integrated, multicultural perspectives throughout(Cordeiro, Reagan, and Martinez 1994).

Establishing Collaborative, School-Linked Services

Clearly, American education functions in a peculiar combination of local, state, and federal jurisdictions. The current intergovernmental collaboration, however, works well for only 20 percent of the nation's students (Hodgkinson 1993). Therefore, the nature of interagency jurisdiction must be redefined to include the private sector and collaboration with business and other community service organizations. This trend is called collaborative, school-linked services, and is based on (Schorr and Schorr 1988):

- Belief in the need for intensive, comprehensive services that address the "whole" child and the community;
- Realization that the family should not be displaced or replaced, but supported by social service agencies; and
- A commitment to change from remediation strategies to earlier ones of intervention and prevention.

Between 1975 and 1989, 20 interagency commissions were formed to foster collaboration between state and local agencies, and 63 such programs were implemented (Levy and Copple 1989). Research by Wang, Haertel, and Walberg (1997) on several hundred collaborative, school-linked services educational sites found three important variations:

- Single versus multisite programs;
- Publicly versus privately sponsored programs; and
- Direct service providers versus referral networks.

The general characteristics important at all of the sites studied include (Wang, Haertel, and Walberg 1997, pp. 42-48):

- A focus on the whole family versus an exclusively student/youth orientation;
- Support from top levels of educational and agency hierarchies;
- Use of case management as opposed to categorizing clients according to separate problems;
- Collaborative outreach to families and students;
- Clearly defined goals; and
- Use of family-based outcomes (e.g., helping family members gain access to basic education, achieve in functional literacy, obtain the GED,

increase income, and obtain employment, along with an overall focus on parental involvement).

Steffy and Lindle (1994, pp.75-77) have developed a 10-step process for developing an interagency improvement plan. The steps are:

(1) Defining the issue/problem/need.
(2) Gathering information about the issue/problem/need.
(3) Diagnosing the problem and analyzing obstacles to achieving the desired state.
(4) Finding general solutions.
(5) Discussing and evaluating the solutions.
(6) Choosing solutions to be implemented.
(7) Presenting completed plans.
(8) Implementing the plans.
(9) Evaluating results.
(10) Summarizing and communicating progress over time.

Because schools are part of wider societal processes, prevailing social practices and beliefs are reproduced in them in countless ways (Cole 1988, Giroux 1994). Laws and customs often cement this correspondence and later have to be overcome. School leaders, therefore, must develop a mind set that sees and works with the countless *communities* working within and around schools to benefit students (Flinchbaugh 1993).

Conclusion

In this chapter, we have examined the American context for the operation and governance of schools and school systems. Our examination of this democratic and highly decentralized system has highlighted the need for educational leaders (superintendents, principals, school board members, site-based teams) to work together and with the community to improve education; for school leaders to be adept at conflict-resolution and consensus-building skills and to value diversity; and for the formulation of effective local school policies to improve operational effectiveness and efficiency. We have seen clearly that even as teachers and parents become increasingly involved in school governance, the leadership of committed educational administrators remains crucial to successful change and restructuring.

Use the following Skill Accomplishment Checklist to assess you skill level on each of the important topics discussed in this chapter.

31

Skill Accomplish Checklist for Chapter 2

Skills	Readings and Activities for Skill Mastery
Understand the system of public school governance in our democracy.	**Readings:** Bell (1988), Finn (1992), Kirst (1984), McAdams (1993), Spring (1986), **Activities:** 1. List strengths and weaknesses of the system of school governance in the United States. 2. Indicate how the three levels of governance have changed over time in the United States.
Describe procedures for effective superintendent/board and principal/site-based team relationships.	**Readings:** Bailey (1991), Blase and Blase (1994), Callahan(1962, 1966), Konnert and Augenstein(1990), Murphy and Beck (1995) **Activities:** 1. Attend a local board meeting and observe how the superintendent and the board relate to one another. Note any areas of conflict or tension. 2. Interview principals functioning under a form of site-based management. Then interview teachers who are members of the site-based team. Discuss your findings.
Formulate and shape policy to provide quality education for children and youth.	**Readings:** Gallagher (1992), Giroux(1994) **Activities:** 1. Obtain a copy of your local school board's policy manual. Interview the superintendent or board president about how the latest adopted policy was developed. 2. Analyze five local board policies. Identify the kind of policy arguments in each.
Demonstrate conflict-resolution and interpersonal sensitivity skills in working with groups whose values and opinions may conflict.	**Readings:** Dyer (1977), Janis and Mann (1979), Nieto (1992), Cordeiro et al. (1994), Steffy and Lindle(1994) **Activities:** 1. Select past areas of conflict in your school district or school and analyze whether they were caused by disagreement over power, resource, or reward disbursement. Write about how they were resolved. 2. Engage in a team-building exercise with a group of colleagues. Try to anticipate obstacles that will have to be overcome to reduce potential sources of conflict.
Establish collaborative, school-linked services.	**Readings:** Kirst (1984) **Activities:** 1. List the advantages and disadvantages of school-linked services in your community. 2. Develop a proposal to pilot school-linked services in your school or district.

Resources

American Association of School Administrators. (1971). *The American School Superintendency*. Edited by S. Knezevich. Washington, D.C.: National Education Association.

American Association of School Administrators. (1958). *School District Organization*. Joint publication of AASA and the National Education Association. Washington, D.C.: National Education Association.

Archbald, D. (October 1993). "Restructuring in the Eyes of Practitioners: An Analysis of 'Next Century' School Restructuring Proposals." *International Journal of Educational Reform* 2,4: 384-398.

Bailey, W. (1991). *School-Site Management Applied*. Lancaster, Pa.: Technomic Pub. Co., Inc.

Beck, L. (1994). *Reclaiming Educational Administration as a Caring Profession*. New York: Teachers College Press.

Bell, T. (1988). *The Thirteenth Man: A Reagan Cabinet Memoir*. New York: The Free Press.

Blase, J., and R. Blase. (1994). *Empowering Teachers*. Thousand Oaks, Calif.: Corwin Press.

Bowman, A., and N. Haggerson. (1992) "Means of Informing Educational Policy and Practice Through Interpretive Inquiry." In *Informing Educational Policy and Practice Through Interpretive Inquiry*, edited by N. Haggerson and A. Bowman. Lancaster, Pa.: Technomic Pub. Co., Inc.

Button, H., and E. Provenzo. (1989). *History of Education and Culture in America*. Englewood Cliffs, New Jersey: Prentice-Hall.

Butts, R., and L. Cremin. (1953). *A History of Education in American Culture*. New York: Henry Holt and Company.

Callahan, R. (1966). *The Superintendent of Schools: A Historical Analysis*. Eugene, Ore.: ERIC.

Callahan, R. (1962). *Education and the Cult of Efficiency*. Chicago: University of Chicago Press.

Chambliss, J. (1987). *Educational Theory as Theory of Conduct*. Albany, New York: SUNY Press.

Clough, D. (1984). *Decisions in Public and Private Sectors: Theories, Practices and Processes*. Englewood Cliffs, N.J.: Prentice-Hall.

Cole, M. (1988). *Bowles and Gintis Revisited: Correspondence and Contradiction in Educational Theory*. London: The Falmer Press.

Conant, J. (1964). *Shaping Educational Policy*. New York: McGraw-Hill Book Company.

Cordeiro, P., T. Reagan, and L. Martinez. (1994). *Multiculturalism and TQE*. Thousand Oaks, Calif.: Corwin Press.

Cubberley, E. (1948). *The History of Education*. Boston: Houghton Mifflin Company.

Cubberley, E. (1929). *Public School Administration*. Boston: Houghton Mifflin Company.

Cunningham, L., and J. Hentges. (1982). "The Superintendency in Brief Historical Perspective." In *The American School Superintendency 1982*, edited by L. Cunningham and J. Hentges. Arlington, Va.: American Association of School Administrators.

Department of Education. *Digest of Education Statistics*. (1989). Washington, D.C.: Author.

Dunham, B. (1964). *Heroes and Heretics: A Social History of Dissent*. New York: Alfred A. Knopf.

Dunn, W. (1981). *Public Policy Analysis*. Englewood Cliffs, N.J. Prentice-Hall.

Dyer, W. (1977). *Team Building: Issues and Alternatives*. Reading, Mass.: Addison-Wesley.

Elmore, R., and M. McLaughlin. (1982). "Strategic Choice in Federal Education Policy: The Compliance-Assistance Trade-Off." In *Policy Making in Education*, edited by A. Lieberman and M. McLaughlin. Chicago: University of Chicago Press.

33

English, F. (1992). *Educational Administration: The Human Science.* New York: Harper Collins.

Finn, C. (September 9, 1997). "Throw These Tests Out of School." *Wall Street Journal* A18.

Finn, C. (1992). "Reinventing Local Control." In *School Boards: Changing Local Control,* edited by P. First and H. Walberg. Berkeley, Calif.: McCutchan Publishing Corp.

Fitzpatrick, J. (October 1996). "Re: Learning: Exposing the Culture." *International Journal of Educational Reform* 5,4: 429-437.

Flinchbaugh, R. (1993). *The 21st Century Board of Education.* Lancaster, Pa: Technomic Pub. Co., Inc.

Futrell, M. (1989). "Mission Not Accomplished: Education Reform in Retrospective." *Phi Delta Kappan* 71, 1: 8-14.

Gallagher, K. (1992). *Shaping School Policy.* Newbury Park, Calif.: Corwin Press.

Gardner, H. (1995). *Leading Minds: An Anatomy of Leadership.* New York: Basic Books.

Getzels, J. (1958). "Administration as a Social Process." In *Administrative Theory in Education,* edited by A. Halpin. New York: MacMillan.

Gibbs, J., K. Basinger, and D. Fuller. (1992). *Moral Maturity: Measuring the Development of Sociomoral Reflection.* Hillsdale, N.J.: Lawrence Erlbaum Associates Publishers.

Giroux, H. (Spring 1994). "Teachers, Public Life, and Curriculum Reform." *Peabody Journal of Education* 69: 35-47.

Giroux, H., and P. MacLean. (April 1992). "American 2000 and the Politics of Erasure: Democracy and Cultural Difference Under Siege." *International Journal of Educational Reform* 1, 2: 99-110.

Glass, T. (1992). *The 1992 Study of the American School Superintendency.* Arlington, Va.: American Association of School Administrators.

Grady, M., and M. Bryant. (1991). "School Board Turmoil and Superintendent Turnover." *The School Administrator* 48, 2: 23.

Greenfield, T., and P. Ribbons. (1993). *Greenfield on Educational Administration.* New York: Routledge.

Greider, C., T. Pierce, and W. Rosenstengel. (1961). *Public School Administration.* New York: The Ronald Press Company.

Guthrie, J. (October 15, 1997). "The Paradox of Educational Power." *Education Week* 17,7: 34.

Hentges, J.(1982). "Superintendent-School Board Relationships." In *The American School Superintendency 1982,* edited by L. Cunningham and J. Hentges. Arlington, Va.: American Association of School Administrators.

Herman, J., J. Herman, and V. Oliver. (October 1995). "A Study of Site-Based Management in Selected Southern States." *International Journal of Educational Reform* 4, 4: 460-466.

Herman, J., and G. Megiveron. (1993). *Collective Bargaining in Education: Win/Win, Win/Lose, Lose/Lose.* Lancaster, Pa.: Technomic Pub. Co., Inc.

Hodgkinson, H. (1993). "American Education: The Good, the Bad, and the Task." *Phi Delta Kappan* 74: 619-623.

Institute for Educational Leadership. (1986). *School Boards.* Washington, D.C.: Author.

Janis, I., and L. Mann. (1979). *Decision Making: A Psychological Analysis of Conflict, Choice, and Commitment.* New York: The Free Press.

Johnson, P., and J. Evans. (January 1997). "Power, Communicator Styles, and Conflict Management Styles: A Web of Interpersonal Constructs for the School Principal." *International Journal of Educational Reform* 6, 1: 40-53.

Kirst, M. (1984). *Who Controls Our Schools?* New York: W.H. Freeman and Company.

Konnert, M., and J. Augenstein. (1990). *The Superintendency in the Nineties.* Lancaster, Pa.: Technomic Pub. Co., Inc.

Kronholz, J. (September 8, 1997). "Opponents Sharpen Pencils Over National Testing Plan." *Wall Street Journal* A20.

Lawton, M. (October 1,1997). "Riley Delays National Tests' Development." *Education Week* 15, 5: 1, 27.

Leithwood, K., P. Begley, and J. Cousins. (1992). *Developing Expert Leadership for Future Schools.* London: The Falmer Press.

Levine, D., and E. Eubanks. (1992). "Site-Based Management: Engine for Reform or Pipedream? Problems, Prospects, Pitfalls, and Prerequisites for Success." In *Restructuring the Schools,* edited by J. Lane and E. Epps. Berkeley, Calif.: McCutchan Publishing Corp.

Levy, J., and C. Copple.(1989). *Joining Forces: A Report from the First Year.* Alexandria, Va.: National Association of State Boards of Education.

Lunenburg, F., and A. Ornstein. (1991). *Educational Administration: Concepts and Practices.* Belmont, Calif.: Wadsworth.

MacRae, D., Jr., and J. Wilde. (1979). *Policy Analysis for Public Decisions.* Belmont, Calif.: Wadsworth.

Madsen, J. (1994). *Educational Reform at the State Level: The Politics and Problems of Implementation.* Washington, D.C.: The Falmer Press.

Malen, B., T. Ogawa, and J. Kranz. (1991). "What Do We Know About School-Based Management? A Case Study of the Literature — A Call for Research." *In Choice and Control in American Education,* edited by W. Clune and J. Witte. New York: The Falmer Press.

Manatt, R. (1995). *When Right Is Wrong: Fundamentalists and the Public Schools.* Lancaster, Pa.: Technomic Pub. Co., Inc.

Martin, W., and D. Willower. (1981). "The Managerial Behavior of High School Principals." *Educational Administration Quarterly* 17, 1: 69-90.

McAdams, R. (1993). *Lessons from Abroad: How Other Countries Educate Their Children.* Lancaster, Pa.: Technomic Pub. Co., Inc.

Murphy, J. (1980). "State Leadership in Education: On Being a Chief State School Officer." Policy Paper 9. Washington, D.C.: The George Washington University.

Murphy, J., and L. Beck. (1995). *School-Based Management as School Reform.* Thousand Oaks, Calif.: Corwin Press.

Nasaw, D. (1979). *Schooled to Order.* New York: Oxford University Press.

Nichols, J. (July 1996). "The Power Behind the Table: A Qualitative Analysis of Two School Board Members." *International Journal of Educational Reform* 5, 3: 318-325.

Nieto, S. (1992). *Affirming Diversity: The Sociopolitical Context of Multicultural Education.* New York: Longman.

Odiorne, G. (1981). *The Change Resisters.* Englewood Cliffs, N.J.: Prentice-Hall.

Ornstein, A. (November 14, 1990). "Dimensions: Tenure of Superintendents." *Education Week* 3.

Parkay, F., J. Shindler, and M. Oaks. (January 1997). "Creating a Climate for Collaborative, Emergent Leadership in an Urban High School." *International Journal of Educational Reform* 6, 1: 64-74.

Radnofsky, M. (April 1994). "Empowerment and the Power Not to Change: Teachers Perceptions of Restructuring." *International Journal of Educational Reform* 3, 2: 154-164.

Ravitch, D. (1974). *The Great School Wars.* New York: Basic Books.

Reitzug, U., and C. Capper. (January 1996). "Deconstructing Site-Based Management: Possibilities for Emancipation and Alternative Means of Control." *International Journal of Educational Reform* 5, 1: 56-69.

Roberts, R., and K. Murray. (April 1995). "State School Reform Legislation and Related Litigation." *International Journal of Educational Reform* 4, 2: 153-161.

Schorr, L., and D. Schorr. (1988). *Within Our Reach: Breaking the Cycle of Disadvantage.* New York: Anchor Books.

Shannon, T. (1992). "Local Control and Organizacrats." *In School Boards: Changing Local Control*, edited by P. First and J. Walberg Berkeley, Calif.: McCutchan Publishing Corp.

Spring, J. (1989). *The Sorting Machine Revisited.* New York: Longman.

Spring, J. (1986). *The American School 1642-1985.* New York: Longman.

Steffy, B., and J. Lindle. (1994). *Building Coalitions*. Thousand Oaks, Calif.: Corwin Press.

Streshly, W., and L. Frase. (April 1993). "School Boards: The Missing Piece of the Reform Pie." *International Journal of Educational Reform* 2, 2: 140-143.

Wang, M., G. Haertel, and H. Walberg. (1997). "Effective Features of Collaborative, School-Linked Services for Children in Elementary Schools: What Do We Know from Research and Practice?" *In Coordination, Cooperation, Collaboration: What We Know About School-Linked Services,* edited by G. Haertel and M. Wang. Philadelphia, Pa.: The Mid-Atlantic Regional Educational Laboratory.

Wardzala, E., and J. Murphy. (Spring/Summer 1994). "School-Based Management and the Role of the Superintendent: Lessons from Coalition Schools." *Planning and Changing 25:1/2,* 18.

Weinberg, M. (1967). *Race and Place: A Legal History of the Neighborhood School.* Washington, D.C. U.S. Government Printing Office.

White, A. (1962). *Local School Boards: Organization and Practices.* Washington, D.C.: U.S. Government Printing Office.

chapter 3 | *Skills in Communication and Community Relations*

Effective communication refers to the school administrator's level of skill in using oral and written language. It involves the ability to present a vision that audiences understand and support, request and respond to community feedback, build consensus, and mediate conflict. Successful school administrators formulate and carry out plans for internal and external communications and build coalitions to gain financial and programmatic support for education.

School administrators, by virtue of their position, are looked upon as leaders. To be a true leader, however, requires more than holding an organizational role. To truly lead, administrators must be more than technically competent in planning, budgeting, curriculum design, scheduling, and facility renovation; they must be able to communicate with their constituencies, and they must have something worthwhile and important to say to them.

A leader's ability to communicate with followers is manifested in the narratives or stories he or she tells. The ability to tell the school story is vital to building support in the community. Howard Gardner (1995) has developed a cognitive approach to studying leadership that focuses on the stories leaders tell. According to Gardner,

> Leaders and audiences traffic in many stories, but the most basic ha[ve] to do with stories of identity . . . the story needs to make sense to audience members at this particular historical moment, in terms of where they have been and where they would like to go (p.14).

Listeners want stories they can relate to and understand, so leaders must call upon familiar, culturally specific signs and symbols. And because audiences hear a lot of stories, which compete with one another for their attention, the simpler the story, the more effective it is likely to be.

This chapter details the skills successful 21st century school leaders must possess to:

• Articulate the district or school vision, mission, and priorities to the community and mass media;

• Write and speak effectively;
• Demonstrate group leadership skills;
• Formulate strategies for passing referenda;
• Persuade the community to adopt initiatives that benefit students;
• Engage in effective community relations and school-business partnerships;
• Build consensus;
• Create opportunities for staff to develop collaboration and consensus-building skills;
• Integrate youth and family services into the regular school program; and
• Promote ongoing dialogue with representatives of diverse community groups.

Articulating the District or School Vision, Mission, and Priorities to the Community and Mass Media

As indicated in Chapter 1, effective school leaders have some concept or view of the future and are able to explain it to others. This explanation of the future usually assumes the form of a narrative. The crux of constructing a story with which audiences identify involves using familiar themes, symbols, and signs. The extent to which audiences identify with a leader's story is the extent to which they will "own" it.

How leaders are able to get their visions accepted is a subject discussed in much of the emerging research regarding successful school restructuring efforts. Parkay, Shindler, and Oaks (1997) report that in the successful restructuring of one urban high school, the principal articulated a clear, concise, compelling vision for what the school might become. Simultaneously, the staff, students, and community had to believe "that it [was] their vision . . . being enacted" (p.72). School leaders must remember that audiences more easily perceive a vision to be their own when it involves a story with which they can relate.

Vision, Mission and Goal Statements

For school leaders, a vision statement has no significance unless it is translated into authentic learning and shared school governance practices (Wallace, Engel, and Mooney 1997). Developing a mission statement is a process in which all or a portion of the vision statement is incorporated into tangible things, tasks, and methods—means that can be scheduled and assigned to persons to perform (Kauffman, Herman, and Watters 1996). The process can be broken into a series of steps:

(1) Construct an ideal vision (often referred to as "practical dreaming"). The vision statement represents a kind of "practical dreaming," usually about why individuals in the schools contribute to the larger society. Such statements are always utopian in some sense.

(2) Derive a mission statement. A mission statement is a general description of what the district or school does and how it carries out its role in society. It should be derived from the "ideal vision."

(3) Develop goal statements. Goal statements are more tangible and measurable than the overall mission statement. They should be stated in terms of results expected and not means to be employed to obtain them (Kauffman et al. 1996).

(4) Create educational functions and tasks related to each goal statement. As goal statements are translated into the life of the organization, they have to be broken into smaller components (i.e., goal indicators and task assignments).

(5) Development, operations, evaluation, renewal. As tasks are assigned, new tasks that are not part of the operations of the organization may have to become part of a training program(s). As people settle down to work, evaluation should take place to determine if the results desired are being obtained, and necessary adjustments should be made.

The importance of the vision from which all planning is generated is underscored by Mintzberg's (1994) critique of classical strategic planning. Mintzberg observes that a plan expressed as a vision is less constraining than a formal plan.

> Moreover, vision as a stimulant to action may be easier to come by, since it emerges from the head of a single leader instead of having to be agreed upon collectively . . . (p.293).

The development of plans cannot produce strategies or evoke a vision. In fact, planning and developing strategy may drive out vision. "Put more boldly, if you have no vision but only formal plans, then every unpredicted change in the environment makes you feel like your sky is falling" (Mintzberg 1994, p. 210). It is up to school leaders to communicate a vision for schools that increases public support and focuses productive action.

Writing and Speaking Effectively

Verbal Communication

For school leaders, linguistic competence is the key to building relationships with staff and constituents. The bulk of a school administrator's communication, both with individuals and groups, is verbal. School leaders speak in a variety of contexts about issues ranging from taxation and finance to collective bargaining disputes and issues of interest to community pressure groups.

Universal principles. Several universal principles exist for verbal interaction. According to DeVito (1983), the universal principles for verbal interaction are:

- Adjustment. Verbal communication is a system of culturally configured signals. For individuals to communicate they must share the same system of signals. Because no two sets of signals are exactly alike, even within the same language system, some adjustment is always necessary for communication to be effective.

- Imminent Reference. All verbal communication takes place in a specific, immediate context, which affects how it is received. This is likely why Lincoln's Gettysburg Address was given on a great battlefield, not in a comfortable parlor.

- Determinism. All messages are determined; that is, all messages have meaning. The full range of human communication is purposeful. Moreover, it is nearly impossible not to communicate. Even silence often sends a message.

- Recurrence. Communication evolves into patterns. School leaders' messages take on familiar themes about the necessity for supporting high-quality schools, including the need to modernize facilities, change curricula, or adopt learning standards.

- Relativity of Signals and Noise. The difference between signals and noise is relative. For example, coughing may be noise during a formal speech, but it is a signal to a school nurse listening for symptoms of an illness.

• Reinforcement/Packaging. A communication package is the complete set of signals given by a speaker, including body posture, gestures, and facial expressions as well as what is expressed verbally. Listeners are acutely aware of dissonance within the communication package, so gestures, facial expressions, and body posture should match the verbal message being conveyed.

Effective speeches. The generic steps in developing a speech are: (1) selecting a topic and purpose, (2) analyzing the audience, (3) gathering materials to support your ideas, (4) organizing the body of the speech, (5) selecting a beginning and an end, (6) outlining the speech, and (7) determining the use of visual aids (Lucas 1986).

School leaders give three general types of speeches — speeches to inform, speeches to persuade, and speeches marking special occasions (Lucas 1986). Speeches designed to inform others might focus on the impact of new state legislation on local school practices, announce the beginning or end of collective bargaining, or explain the pros and cons of strategic planning. Speeches designed to persuade generally convey facts and might be given to build support for a bond issue or tax referendum, a move to site-based management, or adoption of a new discipline code for students. School leaders are also expected to speak at special occasions, including graduations, staff retirement parties, athletic banquets, and even funerals.

Written Communication

The bulk of school administrators' written communication is normally confined to brief messages designed to inform or persuade, namely memoranda and letters to staff, parents, students, citizens, other educational officials, and the board of education. Occasionally, administrators may also develop a longer form of communication, for example, a position paper on the district or school. School leaders must continuously improve their written and verbal communication skills to secure support from within the school district and the community.

Demonstrating Group Leadership Skills

School administrators constantly interact with groups: parent groups, teacher committees, groups of students, citizen groups, and community organi-

zations. A school leader's acceptability to a group is contingent upon his or her credibility, which has at least two elements. The first is competence; the second is trustworthines. Both of these elements are the result of perception. School leaders have credibility when perceived to be knowledgeable about the topic being discussed. Trustworthiness is the perception in the eyes of the group that a school leader is honest, interested in fair play, devoid of hidden agendas, and concerned about others.

Group leadership skills emerge around the needs of groups. Group needs are procedural, task related, and maintenance related. Procedural needs relate to agenda setting, determining when and where groups will meet, preparing minutes, and summarizing the progress made by a group during a meeting. Task-related needs pertain to analyzing the problem(s) facing the group, sorting out work assignments, gathering data, developing criteria for judging potential solutions, and reaching consensus on the final product of the group. Maintenance needs involve the interpersonal dimensions of group membership. Such needs relate to ensuring that all persons contribute and are heard at meetings, gauging the level of satisfaction with the group's accomplishments, and ensuring that members support one another.

In many groups, the administrator may not be the designated leader, or chair. In these circumstances, school leaders must take special care to avoid being perceived as trying to "take over" the meeting. By virtue of being closer to sources of information than many others, administrators may be more knowledgeable than the typical group member. The administrator should be perceived as a helpful group member who is supportive of the designated leader. An administrator can demonstrate support by showing solidarity with the group, raising others' status, helping relieve tension, showing satisfaction, providing suggestions, and accepting others' ideas (Wynn and Guditus 1984).

School leaders encounter certain hazards when working in a group — it can be time consuming; they might feel that essential control is lost; the indecisiveness of the group may delay action; and "groupthink" is possible (Wynn and Guditus 1984) Clearly, group membership poses difficulties for administrators who may be impatient for solutions and hard pressed for timely responses to urgent problems. The fact of the matter, however, is that administrators may have no choice but to spend time with groups whose basic functions they do not control, but by taking the time to allow group members to express diverse ideas, school leaders increase their ability to make informed decisions for students.

Formulating Strategies for Passing Referenda

Formulating strategies for passing referenda involves in-depth planning, the development of a persuasive story to explain the need to the voting public, and extensive and skillful use of written and verbal communication. If trust is low between the public and school officials, attention will have to be paid to these larger issues before requesting financial increases, whether in the form of general tax revenue proposals or bond issues.

Though school leaders might be tempted to focus their persuasive efforts directly on voters within their district, "school officials should not plan elections in ignorance of the dynamics of the power structure" (Nunnery and Kimbrough 1971, p. 19). Within every community certain citizens hold enormous power to influence others and hence to tilt elections. These "top influentials" are surrounded by a variety of other power wielders and grassroots leaders (Nunnery and Kimbrough 1971).

Every community is made of many layers of influence and school leaders cannot afford to ignore how politics operate in the community. A closed system has been defined as a community with a stable population. The power structure in a closed system, especially its top influentials, may not be in tune with popular public thinking. On the one hand, unless the superintendent and the board can find a way to enlist the support of the top influentials, a school initiative may suffer due to these powerful person's opposition. On the other hand, after careful consideration, a well-organized grassroots campaign can be used to overcome latent power centers. An inherent risk, however, is that initial success might lead influentials to mobilize latent power centers into a powerful oppositional force.

Two types of open community systems exist. One has been characterized as pluralistic, the other as a competitive elite. The pluralistic open community is characterized by different groups working on different goals. In such a system, no one group controls the fate of school referenda. Public opinion polls are useful barometers of the sentiment in such communities.

The competitive elite open community contains political power centers opposed to one another. The superintendent must spend time seeking these centers out and building agreement between them to gain support for referenda. This is best accomplished by actively seeking the involvement of the top influentials. When school leaders fail to develop a working compromise in a competitive elite open community, a school referenda can become a pawn in a power struggle (Nunnery and Kimbrough 1971).

A community's power structure can be identified two ways. The first is by reputation, which involves asking persons in a community to provide lists of key, prominent community members (Hunter 1953). The second, decision analysis, involves identifying key decisions made in the area of education that affected the community and then working backwards, using archival data and interviews, to identify leaders who supported those decisions (Dahl 1961).

Voter Behavior

Superintendents should develop a sophisticated view of voting behavior. The following are 10 factors Nunnery and Kimbrough (1971) identify as critical to understanding voter behavior. Lessons for school leaders related to passing referenda are noted after each.

Factor #1: Voters who are members of informal-groups vote alike. Voting is not an individual decision, but a group phenomena. Work with informal groups such as clubs, ethnic associations, and religious groups that support your vision.

Factor #2: There is no substitute for personal leadership. Don't depend simply on the mass media to carry the message. People are influenced by face-to-face interaction. This is particularly true of undecided voters.

Factor #3: The opinion of top influentials can legitimize either a "no" or a "yes" vote. Make every attempt to enlist the support of the community's top influentials for school referenda.

Factor #4: Informal subsystems have the most influence in molding voter attitudes. Formal groups such as Kiwanis, Lions, or Rotary do not have as profound an influence on molding voter attitudes as informal groups and cliques, friendship associations, and the like, and because membership in the community's formal groups is often not contingent on living in the community itself, members may live in other communities.

Factor # 5: Many voters make up their minds early in referenda campaigns. School campaigns must begin early. The success of the campaign may well be decided before the board even announces the official campaign. Initial voter attitudes are influenced by the public relations platform already in the school system.

Factor # 6: Voters who feel pulled in different directions will vacillate, withdraw from voting, or decide late in referenda campaigns. Analyzing the power structure in a community is necessary to determine how to deal with cross-pressured voters. In a stable community with large numbers of voters who traditionally vote "No" on school referenda, a campaign may deliberately try to introduce cross-pressures among the "No" bloc. In a community where the stable bloc has been positive, however, effort should be exerted to play down cross-pressures and preserve voter unity.

Factor # 7: Socioeconomic status influences voter preferences. Typically, voters with a higher socioeconomic status feel more positive about the value of education and the necessity to support the schools. Referenda campaigns should concentrate upon groups of voters most likely to be supportive rather than trying to persuade negative voters to change their minds.

Factor # 8: Family ties are significant in voter behavior. Kinship ties are very significant in influencing voter behavior. School referenda strategies should discern who the leaders are in these subsystems and concentrate on enabling them to understand and support the program.

Factor #9: Citizens active in community affairs often vote independently and in opposition to informal group opinion. The more active individuals are in the community and in school affairs, the more likely they are to be independent of cross-pressures exerted by informal group membership. Cultivate voter independence all year long rather just in the short campaigns for referenda. Developing an informed voter presence is a year-round activity.

Factor #10: The "alienation factor" may have been overemphasized in explaining referenda defeats. The idea of general voter apathy or alien-

ation is a popular but misleading way to explain away referenda defeats. Studies of actual election results point to other factors such as the failure to enlist the support of community influentials (Crain, Katz, and Rosenthal 1969).

The overall lesson to be learned about passing referenda is that developing a positive voter constituency is a full-time, year-round job. A seasoned superintendent was once asked what his school budget was. He answered, "$114 million." He was then asked how much of his budget was spent on public relations. Without hesitation he answered, "$114 million." School leaders must adopt this mindset to pass referenda.

Persuading the Community To Adopt Initiatives that Benefit Students

School leaders face situations in their careers that force them to take an issue to the whole community. Most often, these are issues of finance, such as general tax support or bond issues. Indeed, financing schools has been cited as the number one challenge confronting the superintendency (Glass 1992).

School leaders must persuade citizens to adopt an attitude similar to the position advocated by the board of education. For many citizens this will involve not only a change of attitude but a change in past voting patterns. Changing someone's attitude without changing their voter behavior is possible (Andrews and Baird 1986), but the goal must be to change both, a difficult and complex task.

School leaders should craft their messages for the particular situation (Brewer 1997). Whether through written or oral communication, school leaders must take specific steps to persuade others. To win support for their message, they must heed the following suggestions:

- **ANALYZE THE AUDIENCE**
  The community should be conceived as a series of interrelated and correlative hierarchies. School leaders must take an objective posture, forgetting for the moment what they want and putting themselves in their audience members' shoes. What do they want to hear? Effective communicators build rapport and establish common ground by using signs and symbols of meaning and comfort to audiences and by starting where the audience is and not where the speaker wants to go.

41

.• BUILD CREDIBILITY

Aristotle observed that a speaker's ethos or credibility is the most powerful source of influence for audiences (Andrews and Baird 1986). When working in public, personal appearance is also critical. The way a school leader dresses, sits, walks, smiles, and even shakes hands are important in establishing credibility.

• APPEAL TO AN AUDIENCE'S EMOTIONS

While evidence is important, persuasion involves human emotions. The facts alone will never carry the day. Mahatma Gandhi, one of the most admired and successful leaders of the 20th century, observed about persuading masses of people:

> Nobody has probably drawn up more petitions or espoused more forlorn causes than I, and I have come to the fundamental conclusion that if you want something really important to be done, you must not merely satisfy the reason, you must move the heart also. (Iyer 1973, p.287)

• FOLLOW THE PSYCHOLOGICAL-PROGRESSIVE PATTERN

A good working model for persuasion is the psychological-progressive pattern (Andrews and Baird 1986, p. 428). The pattern involves:

(a) *Arouse:* capture the attention of the audience;
(b) *Dissatisfy:* demonstrate the nature of the problem;
(c) *Gratify:* connect the proposed initiative to solving the problem;
(d) *Picture:* give examples of how the initiative will solve the problem; and
(e) *Move:* use appeals and challenges to move the audience to take action on your proposal by voting or affirming your position in other ways.

Engaging in Effective Community Relations and School-Business Partnerships

Community Relations

The time to think about school-community relations is not when there is a problem. Good relations are not an accident; they are planned. Lober

(1993) identifies the major steps involved in building positive school-community relations as follows:

• IDENTIFY INTERNAL/EXTERNAL TARGET AUDIENCES

School leaders should develop a list of key internal and external audiences to involve in the school-community process.

• IDENTIFY VIABLE CHANNELS OF COMMUNICATION

Community channels of communication include newsletters, calendars, special purpose notices, annual reports, welcome letters and information for new residents, newspaper ads, bumper stickers, board meetings, billboards, town meetings, and recognition ceremonies. Additional school-related communication involves telephone calls, report cards, parent-teacher conferences, back-to-school nights, school assemblies, athletic competitions, coffees, bulletin boards, advisory councils, and home visits.

• ESTABLISH A BUDGET

Planned communications cost money. To ensure that communication is not accidental and haphazard, establish a budget to support it.

• DEVELOP ACTION PLANS

Action plans should be developed that include a statement of objectives to be accomplished and related activities, an evaluation component, persons designated to carry the plans out, timelines, and cost analyses.

• DEVELOP A COMMUNICATIONS GRID

A communications grid is a road map for who will receive which piece of information produced by a school or district. The grid includes all forms of communications, from traditional teacher letters to e-mail for parents and individual school web pages for the entire community (see Duggan 1997, Warner 1997). A simple communications grid is shown in Figure 3.1 on page 44.

• EVALUATE THE EFFECTIVENESS OF THE COMMUNICATIONS EFFORT

As the communication grid is employed, care should be taken to evaluate the effectiveness of each form of communication it contains. Information about effectiveness can be gathered by analyzing response rates, survey returns, requests for additional copies by client groups, and other types of formal and informal feedback.

Glass (1997) identifies four types of opinion surveys typically used in public education: telephone surveys, mail-out surveys, house-to-house interviews, and focus groups. Open forums are not a good way to sample community opinion because they often become the platform for those with special interests, citizens who are angry and upset, and opposition groups. "Ten out of 10,000 citizens can create public opinion if given the opportunity at an open forum" (Glass, 1997, p. 104). (See chapter 9 for more information about survey research.)

School-Business Partnerships

The business community is a natural partner for schools. Warner (1997) notes that the globalization of commerce and industry and the explosive growth of technology are driving business and the schools closer together. Businesses and schools can work together numerous ways. School-business partnerships often involve businesses "adopting" a school, business employees working in schools as volunteers, school-to-work programs, summer employment opportunities for teachers, funding for special school projects, provision of equipment to schools, career exploration days, and grants or gifts to schools.

Another aspect of school-business partnerships is privatization — businesses taking over some instructional functions or services within school systems. Some school districts have contracted out food services, maintenance, or even transportation services. The business sector has two advantages over schools when it comes to providing services. Businesses can depreciate the declining value of a capital asset, and they can include the cost of purchasing new equipment in the price of the product or service they provide (Flam and Keane 1997).

In the area of instruction, it should be remembered that the private sector has long produced most of the textbooks used in the nation's classrooms. In recent years, Channel One, a for-profit cable television company, has also been brought into some schools. In 1994-95, Berlitz operated programs in 41 public schools and districts in 10 states. Sylvan Learning Systems, in 1995, operated on-site learning centers in 23 schools in 5 school systems, including Baltimore and the District of Columbia (Flam and Keane 1997).

Building Consensus

School leaders can choose from three basic decision-making strategies. They can make all the decisions themselves, they can use majority rule within a group, or they can seek support and acquiescence of the total group after debate and discussion. The latter decision-making strategy is known as consensus (Schmuck et al. 1972).

Consensus is a powerful tool. Building consensus in schools and districts:

- Builds trust among individuals and groups;
- Creates an open, problem-solving climate;
- Locates decision-making and problem-solving responsibilities as close as possible to those engaged in the issues being resolved;
- Increases the sense of ownership of goals and objectives among the stakeholders; and
- Moves groups toward more collaborative relationships (Wynn and Guditus 1984, p.170).

The overriding rationale behind building consensus within schools and districts is that it leads to greater clarity about ways to attain all goals and increases the congruence between subordinate goals. Consensus increases motivation because individuals have more control over their jobs and are likely to feel pressure for higher performance from sources other than administrators (House and Mitchell 1977).

Consensus can be facilitated two ways. The first approach is the stimulation of minority viewpoints. The school leader can simply ask silent members of a group to speak on the issue before them or ask someone to represent them in deliberations. This person can be the so-called "devil's advocate."

The second technique to stimulate consensus is to take a survey. After someone in the group presents the issue clearly, every person should be asked to restate it and present personal reactions (Schmuck et al. 1972).

Working by consensus instead of fiat is the hallmark of a school leader committed to improving decisions at every level in a school or district. The idea is to empower people at all levels and is based on the understanding that power is not limited or finite. "Power is a form of human energy, a variable sum without limits . . ." (Wynn and Guditus 1984, p.37) Only under conditions of consensus and collaboration can synergy occur so that the combined energies of a group of people working together become greater than the sum of the energies of each person independently.

43

Figure 3.1 **ABC Public Schools Communications Grid**

TYPE OF INFORMATION	DESIGNATED AUDIENCES				
	Students	**Parents**	**Teachers**	**Community**	**Media**
Newsletters		X	X	X	
News releases					X
Calendars	X	X	X		X
Annual reports		X	X	X	X
Special surveys	X	X	X	X	
Board meetings		X	X	X	X
Program reviews		X	X		X
School tours		X	X	X	X
Advertisements					X
E-mail		X	X	X	X
Internet web page	X	X		X	

Creating Opportunities for Staff to Develop Collaboration and Consensus-Building Skills

Staff-administrator collaborative opportunities are not just "add-ons" to existing schools. Simply tacking on something new leaves the structure of schools unchanged. Providing collaborative opportunities should represent a deliberate effort to build a different kind of school environment, one that enriches teachers and expands pupil achievement and growth.

The collaborative school rests on the belief that:

- Educational quality is site driven and site specific;
- As professionals, teachers should be responsible and held accountable for the process of instruction;
- Many opportunities exist for teachers and administrators to work together;
- The most effective instruction in schools is centered on collegial norms and continuous improvement; and
- Teachers should be involved in goal setting and program implementation at the school level (Smith and Scott 1990, p.2).

What distinguishes collaborative schools from earlier models of democratic administration and supervision is that in these schools, instead of involving teachers because sharing is seen as a "good thing," teachers have greater authority because their roles as professionals have changed. Marks and Louis (1997) note in their study of teacher involvement in school-based decision making that "empowerment works to the academic advantage of students only when it supports teachers in changing their instruction so that it becomes more involving and demanding for students" (p. 266). Frase and Hetzel (1990) point out that staff development efforts that improve instruction in the schools utilize the conceptual framework offered by Rubin (1975, p. 44); that is, they:

- Center on the teacher's sense of purpose,
- Take into account the teacher's perception of students,
- Depend on the teacher's knowledge of subject matter, and
- Involve the teacher's mastery of technique.

When schools are restructured so that teachers have the autonomy to engage in a real examination of their capacities as instructors, collaborative relationships and opportunities occur naturally (Pourdavood and Fleener 1997, Donaldson and Sanderson 1996).

Consensus and Conflict Resolution

As stated in Chapter 2, consensus building is an approach in which all participants contribute their ideas and opinions and all are involved in any final decision. The process "requires a fairly advanced skill in two-way communication, in coping with conflict, and in use of paraphrasing and the survey" (Schmuck et al. 1972, p.258). The keys to conflict resolution are the abilities of those involved to engage in reflective listening to ensure understanding, maintain civility and rapport, separate positions from interests, and define the group's work so that mutual resolution occurs by integrating everyone's interests (Katz and Lawyer 1993). The presence of common interests exists in nearly every situation in schools. An understanding of what these interests are forms the basis for developing skill in consensus building (Maurer 1991). And even in collaborative schools where teachers are more involved in formulating change in schools, the principal's broader knowledge base regarding feasibility is still a necessary component of the consensus-building process (Goldring and Rallis 1993).

Integrating Youth and Family Services into the Regular School Program

The changing nature of families and the effects of those changes on school children has prompted renewed emphasis on partnerships between agencies serving families and schools (Steffy and Lindle 1994, Leuder 1997) The integration of youth family services was one of the hall-marks of the Kentucky Education Reform Act (Steffy 1993). Services provided by the education establishment were to be linked with those of juvenile justice and public health to create systems of interagency collaboration. Centers were established to work with economically disadvantaged families and their children. The objectives of the Kentucky Family Resource Centers were to:

- Promote healthy growth and development of children by identifying and addressing barriers to school success;
- Assist families in developing parenting skills that promote the full development of their children;
- Ensure that families have access to the appropriate community resources; and
- Encourage social support linkages and networks for families in order to reduce isolation and promote family involvement in the community (Steffy 1993, p. 179).

Practical ways school-family-community partnerships connect to the school's curriculum and learning include helping families understand and monitor their children's homework, improving the quality of parent-teacher conferences, and using the home as a classroom support platform (Epstein et al. 1997).

The National Coalition of Advocates for Students (NCAS 1991) has developed a basic set of student entitlements that summarize what equal

---

Figure 3.2 **The Ten Basic Entitlements To Ensure Equal Opportunities for All Students**

All children are entitled to:

(1) Have parents, advocates, and concerned educators included in all decisions affecting their education;

(2) Learn in an integrated, heterogeneous setting responsive to different learning styles and abilities;

(3) Comprehensible, culturally supportive, and developmentally appropriate curriculum and teaching strategies;

(4) Access to a common body of knowledge and the opportunity to acquire higher-order skills;

(5) Broad-based assessment of their academic progress and grading structures that enhance individual strengths and potential;

(6) A broad range of support services that address individual needs;

(7) Attend schools that are safe, attractive, and free of prejudice;

(8) Attend school unless they pose a danger to other children or school staff;

(9) Instruction by teachers who hold high expectations for all students and who are fully prepared to meet the challenge of diverse classrooms; and

(10) An equal educational opportunity supported by the provision of greater resources to schools serving students most vulnerable to school failure: low income, minority, or immigrant students. (NCAS 1991)

opportunity would mean for every student. These entitlements, shown in Figure 3.2, should frame the discourse between school leaders and representatives of other agencies serving children. (See Chapter 2 for information about collaborative, school-linked services.)

Promoting Ongoing Dialogue with Representatives of Diverse Community Groups

Diversity in America is a fact of life. Nearly 40 million people in the United States speak languages other than English, 120 in all. In California, more than 50 percent of the population may be classified as language minority (Delgado-Gaitan and Trueba 1991). A school administrator reflecting majoritarian values may view cultural differences as a problem and language differences as an obstacle. Not all cultural incompatibilities, however, are undesirable, and schools must make accommodations for them (Gutierrez and Larson 1994; Pruyn 1994). The most pernicious obstacle is the mindset of the "deficit model of education." Indeed, school leaders must:

> disregard any line of research or thinking that places the blame for academic failure on the values, the ways of life, and the languages of children. This is the deficit model at its worst, identifying all differences as predictable areas of failure, claiming that the children must compensate for the alleged deleterious effects of home, family, and native language. (Gonzalez 1994, p. 429)

School leaders must take the initiative to promote a dialogue with diverse community groups because many members of those groups do not feel welcome in the schools (Bequer and Bequer 1978, p. 85). Diverse family groups should be approached with respect and objectivity. The motto of the United States, *E Pluribus Unum,* which appears on all of our coins, means *out of many, one.* This motto should be uppermost in the minds of school leaders promoting dialogue with diverse community groups (Hildebrand et al. 1996).

The following excerpts are offered as a brief introduction for practicing school leaders working with families with diverse backgrounds. More in-depth

reading and learning on this subject is required as demographics continue to change. (See Appendix B.)

Black Families

- In 1989, one in seven black families, nearly one million, had annual incomes of $50,000 or more.
- The vast majority of African-Americans believe the criminal justice system is biased against them.
- Negative stereotypes of black men abound in the media.
- Black families are becoming more bipolar, the gap between rich and poor is increasing.
- A majority of black children live in one-parent households.

How To Approach the Black Community

Seek out and cooperate with black churches and other organizations that serve black families. Identify and work with black professionals in affiliated agencies in the black community. (Hildebrand et al. 1996, pp.53-67)

Hispanic-American Families

- Seventy-five percent of the Hispanic community is Mexican, Puerto Rican, or Cuban in origin.
- By the year 2050, there are expected to be 80 million Hispanics in the United States, 21 percent of the U.S. population.
- The majority of Hispanics are Roman Catholic.
- Hispanic individuals find strength in family.
- Twenty-three percent of Hispanic families are headed by females.
- The authority of the father or husband is rarely disputed in Hispanic families.

How to Approach the Hispanic Community

Hispanics place a great deal of emphasis on respect, which has more than 20 different culturally significant meanings. Work is viewed as a means to enhance the family, not as an end in itself. Hispanics respond positively when their culture and language are understood and valued. (Gonzalez et al. 1997)

Asian-American Families

- "Asian American" refers to persons who have origins in 26 different countries.
- Over one-third of the Asian-American population lives in households with an annual income of more than $50,000.

- Asian Americans are the fastest growing minority in the United States (increasing by 95 percent between 1980 and 1990), numbering 7.3 million persons or 3 percent of the total population.
- Most Asian-American households are dominated by male patriarchal models.
- Asian-American families have a group orientation and stress self-discipline, educational achievement, respect for authority, and reverence for the elderly.

How to Approach the Asian-American Community

Asian Americans place a great deal of emphasis on respect and structure. It is wise to use an interpreter when speaking with Asians who are first-generation Americans. (Hildebrand et al. 1996)

Native American (Indian) Families

- There are 300 federally recognized American Indian peoples in the United States; they speak 200 distinctive tribal languages.
- A Native American's primary ethnic identity is with his or her nation (tribe).
- A majority of Native Americans live on only 40 percent of the average national annual income.
- Family practices vary widely with the extended family model the most common.
- Families place high value on interdependence and sharing of resources, which leads to children practicing autonomy at an early age.
- The Native-American culture is concerned with the here and now and fostering traits of self-reliance, noninterference, nonconfrontation, and respect for elders.

How To Approach the Native American Community

When interacting with the Native American community, school leaders should understand that they represent the values of a majoritarian culture, which is sharply at odds with traditional Indian values. Whereas the white, majoritarian, culture is competitive, the Native American culture is communal and cooperative. Contact with elders is vital. (Hildebrand et al. 1996)

Families in communities across the nation belong to many other cultural groups as well. School leaders must shed any naive notions about "the melting pot" analogy used so often to disguise the submergence and submission of ethnicity and cultural identity, which has brought about great resentment and conflict in the schools (Solomon and Ogbu 1992). Their goal should be to prepare students to be cross-culturally competent so that all students can reach their potential in a diverse society and world (Banks 1988).

Conclusion

In this chapter we examined and reviewed skills school leaders need related to communication and community relations. Internal and external constituencies are changing rapidly. Teachers and parents are assuming new roles within the schools; communities and families are changing; and new strains and pressures are emerging within families and communities. These changes present unprecedented challenges for administrators to build coalitions that support schools and school children. Perhaps never before has the diversity of this country's population been so great or the call for full inclusion in preparing an upwardly mobile, technologically competent citizenry been as demanding on the schools as it is on the cusp of the 21st century. School leaders must step up and answer the call.

Use the following Skill Accomplishment Checklist to assess your skill level in each of the important topics discussed in this chapter.

Skill Accomplish Checklist for Chapter 3

Skills	Readings and Activities for Skill Mastery
Articulate district or school vision, mission, and priorities to the community and mass media.	**Readings:** Kauffman, Herman, and Watters (1996), Lober (1993) **Activities:** 1. Develop a vision and mission statement for your school district. 2. Create a logo and motto for your school or district.
Write and speak effectively.	**Readings:** DeVito (1983), Lucas (1986) **Activities:** 1. Compose a five-minute high school graduation speech. 2. Develop a one-page memo for the board of education that explains a complex state or federal law.
Demonstrate group leadership skills	**Readings:** Donaldson and Marnik (1995), Laber (1997), Morse and Ivey (1996), Regan and Brooks (1995), Wynn and Guditus (1984) **Activities:** 1. List the behaviors of group members that most annoy you. Develop effective responses to them.
Formulate strategies for passing referenda.	**Readings:** Herman (1995), Nunnery and Kimbrough (1971) **Activities:** 1. Analyze your community's power structure. Develop a two-page memo about it for the superintendent of schools. 2. Develop a brief matrix of the roles of the key individuals or groups involved in getting a referenda passed. Include the board, superintendent of schools, teachers union, parents, and selected community groups.
Persuade the community to adopt initiatives that benefit students.	**Readings:** Andrews and Baird (1986), Brewer (1997), Ogden and Germinario (1988), Steffy and Lindle (1994) **Activities:** 1. Develop and deliver a three-minute speech about a special service for at-risk students using the psychological-progressive pattern.
Engage in effective community relations and school-business partnerships.	**Readings:** Epstein et al. (1997), Lober (1993), Michel (1997) **Activities:** 1. List the essential steps in building a school-business partnership. Explain which steps will be the easiest and most difficult and why? 2. Develop a job description for a school-community action team and create a preliminary budget for their activities. 3. Develop a communications grid for your school or district.
Build consensus.	**Readings:** Babbage (1997) Katz and Lawyer (1993), Schmuck et. al (1972), Steffy and Lindle (1994), Wynn and Guditus (1984), **Activities:** 1. Identify the most contentious problems in your school. Explain which ones would be most amenable to consensus building and why? 2. Construct a survey to stimulate minority viewpoints on a controversial problem in your school or district.

Skill Accomplish Checklist for Chapter 3—continued

Skills	✓	Readings and Activities for Skill Mastery
Create opportunities for staff to develop collaboration and consensus-building skills.		**Readings:** Donaldson and Sanderson (1996), Frase and Hetzel (1990), Katz and Lawyer (1993), Smith and Scott (1990) **Activities:** 1. Construct a survey/needs assessment to identify teachers' most pressing instructional concerns as a basis for staff development. 2. Identify some ways that common interests are expressed by staff upon which consensus techniques could be developed.
Integrate youth and family services into the regular school program.		**Readings:** Leuder (1997), Steffy (1993), Steffy and Lindle (1994), **Activities:** 1. Ask counselors and other youth workers in your community to identify the problems your students most frequently encounter with the agencies serving them. 2. Develop a collaborative agreement with at least one youth agency in your community to work on a common problem facing your students.
Promote ongoing dialogue with representatives of diverse community groups.		**Readings:** Delgado-Gaitan and Trueba (1991); Gonzalez, Huerta-Macias, and Tinajero (1997); Hildebrand et al. (1996); Shapiro, Sewell, and Ducette (1995) **Activities:** 1. From census data, briefly describe the major types of families in your school district. Do they fit the national picture? 2. Indicate how your school or system has been affected by changing family demographics. What are the trend lines?

Resources

Andrews, P., and J. Baird. (1986). *Communication for Business and the Professions.* Dubuque, Iowa: Wm. C. Brown Publishers.

Babbage, K. (1997). *Meetings for School-Based Decision Making.* Lancaster, Pa.: Technomic Pub. Co., Inc.

Banks, J. (1988). *Multiethnic Education: Theory and Practice.* Boston: Allyn and Bacon, Inc.

Bequer, M., and J. Bequer. (1978). "Community Involvement: A Rich Resource." In *Bilingual Education for Latinos,* edited by L. Valverde. Alexandria, Va.: Association for Supervision and Curriculum Development.

Brewer, E. (1997). *13 Proven Ways to Get Your Message Across.* Thousand Oaks, Calif.: Corwin Press.

Crain, R., E. Katz, and D. Rosenthal. (1969). *The Politics of Community Conflict.* New York: Merrill Company.

Dahl, R. (1961). *Who Governs?* New Haven, Conn.: Yale University Press.

Delgado-Gaitan, C., and H. Trueba. (1991). *Crossing Cultural Borders: Education for Immigrant Families in America.* Bristol, Pa.: The Falmer Press.

DeVito, J. (1983). *The Interpersonal Communication Book.* New York: Harper and Row Publishers.

Donaldson, G., And G. Marnik. (1995). *Becoming Better Leaders.* Thousand Oaks, Calif.: Corwin Press.

Donaldson, G., and D. Sanderson. (1996). *Working Together in Schools.* Thousand Oaks, Calif.: Corwin Press.

Duggan, M. (1997). *Powerful Parent Letters for K-3.* Thousand Oaks, Calif.: Corwin Press.
Epstein, J., L. Coates, K. Salinas, M. Sanders, and B. Simon. (1997) *School, Family, and Community Partnerships: Your Handbook for Action.* Thousand Oaks, Calif.: Corwin Press.

Flam, S., and W. Keane. (1997). *Public Schools and Private Enterprise: What You Should Know and Do About Privatization.* Lancaster, Pa.: Technomic Pub. Co., Inc.

Frase, L., and R. Hetzel. (1990). *School Management by Wandering Around.* Lancaster, Pa.: Technomic.

Gardner, H. (1995). *Leading Minds: An Anatomy of Leadership.* New York: Basic Books, Inc.

Glass, T. (Spring/Summer 1997). "Using School District Public Opinion Surveys To Gauge and Obtain Public Support." *The School Community Journal* 7, 1: 101-116.

Glass, T. (1992). *The 1992 Study of the American School Superintendency.* Arlington, Va.: American Association of School Administrators.

Goldring, E., and S. Rallis. (1993). *Principals of Dynamic Schools.* Thousand Oaks, Calif.: Corwin Press.

Gonzalez, R. (October 1994). "Race and the Politics of Educational Failure: A Plan for Advocacy and Reform." *The International Journal of Educational Reform* 3, 4: 427-436.

Gonzalez, M., A. Huerta-Macias, and J. Tinajero. (1997). *Educating Latino Students: A Guide to Successful Practice.* Lancaster, Pa.: Technomic.

Gutierrez, K., and J. Larson. (January 1994). "Language Borders: Recitation as Hegemonic Discourse." *The International Journal of Educational Reform* 3, 1: 22-36

Herman, J. (1995). *Effective School Facilities.* Lancaster, Pa.: Technomic Pub. Co., Inc.

Hildebrand, V., L. Phenice, M. Gray, and R. Hines. (1996). *Knowing and Serving Diverse Families.* Upper Saddle River, N.J.: Prentice-Hall.

Hunter, F. (1953). *Community Power Structure.* Chapel Hill: University of North Carolina Press.

House, R., and T. Mitchell. (1977). "Path-Goal Theory of Leadership." In *Organizational Behavior,* edited by K. Davis. New York: McGraw-Hill Book Company.

Iyer, R. (1973). *The Moral and Political Thought of Mahatma Gandhi.* New York: Oxford University Press.

Katz, N., and J. Lawyer. (1993). *Conflict Resolution.* Thousand Oaks, Calif.: Corwin Press.

Kauffman, R., J. Herman, and K. Watters. (1996). *Educational Planning: Strategic, Tactical, Operational.* Lancaster, Pa.: Technomic Pub. Co., Inc.

Laber, R. (1997). *Group Process.* Lancaster, Pa.: Technomic Pub. Co., Inc.

Leuder, D. (1997). *Creating Partnerships with Parents.* Lancaster, Pa.: Technomic Pub. Co., Inc.

Lober, I. (1993) *Promoting Your School: A Public Relations Handbook.* Lancaster, Pa.: Technomic Pub. Co., Inc.

Lucas, S. (1986). *The Art of Public Speaking.* New York: Random House.

Marks, H., and K. Louis. (Fall 1997). "Does Teacher Empowerment Affect the Classroom? The Implications of Teacher Empowerment for Instructional Practice and Student Academic Performance." *Educational Evaluation and Policy Analysis.* 19, 3: 245-275.

Maurer, R. (1991). *Managing Conflict: Tactics for School Administrators.* Boston: Allyn and Bacon.

Mercer, R., and R. Berger. (1989). "Social Service Needs of Lesbian Women and Gay Adolescents: Tell It Their Way." *Journal of Social Work and Human Sexuality* 8, 1: 75-95.

Michel, G. (1997). *Building Schools: The New School and Community Relations.* Lancaster, Pa.: Technomic Pub. Co., Inc.

Mintzberg, H. (1994). *The Rise and Fall of Strategic Planning.* New York: The Free Press.

Morse, P., and A. Ivey. (1996). *Face-to-Face: Communication and Conflict Resolution in the Schools.* Thousand Oaks, Calif.: Corwin Press.

Moses, A., and R. Hawkins. (1982). *Counseling Lesbian Women and Gay Men.* Englewood Cliffs, N.J.: Prentice-Hall, Inc.

National Coalition of Advocates for Students. (1991). *The Good Common School: Making the Vision Work for All Children.* Boston: author.

Nunnery, M., and R. Kimbrough. (1971). *Politics, Power, Polls, and School Elections.* Berkeley, Calif.: McCutchan Publishing Corporation.

Ogden, E., and V. Germinario. (1988). *The At-Risk Student.* Lancaster, Pa.: Technomic Pub. Co., Inc.

Parkay, F., J. Shindler, and M. Oaks. (January 1997). "Creating a Climate for Collaborative, Emergent Leadership at an Urban High School." *The International Journal of Educational Reform* 6, 1: 64-74.

Pourdavood, R., and J. Fleener. (Spring/Summer 1997). "Evolution of a Dialogic Community and Teacher Change." *The School Community Journal* 7, 1: 51-62.

Pruyn, M. (January 1994). "Becoming Subjects Through Critical Practice: How Students in One Elementary Classroom Critically Read and Wrote Their World." *The International Journal of Educational Reform* 3, 1: 37-50.

Regan, H., and G. Brooks. (1995) *Out of Women's Experience: Creating Relational Leadership.* Thousand Oaks, Calif.: Corwin Press.

Rubin, L. (1975). "The Case for Staff Development in Professional Supervision for Professional Teachers." In the *1975 ASCD Yearbook,* edited by T. Sergiovanni. Alexandria, Va.: Association for Supervision and Curriculum Development.

Schmuck, R., P. Runkel, S. Saturen, R. Martell, and C. Derr. (1972). *Handbook of Organization Development in Schools.* Eugene: Ore.: National Press Books.

Shapiro, J., T. Sewell, and J. Ducette. (1995). *Reframing Diversity in Education.* Lancaster, Pa.: Technomic Pub. Co., Inc.

Smith, S., and J. Scott. (1990). *The Collaborative School.* Reston, Va.: National Association of Secondary School Principals.

Solomon, R., and J. Ogbu. (1992). *Black Resistance in High School.* Albany, New York: SUNY Press.

Steffy, B. (1993). *The Kentucky Education Reform.* Lancaster, Pa.: Technomic Pub. Co., Inc.

Steffy, B., and J. Lindle. (1994). *Building Coalitions.* Thousand Oaks, Calif.: Corwin Press.

Wallace, R., D. Engel, and J. Mooney. (1997) *The Learning School.* Thousand Oaks, Calif.: Corwin Press.

Warner, C. (1997). *Everybody's House — The Schoolhouse.* Thousand, Oaks, Calif.: Corwin Press.

Wynn, R., and C. Guditus. (1984). *Team Management: Leadership by Consensus.* Columbus, Ohio: Charles E. Merrill Publishing Company.

chapter 4 | *Skills in Organizational Management*

The job of all educational leaders, whether their primary responsibility is to a single school or a school district, is to create highly reliable organizations in which all children can be successful. Effective organizational management is the key to developing such organizations. When calculating the costs of such a task, Stringfield (1994, p. 293) reminds us, "It will cost less to provide highly reliable schools for students at risk than to pay for continued expansion of welfare, police, and prison programs."

This chapter details the skills successful 21st century school leaders must possess to:

- Gather, analyze, and use data to inform decision making;
- Delegate decision-making responsibility;
- Ensure adherence to legal concepts, regulations, and codes for school operations;
- Use technology to enhance administration;
- Engage in financial planning and cash flow management;
- Establish procedures for budget planning, accounting, and auditing;
- Administer auxiliary programs;
- Develop a plan for maintaining the school plant, equipment, and support systems;
- Apply appropriate components of quality management; and
- Implement a systems approach to monitoring all components (subsystems) of the school system for efficiency.

Gathering, Analyzing, and Using Data To Inform Decision Making

The components of informed decision making can be divided into two parts:(1) understanding, which involves perception, definition, and data gathering; and (2) problem solving, which involves choices and consequences (Taylor 1984).

Understanding

Perception. Kaufman(1988) describes a problem as a gap or "need" selected for reduction or elimination. To undertake effective decision making, school leaders, like other organizational executives, must first recognize that a problem exists.

Definition. The definition of problems involves cultural, political, and economic factors. For example, for a time, it was acceptable to school executives that large numbers of minority children failed at school (Pinkney 1988). This is no longer politically acceptable. The problem now is reducing minority dropout rates.

Data gathering. Perception and definition must be followed by data gathering. Decision makers must know what information is relevant to a given decision.

Problem Solving

Choices. Once data about a problem have been gathered, school leaders must make choices about which solutions to try and the best ways to proceed. Choice, of course, becomes difficult when a decision is likely to lead to more than one outcome. School leaders often must consider the probable results of decisions according to potential impact and cost on a scale of desirability, and eliminate unsatisfactory alternatives (Clough 1984).

Consequences. Calculating the consequences of a decision requires an understanding of what outcomes are being sought. Such calculations require clarity of goals and expectations because "without clearly defined purposes, no basis exists for taking any action" (Watson 1981, p.7).

The Decision Structure

Defining processes for informed decision making requires knowing the way individuals process information and the communication structure of the system itself (Alexis and Wilson 1967). In schools, superintendents and principals often function as line officers, relying upon assistant superintendents, assistant principals, coordinators, and supervisors (staff officers) for information.

Limited time and inaccessible information limit school leaders' ability to make optimal decisions. Therefore, the general rule for efficient decision making is to assign decisions to those individuals who require the least additional information. This principle is based on the belief that those closest to a decision should make it because the higher up a decision is made in an organization, the more general (less specialized and departmentalized) it becomes. General decisions are "good enough," but far from perfect. And almost any decision made under the stress of limited data and time can be criticized by opponents as inadequate.

Delegating Decision-Making Responsibility

Enabling staff members in schools and school systems to engage in decision making is one of the hallmarks of site-based management (SBM) (Babbage 1997). Moving the responsibility for such decisions to various areas of a school system, such as parent-based councils, is believed to be good practice (Batey 1996). Emerging research regarding the process of involvement, however, does not support the idealism of SBM advocates who believe it will improve the school achievement of low-income students and increase parental involvement. Unless existing power relations are changed, delegation alone will not usher forth true educational reform (Lipman 1997, Hayes 1978).

Though delegating the responsibility for decision making does not guarantee that problems will be defined, analyzed, or attacked better, it is entirely consistent with ideas concerning decision processes and management structures. Management, some now say, is about managing processes, not decisions. "The importance of this management/decision making distinction is that [top-level] management does not actually manage the organization . . . it designs decision structures" (Weick 1985, p. 114). But it bears repeating that unless power is shared in schools, delegation alone will not lead to real reform. (See Chapter 1 for more about delegation.)

Ensuring Adherence to Legal Concepts, Regulations, and Codes for School Operations

Schools function within a complex and overlapping matrix of federal, state, and local laws. The increased activism of state legislatures and Congress has led to an increase in education laws and the subsequent judicial rulings that inevitably follow their implementation. "School law has been a growth industry for more than two decades" (Sergiovanni et al. 1980, p.308).

Today, the major education issues apt to wind up in the U.S. Supreme Court are those related to school district finance and organization, church-state relations, student and employee rights and responsibilities, school board elections and liability, and race, language, and sex discrimination (Sergiovanni et al. 1980). Figure 4.1 (opposite) is a sample of the major legal issues facing school leaders today.

KEY LEGAL TERMS

The Rule of Law and Due Process

The rule of law and due process apply to students and teachers. The rule of law is a restraint on the conduct of school officials, which makes them accountable to the law. Due process means that before any teachers, staff, students, or parents can be denied or deprived of rights, privileges, or employment, stipulated procedures and processes must be followed to ensure fairness and equity.

Negligence

School administrators can be considered negligent when they fail to take reasonable precautions to prevent injury to students, teachers, or citizens.

(Streshly and Frase 1992)

Figure 4.1 **Contemporary Legal Issues Related to Education**

Area	Current Status
Equality	• Separate but equal is unconstitutional • Racial and gender discrimination are illegal • Discrimination against handicapped persons outlawed • Tracking based on group intelligence tests abolished
Human Rights	• Students have the right to free speech as guaranteed by the Constitution • Parents have the right to inspect school records • Teachers have due process rights
Church and State	• School prayer banned as an official act of the school district • Prayer meetings acceptable at school as long as they are not sponsored by the school district
Compulsory education	• Discrimination against married or pregnant students outlawed • Children with AIDS must be allowed to attend school • States may require immunization of students, except those whose refusal is based on religious beliefs • Private schools must meet states' minimum standards • States may place limitations on home schooling
Curriculum	• States may set curricular requirements • Local school boards may set attendance and other program requirements related to granting a diploma • Local school boards have the power to place students
Managing grades, tests, and records	• Teachers' grades may not be changed by school officials unless shown to be arbitrary or capricious • The use of standardized IQ tests for placement of mentally retarded students is unconstitutional • Student records must be kept confidential
Search and seizure	• Searches of students and their belongings must be reasonable and not excessively intrusive
Special education	• Equal access to schools must be guaranteed • All children are entitled to a free, appropriate education in the least restrictive environment

Adapted from Streshly and Frase 1992

Law-Based Reform

Reformers have begun seeking to bring about changes in schools through the legislative and judicial processes. Wise (1979), however, has presented a highly critical view of school reform via legislation. Wise coined the term *hypernationalization* to point out that educational reform mandated by government leads to increased centralization and bureaucratization. Enactment of such laws assumes that teachers and students are infinitely pliable and that a "science of education" exists. According to Wise (1979, p. 59), neither of these assumptions is correct; "in the drive to make educational institutions accountable, goals have become narrow, selective, and minimal."

DeMitchell and Fossey (1997, p. 184) conclude that "litigation . . . has utterly failed to fulfill its promise of improving educational opportunities." They also assert that of "the hundreds of educational reform laws passed by the states over the past 20 years, not one has altered the fundamental way children are educated" (p. 185).

Law-based reform efforts have been unproductive for three reasons. First, reform legislation has avoided encroaching on the interests of teachers unions or school board power. "Not only have the unions often opposed substantive reform proposals, they have clung tenaciously to an industrial model of labor relations, which is a serious barrier to improving school environments" (DeMitchell and Fossey 1997, p. 185). Second, such reform attempts have not dealt with the issues of teacher quality or professional malpractice. And third, while law-based reforms often use the phrase "all children can learn," the actual socio-economic conditions of some children have worsened, making it unlikely that any single school reform can overcome the stark landscape (DeMitchell and Fossey 1997, pp.186-7).

Using Technology To Enhance Administration

School leaders apply technological applications to improve processes related to budgeting, policy development, enrollment projections, employee compensation, cash flow and investments, lease-purchase arrangements, revenue projections, and retirement options (see Chambers 1994). Technology can be used to build different budgets based on varying assumptions of revenue streams and expenditure decisions, to forecast enrollment for bond issues and school facility renovation, and in collective bargaining to assess teachers union proposals and develop fair counter proposals in a short time.

School leaders applying technology to business administration and support systems must carefully choose the proper database for informing each decision. They must also know how to construct and present informative databases that allow for the construction of alternative scenarios. The use of spreadsheets and accounting software offer excellent examples of ways computers' calculating capacity can be used to promote greater public understanding of a school system's financial condition (Poston, Stone, and Muther 1992).

Engaging in Financial Planning and Cash Flow Management

Financial Planning

The basis for sound financial planning begins with accurate pupil enrollment forecasting. This requires a summary and analysis of the U.S. and school census and migration data, annual resident birth rates, new residential dwelling construction rates, private and parochial enrollments, the enrollment density of pupils attending public schools by residential sectors, and an index of school plant use (Hack, et al. 1995). These documents are the basis for the most common enrollment projection, the cohort survival method (CSM) (see Herman 1995). When sizeable demographic changes are occurring in a district, the CSM can and should be adjusted and updated annually.

In addition to enrollment information, financial planning requires:

- *Pupil data:* including pupil demographics and projections;
- *Program data:* including information about program, curricular, and instructional goals and objectives;
- *Personnel data:* payroll and assignment information;
- *Facilities data:* information about the expenses involved in operating school plants, including overhead, inventory supplies, equipment, maintenance, and construction projects; and
- *Financial data:* forecasts of revenues and expenditures, taking into account enrollment, teacher compensation, and capital funding analyses and requirements (Hack et al. 1995, pp.135-6).

Cash Flow Management

Cash flow management has become critical for school leaders as tax revenues have not expanded to meet rising costs or dried up altogether. Because state aid based on enrollment and local tax revenues often comes in lump-sum payments that exceed monthly expenditure levels, school systems from time to time have more cash on hand than they need to expend. The excess cash is available for short-term investments that can produce additional revenue for educational purposes. The options for investment include U.S. Treasury bills, bonds, and notes; U.S. government agency bonds; certificates of deposits; repurchase agreements; money market certificates, money market funds, and passbook savings; and commercial paper (Hack et al. 1995). Some school districts practice cash investment pooling by working with their banks to roll monies from various accounts into one for purposes of investing (Dembroski and Biros 1981).

It is critical that cash flow management and the subsequent investment strategies be guided by state law and regulation and a definitive local school board policy. Such a policy should stipulate the following: (1) the objectives of the investment program; (2) the designated administrator accountable for the program and the contracted investment counsel or services to be used; (3) the authority and responsibility of the designated administrator; (4) the procedures to be used to project cash flow and the sources and level of cash to be used for investment; (5) the designation of minimum and maximum maturities; and (6) the investment instruments to be employed (Hack et al. 1995).

SAFETY, YIELD, AND LIQUIDITY

When selecting investments, safety, yield, and liquidity must be considered. *Safety*, as applied to investing, is a relative term that is defined in different ways. For example, one school system's policy specifies safety as "the certainty of receiving full par value plus accrued interest at the security's legal final maturity" (Hack et al. 1995, p.299). *Yield* refers to the income derived from interest or appreciation of the principal on the investment. *Liquidity* refers to how soon the district may have its investment back if there is a fiscal emergency and the penalties, if any, involved in the process.

School district officials dare not take chances with investments. In Pennsylvania, two investment companies that claimed to provide full protection to school districts have been criminally investigated for fraud. Seventy-five school districts were involved in the scam and lost more than $70 million (Beckett 1997).

Establishing Procedures for Budgeting, Accounting, and Auditing

Budgeting

A budget has been defined as "a set of data that record proposed or adopted allocation decisions in terms of goals to be accomplished (program plan), resources available (revenue plan), and anticipated services and materials to be acquired (expenditure plan) during a specified period of time (fiscal period)" (Sedenburg 1984, p.60). Budgeting involves four elements: (1) planning, (2) receiving funds, (3) spending funds, and (4) evaluating results.

School district budgeting performs the following important functions:

- It requires that school programs be planned will in advance;
- It delineates funding sources, anticipated expenditures, and preliminary decisions regarding allocations;
- It serves as a public information tool about the district's finances and educational priorities;
- It provides a focal point for a year-to-year comparison of programs, priorities, and related decisions;
- It provides incentives for good annual planning; and
- It reflects the mix of federal, state, and local funds and authority regarding their distribution at the local level (Burrup, Brimley, and Garfield 1993, p.317-8).

Types of Budgets

The four basic types of budgets are (1) traditional, line-item budgets, (2) performance budgets, (3) program budgets, and (4) zero-based budgets.

Traditional budgets. Traditional, line-item budgets are the most common form of school system budgeting. They show expenditures such as instruction, transportation, and administration. These "objects" of expenditures form generic themes within which to group costs, but are not summarized by program (i.e., reading, music, middle school social studies teachers' salaries, etc.). Therefore, the way the public often thinks about schools does not usually coincide with the way costs are calculated or discussed. Traditional budgeting also does not accurately reflect changes within categories based on reaching specified objectives or results obtained from one year to the next. For example, if reading test scores prompt the hiring of additional reading teachers, their retention is usually not tied to attaining better reading scores.

Performance budgets. Performance budgets are developed based on the assumptions that assessment data and other forms of feedback should shape budgetary priorities; budgetary decisions should be driven by curricular requirements and their attendant value for learning; curricular and instructional program outcomes can be defined; levels of achievement for programs can be measured; assessment results can be translated into educational needs; needs and program priorities change over time; program needs can be expressed or translated into budgetary requests; and budgetary requests usually exceed resources (see Poston et al. 1992). Performance budgets are feasible for school use.

Program-based budgets. Planning, programming, budgeting systems (PPBS), or program-based budgeting, was initiated in the 1960s by the U.S. Department of Defense. One advantage of PPBS is that it extends the planning period for budgeting beyond the year-to-year basis of traditional budgets. PPBS uses a cycle of budget development based on establishing objectives, determining the costs of reaching the objectives, evaluating the results of efforts to reach the objectives, improving or upgrading the objectives, and improving the planning processes to reach revised objectives (Burrup et al. 1993). Program-based budgets are clear and provide a key tool for school finance.

Zero-based budgeting. Zero-based budgeting throws out one of the major premises of budgeting, which is that certain expenditures or expenditure levels are givens. The idea behind zero-based budgeting is that every program and expenditure level within a program must re-establish itself every year. Therefore, budget developers do not begin constructing a budget by looking at the previous year's. The starting point instead for each new budget is zero, and every program must compete anew for allocations (Stonich 1977).

In reality, true zero-based budgeting is very difficult to use for developing public school budgets. Unlike governmental or private sector organizations, no matter how poor the English or math programs might be, they are not likely to be abolished. Teachers' salaries and fringe benefits cannot drop to zero; nor are the costs associated with mandatory state transportation or heating or cooling school buildings liable to be zeroed out. Public schools provide mandatory services for a clientele compelled to partake of them. Therefore, instituting zero-based budgeting in schools would be next to impossible. (See Chapter 6 for information about assigning financial resources.)

SITE-BASED BUDGETING

With the advent of SBM has come the call for site-based budgeting (SBB) (Poston et al. 1992, Odden and Wohlstetter 1995). The following are the major phases and steps of SBB (Herman and Herman 1997, pp. 45-68).

Phases and Steps of SBB

PHASE 1: Engaging in Budget Planning
Major Steps
- Develop a budget calendar
- Project enrollment by class
- Project the number of employees
- Project expenditures for supplies and equipment
- Conduct a needs assessment

PHASE 2: Calculating Expenditures
Major Steps
- Develop expenditure estimates

PHASE 3: Determining Accounting and Budgetary Controls
Major Steps
- Identify the necessary accounting and budgetary controls (transfers, expenditures, reporting of balances, use of purchase orders, bidding rules, etc.)

PHASE 4: Undertaking Financial Review: Audits
Major Steps
- Employ an external or internal auditor to examine the financial records to determine accuracy and adherence to generally accepted accounting principles.

Accounting

Accounting is concerned with recording transactions and processing account data (see Tidwell 1974). School accounting deals with "recording and reporting activities and events affecting the personnel, facilities, materials, or money of an administrative unit and its programs" (Adams et al. 1967, p.260).

Auditing

The purpose of financial auditing has moved beyond detecting fraud or finger pointing at poor financial decisions, though these remain in some cases where district or school finances run aground. The primary purpose of auditing is to ensure that the financial reports issued by school system administrators are factual and truthful and accurately portray the financial condition and transactions that have occurred during a specified period. The three types of audits are internal, external, and continuous. The first two types refer to the position of the auditor vis-a-vis the organization. The last type is used to determine net worth or cash flow at a specific time and can be accomplished by either an internal or external auditor.

Administering Auxiliary Programs

Auxiliary services or programs include "any activity or resource subordinate to or supportive of the design and delivery of instructional services or programs in a school system"(Poston et al. 1992, p.44). These programs include risk management, food services, and facility construction and renovation.

Risk Management

Risk management involves reducing the chance of harm, injury, or liability due to hazardous or dangerous practices or actions. When practices or actions that may contain liability components cannot be eliminated, school leaders must consider purchasing insurance for protection (Poston et al. 1992).

Food Services

Nearly four billion meals are served annually in the nation's public school cafeterias. While most school food service operations are delegated to qualified managers, school leaders should know that the managerial responsibilities include meal planning and delivery, facilities support, and meal counting and claiming (Poston et al. 1992).

Cafeterias are one of the principal school operations that can be contracted out or privatized. The Marriott Corporation estimates that 11 percent of the nation's public schools have privatized their food service operations (Flam and Keane 1997). The major rationale for privatization is to reduce cost (see AASA 1995). The privatization of food services, however, may be a quick fix as opposed to a long-term solution. Once a private company comes into a school district, which then lets employees go, the company may raise prices knowing that the district will probably not rehire its old staff. Privatization also has political consequences inasmuch as cafeteria workers and other noninstructional staff frequently live in the community.

Facility Construction and Renovation

Current thinking calls for configuring school facilities in line with recent ideas regarding learning while saving on construction costs. One high school was recently built in the Henry Ford Museum in Dearborn, Mich., at a cost of $5,500 per student, well below the median cost for school construction. Architect Steven Bingler calls this concept the "hermit crab" model because the school is fit into a structure that already exists. Such schools promote active learning and reject the traditional "cells and bells" models of their predecessors. The idea, however, is not new. Many such schools were piloted by John Dewey at the turn of the century (Tanner 1997).

Herman (1995, p. 1-9) identifies the following variables as critical in designing school facilities:

- Students' developmental and interest patterns;
- Students' varying learning styles;
- Teachers' instructional styles;
- The variance in programs and instructional delivery methods required to accommodate various grade levels and specialized instructional programs; and
- The space needs of students, teachers, programs, and instructional delivery methods.

Health and safety factors have traditionally been the reason for school renovation. However, technological advances and the burgeoning use of the Internet and two-way interactive video instruction are increasingly making instructional obsolescence a reason for renovation.

Developing a Plan To Maintain the School Plant, Equipment, and Support Systems

School buildings, the equipment in them, and the land upon which they are constructed are a school system's largest capital investment. Evaluation of a school plant's condition may involve questionnaires, observations, focus groups, personal interviews, and a review of safety and accident records (Herman 1995).

Important questions to ask regarding the long-term adequacy of the school plant are:

(1) Is the plant safe and can it provide an optimal learning place for students?
(2) Is the full range of student activities possible at the plant?
(3) Is the plant energy efficient?
(4) Are the heating and ventilating systems adequate?
(5) Is the current level of maintenance adequate to meet learner needs within reasonable cost levels?
(6) Is the plant free of noise and void of Occupational Safety and Health Administration violations?

(7) Is the electrical system adequate to keep up with changing technologies?
(8) Are there any places where normal wear and tear are becoming serious problems?
(9) Is the roof in adequate condition and what kind of maintenance is required to keep it functional for all kinds of weather? (Herman, 1995, pp. 128-9)

Accurate records are an important part of planning for the maintenance needs of a district's school plants and uncovering threats to school safety (Lane, Richardson, and Van Berkum 1996). One way for school leaders to keep tabs on school plants is to develop a school plant inventory. A sample is provided in Figure 4.2.

Applying Appropriate Components of Quality Management

Quality management (QM) has become widespread in U.S. business and industry. QM was pioneered by Shewhart (1931) and later by Juran (1979) and Deming (1986).

Quality has been defined as "an offering (product or service) that meets or exceeds customer requirements" and *quality management* as:

Figure 4.2 A Sample School Plant Inventory

Legend

A= name of school
B= date constructed
C= pupils currently enrolled

D= building capacity
E= square feet
F= square feet per pupil enrolled

G= square feet per pupil capacity
H= percentage above or below capacity
I= year(s) renovated

A School	B Date Const.	C Pupils Enrolled	D Capacity	E Sq. Ft.	F Sq.Ft./ Pupil Enrolled	G Sq.Ft. Pupil Capacity	H % +/- Capacity	I Years Renov.
Elementary								
Adams	1929	509	565	77,002	151	136	-9.91	'58,'69
Hale	1922	659	752	118,743	180	158	-12.37	'96
North	1959	284	429	51,286	181	120	-33.80	'94
Oak	1963	192	215	26,534	138	123	-10.70	'72
Middle								
South	1958	616	840	100,000	162	119	-26.67	
West	1951	489	1,204	139,680	286	116	-59.39	'87
High								
Monroe	1972	1403	2,212	303,000	216	137	-36.57	'89
Alt.HS	1924	160	588	39,246	245	67	-72.79	'63

60

developing and operating work processes that are capable of consistently designing, producing, and delivering quality offerings. Central to this definition is the focus on process (versus functional) management as a primary means of continuous improvement. (Heilpern and Nadler 1992, p.138)

The core concepts of QM are process control and capability, management by fact, employee involvement, and teamwork (Heilpern and Nadler 1992). The transfer of quality management concepts to education has its advocates and critics. Kaufman and Zahn (1993) argue that QM is appropriately applied to education because, like businesses, schools have external clients (parents and taxpayers); must demonstrate results(student achievement); operate using processes (teaching, learning, activities, and curriculum); and include inputs (facilities and other capital resources) and outputs (graduates). Bradley (1993) sees another parallel between school and businesses that suggests the transferability of QM, noting that schools and busi-

nesses as service organizations have similar characteristics, such as direct transactions with masses of people, large volumes of paperwork, large amounts of processing, an extremely large number of ways to make errors, and the need to handle huge numbers of small items related to communication.

Henry Giroux (1997), on the other hand, has been critical of the impact of transferring Deming's work to education, which he believes defines "young people in terms of market values — as either consumers or commodities." Pallas and Neumann (1993) assert that QM places a heavy emphasis on "tight couping," which does not exist in schools. English (1994) sees similar themes in Frederick Taylor's scientific management and Deming's total quality management and views the latter as the reincarnation of an emphasis on efficiency in education.

Despite these conflicting views of its value for education, there can be no doubt that QM has had an impact on school leaders' thinking. Some of the emerging positive and negative aspects of quality management are summarized in Figure 4.3.

Figure 4.3 **Positive and Negative Consequences of Quality Management in Education**

Positive Effects

(1) Greater employee involvement in management is encouraged.

(2) Improved clarity of purpose occurs, allowing means to be related to ends.

(3) The importance of students as learners is re-emphasized as the core of the enterprise.

(4) The importance of using assessment results as a tool for system feedback and improvement is stressed.

(5) The importance of top management serving as leaders is underscored.

(6) The fact that objectives change is emphasized so improvement is seen as a continuous process.

Negative Effects

(1) While stressing involvement, the actual power sharing of employees is often not changed (i.e., the organization does not become more democratic).

(2) Efficiency is always a possible hidden goal (i.e., cheaper is often viewed as better and can replace effectiveness as a goal).

(3) The emphasis on goal and objective clarity skews the emphasis to trivial goals and objectives that are always measurable and reinforces the status quo.

(4) The primary approach to attaining efficiency is the relentless and ruthless elimination of variance in all forms, yet education is about fostering individuality in learners and teachers.

(5) By emphasizing the importance of customers, the implicit goal is on consumerism and marketing.

(6) The context of leadership in QM emphasizes stability, control, prediction, and hierarchy, not creativity.

Implementing a Systems Approach to Monitoring All Components (Subsystems) of the School System for Efficiency

The curriculum management audit is an excellent approach to monitoring school district performance (Frase, English, and Poston 1995). The curriculum management audit process examines the capability of a school system to attain agreed-upon objectives within the policy and cost parameters under which it must function. The following five standards for a curriculum audit embrace the concept of quality control (English and Larson 1996, pp.232-247).

Standard 1: The school system exercises control over its major functions
Applicable Board Policies and Practices
• An aligned written, taught, and tested curriculum
• Statements on curriculum framework approach
• Board adoption of curriculum
• Accountability through roles and responsibilities
• Long-range or strategic planning

Standard 2: The school system has developed clear directions regarding desired learner outcomes
Applicable Board Policies and Practices
• Written curriculum for all subject/learning areas
• Periodic and systematic review of curriculum
• Formal textbook/resource adoption by the board
• Indication of content area emphasis (priorities)

Standard 3: The school system provides for connectivity and equity of the delivered curriculum
Applicable Board Policies and Practices
• Curriculum predicts content from one level to the next (vertical connectivity)
• Staff training in the delivery of curriculum
• Curriculum monitoring
• Equitable access to the curriculum

Standard 4: The school system uses feedback to improve its pupil performance
Applicable Board Policies and Practices
• Rationale for selection of tests provided
• A multifaceted assessment program
• Assessment data help determine program/curricular effectiveness and efficiency
• Regular reports to the board regarding effectiveness

Figure 4.4 Frequency and Percentages of Positive and Negative Curriculum Management Audit Findings 1988–1994

Standard/Indices	Positive	%	Negative	%	Total (n)
Standard 1: Control					
-Policy design	3	5	56	95	59
-Policy implementation	0	0	13	100	13
-Planning design	4	7	51	93	55
-Planning implementation	1	11	8	89	9
-Organizational structure	2	4	45	96	47
-Org. implementation	4	24	13	76	17
-Personnel practices	0	0	20	100	20
-Personnel supervision	3	16	16	84	19
Standard 2: Direction					
-Goals and objectives	2	6	29	94	31
-Curricular scope	8	26	23	74	31
-Curricular design	1	2	55	98	56
-Curricular delivery	0	0	18	100	18
-Curr. mgmt. structure	2	4	52	96	54

Standard 5: The school system is able to improve productivity

Applicable Board Policies and Practices

- A curriculum-driven budget
- Resource allocations tied to curricular priorities
- Data-driven decisions used to improve student learning

English, Vertiz, and Bates (1995) analyzed the results of 59 audits conducted by the American Association of School Administrators between 1988 and 1994. Few of the 59 school systems audited met audit standards (see Figure 4.4).

The standards and indices were derived from a broad range of educational and business publications (see English 1988), and though widely acknowledged in the literature, they were rarely followed in practice. The reasons for this discrepancy include:

- School board instability and lack of attention to policy development;
- Superintendent indifference to planning;
- Superintendent insensitivity to or lack of knowledge about necessary vertical linkages within the system;
- Inequitable resource allocation practices based on formulaic approaches;

- Failure to use test data to improve student performance;
- The failure of typical school budgeting practices to link costs to benefits or results (English et al. 1995, p. 15).

The curriculum management audit remains a powerful tool for monitoring how well all the components of a school system reach a variety of local, state, and federal goals and objectives.

Conclusion

This chapter has reviewed the school leader's organizational management responsibilities. Successful organizational management requires school leaders to be knowledgeable about and skilled in decision making and delegation; to have a thorough knowledge of budgeting, finance, and legal issues and a systemic view of quality; to effectively use technological applications; and to manage auxiliary programs to support school missions and goals.

Use the following Skill Accomplishment Checklist to assess your skill level on each of the important topics discussed in this chapter.

Figure 4.4 Frequency and Percentages of Positive and Negative Curriculum Management Audit Findings 1988–1994

Standard/Indices	Positive	%	Negative	%	Total (n)
Standard 3: Connectivity and Equity					
-Internal consistency	1	3	28	97	29
-Equity: design	3	6	45	94	48
-Equity: implementation	1	4	22	96	23
-Monitoring practices	2	4	47	96	49
-Staff development: design	1	3	39	98	40
-Staff development: delivery	0	0	10	100	10
-Articulation/coordination	1	3	36	97	37
Standard 4: Feedback					
-Testing program: scope	1	2	44	98	5
-Testing program: quality	1	3	32	97	33
-Use of testing data	1	2	52	98	53
-Use of program eval. data	0	0	19	00	19
Standard 5: Productivity					
-Curriculum-driven budget	0	0	56	100	56
-Cost effectiveness	1	5	21	95	22
-Organizational improvement	0	0	22	00	22
-Facility safety	18	35	34	65	52
-School climate	5	83	1	17	6
-Support system functions	2	29	5	71	7

Skill Accomplish Checklist for Chapter 4

Skills	Readings and Activities for Skill Mastery
Gather, analyze, and use data for informed decision making.	**Readings:** Clough (1984); English, Frase, Arhar (1992); Glasman (1994); Kaufman (1988); Schmieder and Cairns(1996) **Activities:** 1. Take the most controversial decision made recently in your school system and analyze the definition of the problem and the solutions explored. How were the decision processes related to the controversy? 2. Analyze several school board meetings. Upon what items does the board spend the most time? Why?
Delegate decision-making responsibility.	**Readings:** Chapter 1 of this book; Candoli (1991); Harvey, Bearley, and Corkrum(1997); Herman and Herman (1997); Reavis and Griffith (1992) **Activities:** 1. List the major reasons why some school administrators are reluctant to delegate. 2. Describe a decision that has been delegated in your school or district and the process for delegation.
Ensure adherence to legal concepts, regulations, and codes for school operations.	**Readings:** DeMitchell and Fossey (1997), Streshly and Frase(1992) **Activities:** 1. Inventory the most common legal issues facing your school or district. What are the possible reasons for these issues? 2. What reforms in your school system have been initiated by laws or judicial opinions?
Use technology to enhance administration.	**Readings:** Chambers (1994), Hobbs and Christianson (1997), McKenzie (1993), Poston et al. (1992) **Activities:** 1. Perform a technology inventory of your school or district. Identify the critical shortages. List areas where technologies could be used to improve productivity.
Engage in financial planning and cash flow management.	**Readings:** Hack, Candoli, and Ray (1995, pp. 290-308) **Activities:** 1. Describe your local board's policy on cash flow planning and investment. Then list the most common investments made in the past five years. 2. Estimate the extra income earned over the past five years from investments and where it was spent. What things would not have happened without these funds?
Establish procedures for budgeting, accounting, and auditing.	**Readings:** Burrup et al.(1993), Herman and Herman (1997), Poston et al. (1992) **Activities:** 1. Identify the most difficult issues involved with site-based budgeting. How were these issues resolved in your district or how can they be? 2. Review the management letters of your district's CPA for the past five years. What areas were cited as excellent and as needing improvement.
Administer auxiliary programs.	**Readings:** Flam and Keane (1997), Hack et al. (1995, pp. 334- 358), Herman (1995), Poston et al. (1992) **Activities:** 1. Develop a maintenance inventory of the most common problems in your schools over the past five years. 2. Evaluate the impact of the hypothetical privatization of an auxiliary program in your school district.

Skill Accomplish Checklist for Chapter 4—continued

Skills	Readings and Activities for Skill Mastery
Develop a plan to maintain the school plant, equipment, and support systems.	**Readings:** Readings: Herman (1995); Lane, Richardson, and Van Berkum (1996) **Activities:** 1. Construct a plant inventory for your schools as shown in Figure 4.3.
Apply appropriate components of quality management.	**Readings:** Bradley (1993); Downey, Frase, and Peters (1994); Kaufman and Zahn (1993) **Activities:** 1. Reassess the basic parallel between schools and business related to QM. Is it a perfect fit? If not, why? 2. Which are the easiest and hardest areas to apply QM to in schools? Speculate on the reasons.
Implement a systems approach to monitor all components (subsystems) of the school system for efficiency.	**Readings:** Frase et al. (1995); Kaufman and Grime (1995) **Activities:** 1. Conduct a preliminary curriculum management audit, applying the five standards the chapter identifies as critical. How many are present in your school(s)? 2. Identify the risks in conducting an audit and determine whether it would be a good idea to have one in your school district.

Resources

Adams, B., Q. Hill, A. Lichtenberg, J. Perkins, and P. Shaw. (1967). *Principles of Public School Accounting. State Educational Records and Reports Series: Handbook II-B.* Washington, D.C.: U.S. Government Printing Office.

Alexis, M., and C. Wilson. (1967). *Organizational Decision Making.* Englewood Cliffs, N.J.: Prentice-Hall.

American Association of School Administrators. (1995). *Guidelines for Contracting with Private Providers for Educational Services.* Alexandria, Va.: author.

Babbage, K. (1997). *Meetings for School-Based Decision Making.* Lancaster, PA.: Technomic Pub. Co., Inc.

Batey, C. (1996). *Parents as Lifesavers.* Thousand Oaks, Calif.: Corwin Press.

Beckett, P. (November 24, 1997). "U.S. Launches Criminal Probe in Schools' Case." *The Wall Street Journal* B5A.

Bradley, L. (1993). *Total Quality Management for Schools.* Lancaster, Pa.: Technomic Pub. Co., Inc.

Burrup, P., V. Brimley, and R. Garfield. (1993). *Financing Education in a Climate of Change.* Boston, Mass.: Allyn and Bacon.

Candoli, C. (1991). *School System Administration.* Lancaster, Pa.: Technomic Pub. Co., Inc.

Carrns, A. (November 12, 1997). "Schools Aren't Brick Boxes Anymore." *The Wall Street Journal* B1-B10.

Chambers, B. (1994). *Computer Applications for School Administrators.* Lancaster, Pa.: Technomic Pub. Co., Inc.

Clough, D. (1984). *Decisions in Public and Private Sectors.* Englewood Cliffs, N.J.: Prentice-Hall.

Darling-Hammond, L. (1997). *The Right To Learn.* San Francisco: Jossey-Bass.

Dembroski, F., and J. Biros. (1981). *Handbook of School/Banking Relations.* New York: State Association for School Business Officials.

Deming, E. (1986). *Out of the Crisis.* Cambridge, Mass.: MIT Press.

DeMitchell, T., and R. Fossey. (1997). *The Limits of Law-Based School Reform.* Lancaster, Pa.: Technomic Pub. Co., Inc.

Downey, C., Frase, L., and Peters, J. (1994). *The Quality Education Challenge.* Thousand Oaks, Calif.: Corwin Press.

Earthman, G. (1994). *School Renovation Handbook.* Lancaster, Pa.: Technomic Pub. Co., Inc.

English, F. (1994). *Theory in Educational Administration.* New York: Harper Collins.

English, F. (1988). *Curriculum Auditing.* Lancaster, Pa.: Technomic Pub. Co., Inc.

English, F., L. Frase, and J. Arhar. (1992). *Leading Into the 21st Century.* Newbury Park, Calif.: Corwin Press.

English, F., and R. Larson. (1996) *Curriculum Management for Educational and Social Service Organizations.* Springfield, Ill.: Charles C. Thomas Publisher.

English, F., V. Vertiz, and G. Bates. (Fall 1995). "Gauging the Impact of the Curriculum Management Audit Catalyst." *Catalyst for Change* 25, 1: 13-15.

Flam, S., and W. Keane. (1997). *Public Schools: Private Enterprise.* Lancaster, Pa.: Technomic Pub. Co., Inc.

Frase, L., F. English, and W. Poston. (1995). *The Curriculum Management Audit.* Lancaster, Pa.: Technomic Pub. Co., Inc.

Giroux, H. (1997). *Pedagogy and the Politics of Hope.* New York: Westview Press.

Glasman, N. (1994). *Making Better Decisions About School Problems.* Thousand Oaks, Calif.: Corwin Press.

Hack, W., I. Candoli, and J. Ray. (1995). *School Business Administration: A Planning Approach.* Boston, Mass.: Allyn and Bacon.

Harvey, R., W. Bearley, and S. Corkrum. (1997). *The Practical Decision Maker.* Lancaster, Pa.: Technomic Pub. Co., Inc.

Hayes, J. (1978). *Cognitive Psychology: Thinking and Creating.* Homewood Ill.: Dorsey.

Heilpern, J., and D. Nadler. (1992). "Implementing Total Quality Management: A Process of Cultural Change." In *Organizational Architecture: Designs for Changing Organizations,* edited by D. Nadler, M. Gerstein, and R. Shaw. San Francisco: Jossey-Bass.

Herman, J. (1995). *Effective School Facilities.* Lancaster, Pa.: Technomic Pub. Co., Inc.

Herman, J., and J. Herman. (1997). *School-Based Budgets.* Lancaster, Pa.: Technomic Pub. Co., Inc.

Herman, J., and J. Herman. (1995). Effective Decision Making. Lancaster, Pa.: Technomic Pub. Co., Inc.

Hobbs, V., and J. Christianson. (1997). *Virtual Classrooms.* Lancaster, Pa.: Technomic Pub. Co., Inc.

Hoy, W., and C. Tarter. (1995). *Administrators Solving the Problems of Practice.* Boston, Mass.: Allyn and Bacon.

Juran, J. (1979). *Quality Control Handbook.* New York: McGraw-Hill.

Kaufman, R. (1988). *Planning Educational Systems.* Lancaster, Pa.: Technomic Pub. Co., Inc.

Kaufman, R., and P. Grime. (1995). *Auditing Your Educational Strategic Plan.* Thousand Oaks, Calif.: Corwin Press.

Kaufman, R., and D. Zahn. (1993). *Quality Management Plus: The Continuous Improvement of Education.* Newbury Park, Calif.: Corwin Press.

Kuhn, A., and R. Beam. (1982). *The Logic of Organization.* San Francisco: Jossey-Bass.

Lane, K., M. Richardson, and D. Van Berkum. (1996). *The School Safety Handbook.* Lancaster, Pa.: Technomic Pub. Co., Inc.

Lipman, P. (Spring 1997). "Restructuring in Context: A Case Study of Teacher Participation and the Dynamics of Ideology, Race, and Power." *American Educational Research Journal* 34, 1: 3-37.

McKenzie, J. (1993). *Selecting, Managing, and Marketing Technologies.* Thousand Oaks, Calif.: Corwin Press.

Odden, E., and P. Wohlstetter. (1995). "Making School-Based Management Work." *Educational Leadership* 52, 5: 32-36.

Pallas, A., and A. Neumann. (March 1993). "Blinded by the Light: The Applicability of Total Quality Management to Educational Organizations." Paper Presented at the American Education Research Association, Atlanta, Ga.

Pinkney, A. (1988). *The Myth of Black Progress.* New York: Cambridge University Press.

Poston, W. Jr., P. Stone, and C. Muther. (1992). "Making Schools Work: Practical Management of Support Operations." In *Successful Schools: Guidebooks to Effective Educational Leadership,* edited by F. English. Newbury Park, Calif.: Corwin Press.

Reavis, C., and H. Griffith. (1992). *Restructuring Schools.* Lancaster, Pa.: Technomic Pub. Co., Inc.

Schmieder, J., and D. Cairns. (1996). *Ten Skills of Highly Effective Principals.* Lancaster, Pa.: Technomic Pub. Co., Inc.

Sedenburg, C. (1984). "Budgeting." *In Managing Limited Resources: New Demands on Public School Management: Fifth Annual Yearbook of the American Education Finance Association,* edited by L. Webb and V. Mueller. Cambridge, Mass.: Ballinger.

Sergiovanni, T., M. Burlingame, J. Coombs, and P. Thurston.(1980). *Educational Governance and Administration.* Englewood Cliffs, N.J.: Prentice-Hall.

Shewhart, W. (1931). *Economic Control of Quality of Manufactured Product.* New York: Van Nostrand.

Stonich, P. (1977). *Zero-Based Planning and Budgeting.* Homewood, Ill.: Dow Jones-Iorwin.

Streshly, W., and L. Frase. (1992). *Avoiding Legal Hassles.* Thousand Oaks, Calif.: Corwin Press.

Stringfield, S. (1994). "Identifying and Addressing Organizational Barriers to Reform." In *Schools and Students at Risk,* edited by R. Rossi. New York: Teachers College Press.

Taylor, R. (1984). *Behavioral Decision Making.* Glenview, Ill.: Scott Foresman and Company.

Tanner, L. (1997). *Dewey's Laboratory School.* New York: Teachers College Press.

Tidwell, S. (1974). *Financial and Managerial Accounting for Elementary and Secondary School Systems.* Chicago: Ill.: Association for School Business Officials.

Watson, C. (1981). *Results-Oriented Managing.* Reading, Mass.: Addison-Wesley.

Weick, K. (1985). "Sources of Order in Underorganized Systems: Themes in Recent Organizational Theory." In *Organizational Theory and Inquiry,* edited by Y. Lincoln. Beverly Hills, Calif.: Sage.

Wise, A. (1979). *Legislated Learning: The Bureaucratization of the American Classroom.* Berkeley, Calif.: University of California Press.

chapter 5 | Skills in Curriculum Planning and Development

Curriculum is "any document or plan in a school or school system that defines the work of teachers, at least to the extent of identifying the content to be taught children and the methods to be used in the process" (English 1992, p. 2). Over the past century, textbooks have been the most commonly used curriculum documents (Perkinson 1985). Today, however, there is an increasing movement away from the use of textbooks as the curriculum and toward the use of textbooks and other print and nonprint materials as vehicles for teaching higher-order thinking skills and applications-based problem solving. This trend makes it especially important for school leaders to have a sound knowledge of curriculum development and management.

"Any new effort in curriculum thought and action must treat the persistent questions of purpose, activity, organization, and evaluation" (McNeal 1996, p. 427). Even at the end of the 19th century, when there were no curriculum experts in the United States — no curriculum development committees, no state frameworks, and no national standards — there was still controversy. In the mid-1980s, Kliebard (1986) identified four groups with varying orientations who took four different approaches to curriculum development: (1) classical humanists who focused on the liberal arts and perpetuating cultural values and traditions, (2) child-centered theorists who believed that the school should fit the child rather than the child fitting the school, (3) social efficiency proponents who saw the school as a vehicle for the preparation of children for adult life and work, and (4) social reconstructionists who looked to the schools to provide social change. These competing views still affect curriculum development and delivery today.

Successful school administrators must be able to oversee the design of curriculum and the development of a strategic plan that enhances teaching and learning in multiple contexts. This chapter details the skills successful 21st century school leaders must possess to:

- Develop curriculum design and delivery systems for diverse school communities;
- Create developmentally appropriate curriculum and instructional practices;
- Assess students' present and future learning needs;
- Demonstrate an understanding of curricular alignment to ensure improved student performance and higher-order thinking;
- Design, evaluate, and refine curricular, co-curricular, and extracurricular programs;
- Create curricula based on research, applied theory, informed practice, recommendations of learned societies, and state and federal policies and mandates; and
- Use technology, telecommunications, and information systems to enrich curriculum development and delivery.

Developing Curriculum Design and Delivery Systems for Diverse School Communities

Types of Curriculum

Choate and colleagues (1995) distinguish between four categories of curriculum. These categories are core curriculum, collateral curriculum, support curriculum, and enrichment curriculum. *Core curriculum* has three components: (1) reading, made up of word recognition and comprehension; (2) written expression; and (3) arithmetic, made up of computation and problem solving. These components are the foundation for the other curriculum categories. Social studies and science are considered the *collateral curriculum* because of their importance and because they require students to apply the core curriculum subject areas. The *support curriculum* includes the skills necessary to support learning, such as social interaction skills, study skills, computer literacy, and word-processing skills. Creative arts and physical education are the *enrichment curriculum.*

Reading and writing. The development of reading and writing skills is inextricably linked to language development. Current thinking regarding the teaching of language arts incorporates both a whole-language and a traditional phonics approach. The whole-language approach integrates instruction in reading, writing, speaking, and listening (Mills, O'Keefe, and Stephens 1992). The traditional phonics or basal approach teaches discrete skills such as grammar, spelling, and decoding skills.

Arithmetic. Success with arithmetic, a subset of mathematics, is influenced by language arts skills and the ability to reason. The mathematics community is divided about whether the focus of instruction should be on the basic skills of computation or on problem solving. The authors of this book believe both are required.

Inclusive Classrooms in a Multicultural Context

The concept of full inclusion is replacing the concept of integration in U.S. schools today. Full inclusion refers to meeting the needs of all children and is based on the belief that "all children need to be included in the educational and social life of their neighborhood schools and classrooms, not merely placed in the mainstream" (Stainback and Stainback 1992). In inclusive schools, students are grouped heterogeneously in classrooms; students and staff are empowered to support one another; there is a belief that all children belong and can learn; classroom rules accommodate the rights of each member; support and assistance are provided to help everyone achieve; support networks include peer tutoring, buddy systems, circles of friends, and cooperative learning; and the curriculum is modified when necessary to meet students' unique needs.

Inclusion means serving the needs of all children. Black children make up about 16 percent of the student population of public schools. The percentage of black children is around 90 in cities such as Atlanta, Detroit, and Washington D.C. And in most urban school districts in the nation, the percentage of back students is on the rise (National Center for Education Statistics 1989). Many black families view education as the vehicle for eliminating discrimination and providing a certain measure of economic security (Hildebrand et al. 1996).

In 1992, Hispanics represented 9.5 percent of the U.S. population. This percentage is expected to rise to at least 21 by the year 2050, according to the U.S. Bureau of Census. Hispanic students have been shown to make the most academic progress when the school environment is accepting, when students work with peers in small groups, and when there is a strong interpersonal relationship between the student and teacher (Hildebrand et. al. 1996).

Asian Americans are the fastest-growing minority group in the United States today. This group includes persons whose families come from China, Japan, Korea, the Philippines, and Viet Nam (O'Hare and Felt 1991). Asian Americans are viewed as a population that has been able to overcome racism through hard work and strong family support. (See Chapter 3 and Appendix B for more demographic information about these groups.)

In addition to these growing enrollments, public schools are seeing an influx of Arab, Indian, and Amish children. Each group brings a different cultural orientation to school. Therefore, instructional delivery systems that meet the needs of the white middle-class are no longer sufficient. According to Ramsey (1987, pp. 3-5), the following are eight goals for teaching from a multicultural perspective in inclusive classrooms:

- To help children develop positive identities and become effective members of diverse groups;
- To enable children to see themselves as part of the larger society that involves equal membership from a variety of groups;
- To respect diversity in how people live;
- To encourage cooperation among diverse student groups;
- To help students develop a sense of social responsibility beyond their own cultural group;
- To empower students to be critical social activists;
- To promote the development of educational and social skills needed to effectively live in the larger society; and
- To develop positive school–family relationships.

Meeting these goals requires changes in our approach to curriculum delivery — changes that school leaders must encourage and guide. Because traditional delivery systems that deliver predetermined curriculum in lock-step fashion disempower students there is a movement away from delivering a single, discrete body of information toward teaching students how to access and learn relevant information and skills when placed in a new learning situation. School leaders must guide this movement and help schools adopt a full inclusion delivery approach.

Creating Developmentally Appropriate Curriculum and Instructional Practices

Choate and colleagues (1995) have designed a process for personalizing the instruction embedded in a district curriculum. The process begins with the teacher following the scope and sequence of the general educational curriculum. This is an important first step; it means that teachers are not free to choose whatever curriculum they want. The basic parameter is the district curriculum. The teacher's charge is to differentiate pacing, materials, instructional strategies, and whatever else is necessary to ensure student growth and achievement with that curriculum. "The individualization of curriculum to a specific student's needs depends upon the instructional delivery system, the teacher's resources, organization, and adjustments to methods and materials" (Choate et al. 1995, p. 43).

All children do not learn in the same way and on the same day, so it is necessary to set content priorities for students so that they can achieve success. The pacing of the curriculum is also critical. Some children need to spend extra time achieving the basic content and skill objectives of a unit, while others will quickly accomplish the basics and need enrichment activities. And because students learn in diverse ways, they need access to materials that capitalize on several modalities (e.g., auditory, visual, and kinesthetic). Instruction should to be delivered in a way that capitalizes on each student's strongest learning style, while helping students strengthen other styles. During instruction, teachers must be aware of students' level of engagement and modify and adjust the delivery to ensure student mastery. To effectively monitor students' achievement and the program requires both formative and summative evaluation.

Research has identified numerous effective teaching strategies for working with diverse students (Saravia-Shore and Garcia 1995). According to Zeichner (1992), ethnic and language minority students are best served when:

- Teachers have a clear sense of their own identity;
- Teachers set high expectations for all students and truly believe that all students can achieve at high levels;
- Teachers have a personal commitment to equity and believe they can make a difference in their students' lives;
- Teachers form a close bond with their students;

- Students are provided with a challenging curriculum, focusing on the development of higher-order thinking and problem-solving skills;
- Instruction focuses on students making meaning from their learning experiences;
- Students view their learning tasks as meaningful;
- Instructional content is representative of the contributions of individuals from diverse cultures;
- Teachers link instructional content to the knowledge base and students' cultures;
- Teachers teach the culture of the school while maintaining respect for students' ethnic pride;
- Community members and parents are encouraged to participate in students' education; and
- Teachers are politically active in efforts to provide a more just, humane society.

Educating Everybody's Children: Diverse Teaching Strategies for Diverse Learners (Cole 1995) lists 19 strategies and supporting examples to assist teachers in understanding ways to educate diverse groups of learners. The book asserts that diverse learners are most likely to reach their potential when teachers:

- Maintain high standards and offer challenging and advanced coursework;
- Learn about their students' cultures in order to better understand behavior in and out of the classroom;
- Remind parents of the importance of talking with their children, reading to them, sharing family stories and traditions, and talking about objects and events around the home;
- Recognize that students come to school with different skills and use the cultural background of each child to teach new skills;
- Use curriculum and instructional materials that are culturally relevant to students;
- Use nonsexist, nonracist, nonethnocentric language and instructional resources;
- Are sensitive to and recognize students' learning styles;
- Use cooperative learning approaches that include group goals and individual accountability;
- Design instruction to capitalize on students' cultures and native languages;
- Provide instruction in a student's native language while they are learning English;
- Use dual-language approaches;
- Use integrated, holistic approaches to language experiences;

- Use subject matter to teach English to students with limited proficiency in English;
- Embed English as a second language in multilingual schools too linguistically diverse to form bilingual classrooms;
- Organize classrooms into flexible, heterogeneous, cooperative learning groups with native English speakers and limited English speakers;
- Use cross-age and peer tutoring;
- Demonstrate respect for each student's native language;
- Use themes to integrate the learning of subject matter and second-language acquisition; and
- Allow students to use computers to learn English as a second language.

School leaders must provide opportunities for teachers to learn the strategies listed here and then monitor their implementation.

Assessing Students' Present and Future Learning Needs

According to Barrow (1988), school leaders and others can decide whether an educational curriculum is worthwhile using philosophical inquiry, democratic consensus, and empirical assessment of need. Each of these approaches should be a component of a needs assessment — a future-focused information-gathering and analysis process (Suarez 1991). A curriculum needs assessment reveals the "gap between where the learner is now and where we would want the learner to be" (Pratt 1994, p. 37). Pratt recommends that school leaders consult three main groups — specialists, clients, and gatekeepers — when planning a new curriculum.

Specialists. Specialists should be consulted to ensure that the new curriculum represents the most current thinking of experts and learned societies in a particular content area. The recent proliferation of standards documents published by national associations is an example of the work of specialists. All of the committees working on these documents were made up of individuals believed to be expert in their fields. During deliberations, these groups attempt to define "world-class standards" so schools can ensure that U.S. students meet the highest expectations found around the world.

Clients. Students are the most obvious and most important clients of the curriculum. Teachers, parents, employers, and the community are also clients. "There is no other place to begin instruc-

tion than where students already are. Ascertaining their backgrounds, their interests, their aspirations and motivations, their preferences and aversions, and their histories of success and failure is essential if curricula are to meet their needs rather than those of teachers or curriculum planners" (Pratt 1994, p. 41).

Gatekeepers. Gatekeepers are those individuals who can affect the implementation of a curriculum; they can be school board members, parent groups, opinion leaders, or business notables within a community. It is imperative to include gatekeepers in the curriculum development process, perhaps not as producers, but certainly as reviewers of the emerging document. Having them involved in the process so their questions can be answered during curriculum development is better than attempting to deal with their concerns in a public arena afterward.

Curriculum Selection

Currently, our knowledge base is doubling every three to five years, yet the amount of instructional time available in schools is not increasing. Deciding what are the most important processes, skills, attitudes, content, and concepts to teach is difficult. English (1992) suggests the use of a content validation matrix to assist in selecting the most appropriate curriculum. English proposes the construction of a matrix with content proposed to be included in the curriculum listed vertically on the left side, and columns labeled "state law," "state test," "national task forces," "local policy," "local teacher poll," "textbooks," and "futurists" across the horizontal axis. Different labels can be added to the matrix throughout the process.

Completion of the validation matrix provides a picture of the degree of consensus among various groups and documents regarding the proposed curriculum as various topics, skills, and concepts can be placed according to the group(s) who advocate them. Curriculum developers can then answer questions about each topic, skill, and concept. For instance, does current state law require that the topic/skill/concept be taught? Is it assessed on the state test? Is it included as part of the recommended curriculum by a national task force or association? Is it included as part of local school policy? Do teachers view it as a priority? Is it included in current instructional text and supplementary materials? Do futurists view it as important? Interpretation of the matrix must be guided by school officials and curriculum development committees.

Assessments

Student assessment can be used for screening, determining eligibility for special education, and instructional assessment.

Screening. Screening is used to determine which students need a particular program, and is most often done through formal, standardized tests administered to groups of students. These tests are generally supplemented with rating sheets based on teacher observations and parent observation information. The results of these assessments are used to provide students with programs, activities, and services designed to ameliorate perceived learning deficiencies.

Eligibility for special education services. The 1992 Individuals with Disabilities Education Act (IDEA), which was reauthorized in 1997, sets forth evaluation standards to guide the assessment of children with disabilities. Under IDEA, children with disabilities are assured of an appropriate education, the rights of the children and their parents are protected, and assessments are required to determine the effectiveness of the educational program for each child. While developed primarily for children with disabilities, these standards can be applied to all children.

Instructional assessment. Assessment of instruction is routinely conducted through informal inventories and teacher-made and criterion-referenced tests. Traditional teacher-made tests have included multiple-choice, completion, short answer, and true-and-false tests. Recently, an increased demand has risen for alternative forms of assessments. These alternative forms of assessment include open-ended response items, performance events, and portfolios. All of these assessments can be used to determine student learning needs.

Curriculum-based assessment (CBA) is another part of the instructional assessment mix. CBA is "the process of determining students' instructional needs within a curriculum by directly assessing specific curriculum skills" (see Choate et al. 1995). CBA helps educators determine what to teach, is efficient, facilitates evaluation of student progress, is valid and reliable, increases student achievement, can be used to help make referral decision, and complies with the requirements of IDEA.

The curriculum-based assessment/programming model (CBA/P) extends the CBA model and "contains procedures to assess and program for a student's needed skills, as well as to ensure that tar-

get tasks are mastered on both short-and long-term bases" (Choate et. al. 1995, p. 50). CBA/P begins with an analysis of the curriculum, continues with the assessment of student performance followed by the development of instruction to meet the student's assessed needs, and then repeats the cycle. At the end of each cycle, student progress is communicated to relevant stakeholders.

School leaders must ensure that all assessment practices adhere to the basic principles of assessment. That is, administrators must:

- Ensure that the assessment process is efficient and purposeful;
- Relate assessment to the requirements of the curriculum;
- Set priorities for assessment;
- Use only appropriate tools and techniques;
- Proceed from broad, general areas to specific skills;
- Analyze all errors;
- Determine the strategies a student uses to do tasks;
- Substantiate assessment findings;
- Record and report results of assessment; and
- Continually improve assessment practice (Choate et al. 1995, p. 22).

Demonstrating an Understanding of Curricular Alignment To Ensure Improved Student Performance and Higher-Order Thinking

Curriculum Alignment

Curriculum alignment refers to the relationship among the written, taught, and tested curriculum. When curriculum is truly aligned, school districts define the curriculum and write it down; teachers use these curriculum documents to plan and deliver instruction; students are taught in a manner that enables them to reach mastery of the curriculum; and students are then able to demonstrate that mastery on teacher-made tests and district, state, and national assessments. Three pairs of key concepts impact curriculum alignment: design and delivery, articulation and coordination, and focus and connectivity (English and Larson 1996). Effective curriculum management alignment systems must address all six components (English 1992, pp. 2-6).

Design alignment refers to the relationship between the written curriculum and the tested curriculum. Because the tested curriculum used for accountability purposes in most districts is the state assessment system, it is imperative that the local written curriculum reflect the competencies assessed on state tests. While this sounds simplistic, most district curriculum guides do not make this relationship clear to teachers. *Delivery alignment* refers to teachers' ability to present instruction to ensure that students achieve mastery of the skills to be assessed.

Articulation refers to the curriculum connectivity between grades and levels within the system. Does the 3rd grade mathematics curriculum build on the 2nd grade curriculum? Does the middle school science curriculum extend and progress from the elementary science curriculum? In other words, does curriculum articulation exist K-12 within the system in all content areas?

Coordination refers to the consistency across grade or course levels. Curriculum coordination is a particular problem in large schools where several teachers teach the same subject but each focuses on different content and skills. If the high school has five Algebra I teachers, are all five teachers teaching the same curriculum? Curriculum coordination is also a problem across elementary schools.

Implementation of a coordinated and articulated curriculum designed to link the written curriculum with the tested curriculum and delivered to ensure student mastery brings *focus* and *connectivity* to the system.

Teaching for Understanding

"The relative absence in schools of a concern with deep understanding reflects the fact that, for the most part, the goal of engendering that kind of understanding has not been a high priority for educational bureaucracies" (Gardner 1991, p. 8). Public education during the 20th century has not produced a widespread pedagogy for understanding, one that provides students with opportunities to test and apply their ideas, to look at concepts from many points of view, and to develop proficient performance.

Students taught for understanding can evaluate and defend ideas with careful rea-

soning and evidence, independently inquire into a problem using a productive research strategy, produce a high-quality piece of work, and understand the standards that indicate good performance. (Darling-Hammond 1997, p.96)

Teaching for understanding requires a focus on problem-solving skills. A general problem-solving strategy can be reduced to five stages (see Derry 1991, Gallini 1991). Bransford and Stein (1993) use the acronym IDEAL to identify the five steps:

I   Identify problems and opportunities
D   Define goals and represent the problem
E   Explore possible strategies
A   Anticipate outcomes and act
L   Look back and learn

The process begins by identifying a problem and recognizing the problem as an opportunity for creating a solution. To define the goals for action and represent the problem in a solvable manner, students must focus on relevant information, understand the elements of the problem, and develop the right schema to comprehend the problem. This requires focusing attention on the problem and understanding the work.

Without linguistic comprehension a problem cannot be fully understood. Mayer (1992) recommends providing students with practice recognizing and categorizing a variety of problems, presenting problems in a variety of ways using items such as pictures, symbols, or graphs, and selecting relevant and irrelevant information in problems. In this way students learn about the process of problem solving and develop understanding.

Designing, Evaluating, and Refining Curricular, Co-Curricular, and Extracurricular Programs

In 1994, the Joint Committee on Standards for Educational Evaluation published a comprehensive listing of program evaluation standards categorized in four areas: utility standards, feasibility standards, propriety standards, and accuracy standards (See chapter 9 for more detail.). In order to evaluate the effectiveness of a program, the program must be designed in such a way that the goals and objectives are clearly defined, the program's purpose is explained, and the program is described in sufficient detail to enable a program evaluation to be constructed (Steffy and English 1997). Program designers must determine a need to be addressed and be specific about what the newly designed program will try to accomplish relevant to that need. Attention should first be given to whether the need calls for a new program design or whether an existing program can be modified and used.

It is important to determine what clients perceive they need from a new program. In particular, staff should be surveyed about what problems they perceive and how effective the organization has been in addressing these perceived problems. Also, an effort should be made to determine the areas in which the organization is most seriously failing to achieve its goals. Then plans can be made to design special programs or to revise old ones. The design of a new program must fit within the goals of the organization and community, which must be agreed upon by all stakeholders.

Once all of the goals and needs are determined, program goals and objectives should be developed. The program's most important characteristics, materials, activities, and administrative arrangements should be determined. Also, a careful analysis of how the program's activities are supposed to lead to attainment of the objectives should be documented. Formative and summative evaluation procedures should also be planned during program design. Formative evaluation should answer questions regarding whether the program is being implemented as designed and whether the program needs to be modified along the way. Summative evaluation procedures should determine whether the program has been effective in accomplishing its objectives. Figure 5.1 on page 76 is a comparison of formative and summative evaluation for a number of criteria adapted from the work of Herman, Morris, and Fitz-Gibbon (1990, p. 26)

Program design involves building a bridge between planning and doing through a methods-means analysis (Kauffman, Herman, and Watters 1996). Before beginning a methods-means analysis, those conducting it must have a copy of the program mission objectives, including performance requirements for achieving the ideal mission; the functions to be performed and their performance requirements; and the tasks and their performance requirements (if a task analysis was completed). With these data, those conducting the analysis are ready to identify possible ways and means to accomplish each function and task, identify advantages

and disadvantages of each possible method and the means available to get the job done, and identify constraints and eliminate them if possible.

Creating Curricula Based on Research, Applied Theory, Informed Practice, Recommendations of Learned Societies, and State and Federal Policies and Mandates

The work of Venezky (1989, 1992) shows how curricula in any content area falls into five categories: needed, desired, prescribed, delivered, or received.

Needed. The needed curriculum represents the recommendations of curriculum specialists, commissions, blue-ribbon panels, and politicians. It is the ideal and is often suggested without consideration of time, resources, or delivery systems.

Desired. The desired curriculum is represented by state frameworks and sometimes by district curriculum guides. The recent proliferation of national standards is an example of desired curriculum. NCTM was credited with one of the first iterations of a desired curriculum with its publication of national mathematics standards in the late 1980s. While desired curriculum documents tend to be developed by specialists in their respective fields, they are not devoid of the influence of politicians, textbook publishers, or special interest groups.

Prescribed. The prescribed curriculum refers to the textbooks and other instructional materials placed into teachers' hands. Generally, new textbooks are purchased on a five- to six-year cycle with funds supplied by the state, and many states have state-approved textbook lists from which local districts may choose. Textbook publishers lobby feverishly to be sure their texts appear on these lists.

Delivered. The delivered curriculum is what teachers teach.

Received. The received curriculum is what students acquire.

Many variables affect what gets taught in schools. Teachers and school districts decide what is important to teach and test based on: their own professional judgment; the culture, norms, and history of the environment in which they work; their professional networks; and the influence of the institutions that trained them (Elmore and Sykes 1992). State and national policies, frameworks, and regula-

75

Figure 5.1 Comparative Indicators in Formative Versus Summative Evaluation

Criteria	Formative	Summative
Primary audience	Program developers/ managers Program implementers	Policymakers Interested publics Funders
Primary emphasis in date collection	Clarification of goals	Documentation of outcomes
	The nature of the program process/implementation	Documentation of implementation
	Clarification of problems in implementation and in progress on outcomes	
	Micro-level analyses of implementation and outcomes	Macro-level analyses of implementation and outcomes
Primary role of program developers and implementers	Collaborators	Data provider
Primary role of evaluator	Interactive	Independent
Typical methodology	Qualitative and quantitative, with more emphasis on qualitative	Quantitative, sometimes enriched with qualitative
Frequency of data collection	Ongoing	Limited
Primary reporting mechanisms	Discussion/meetings Informal interaction	Formal reports
Reporting frequency	Frequent throughout	At conclusion
Emphasis in reporting	Micro-level relations among context, process, and outcome	Macro-level relations among context, process, and outcomes
	Implications for program practices and specific changes in operations	Implications for policy, administrative controls, and management
Requirements for	Understanding of program rapport with developers/ implementers Advocacy/trust	Scientific rigor Impartiality

tions, as well as the work of national learned societies and textbook publishers also alter the curriculum.

The government influences curriculum by setting guidelines and funding research and development projects, by endorsing the ideas of professional organizations (e.g., funding the development of national standards for math, technology, and science), and by framing policies in particular ways. Attempts via state and national policies to bring about dramatic change in the classroom, however, have produced limited positive results. Often, these policies are symbolic rather than substantive. "In fact, policymaking often has little to do with instrumental action. . . . because political circumstances often force policymakers to act even though they have no idea what the correct action is" (Elmore and Sykes 1992, p.187).

Control of the Curriculum

Curriculum development is complicated by the concept of local control where ostensibly important decisions about what should be taught in local schools is a local decision made by the local school board upon the recommendation of the superintendent. In reality, local control is often replaced by state and national control, and by the control of private corporations such as test developers. Local control can also have its dark side when the educational needs of students are put aside by political patronage, corruption, and discrimination.

"The time is short and there is much to teach" is a simplistic statement, but a description of why the curriculum has become a battleground of conflicting ideas about what is worthwhile knowledge. Kliebard (1986) identified four conflicting forces that drive curriculum development: adherence to the traditional liberal arts, cognitive-developmentalist approaches to learning, the desire to create efficient systems of instruction, and social reconstruction. Currently, a powerful trend exists toward state control of the curriculum through increased course credit requirements, professional development requirements for educators, and state assessment. This trend has heightened interest in who controls the curriculum and what that means to our society. Some view control of the curriculum as transmitting privilege and reproducing inequity (Apple 1979). This view holds that the organization of knowledge and the mechanism for its transmission limit access for some and provide privileges for others. Knowledge is seen as "cultural capital," a lack of which disadvantage some groups (Bernstein 1977).

Still, public schools continue to do what they have been doing for a very long time. Some of this is related to the decentralization of schools into 50 states and more than 15,000 school districts. Because of this decentralization of power and authority, schools have been referred to as "loosely coupled" both in terms of the linkage among districts within the nation and the linkage among schools within a district. In addition, all schools are vulnerable to externally imposed changes — demographic, cultural, political, social, and economic — and, therefore, establish mechanisms to protect themselves from these influences. In this buffering process, policy change mandates are filtered and diffused through many layers. As policy changes move through the layers, controversy arises, compromises are made, and the day-to-day business of the classroom continues relatively unchanged. Schools maintain internal processes for preserving their stability, and teachers are adept at recognizing early warning signs of impending change and have many strategies for maintaining the status quo. Proposed changes typically follows the same cycle. The change usually begins with the advocacy of the new program or approach; public interest is heightened; politicians go for the quick fix; and when dramatic results are not forthcoming in a year or two, another solution is sought and the cycle of innovation repeats itself.

In the end, teachers control the curriculum. They each make the final determination about what to teach, in what order, for how long, using what materials and instructional strategies, and how to assess what students have learned. Teachers rely heavily on district-provided textbooks in making these determinations. "A textbook exists both as a cultural artifact and as a surrogate curriculum" (Venezky 1992, pp. 436-461). Textbooks carry with them both manifest and latent curricula. That is, they cover a specific content in a specific order, and instruct the teacher to deliver the content in a specific way. Content is presented at a specified level of difficulty (readability), and, often, through the use of pictures, examples, and content omissions, the selective traditions of the dominant society are transmitted.

Research

Since the mid 1960s, educational research has been funded by the federal government as well as a number of foundations. The results of these research studies appear in numerous journals and

77

become the topic of professional books and the basis for refereed papers presented at national conferences. Because literally hundreds of research studies are conducted dealing with any one area using a variety of methodologies and resulting in a variety of often conflicting results, it is possible to find support for almost any position an educator wants to take grounded in some research project. "Educational research centers, under the requirement of dissemination, are as apt as commercial institutions to propagandize their results, often suggesting directly to textbook publishers what they should be doing" (Venezky 1992, p. 440).

It is imperative that school leaders use their professional judgment to ensure that curriculum is based on best practice and students' present and future needs.

Using Technology, Telecommunications, and Information Systems To Enrich Curriculum Development and Delivery

Today, there is a rapid movement toward use of the Internet in education, which brings with it access to a phenomenal knowledge base that can be retrieved through a vast array of digital technologies such as bulletin boards, teleconferencing, interactive networks, and multimedia systems. "In the very near future, we will have the needed links to bring the community, home, school, and business together in a lifelong interactive education experience" (Hirschbuhl and Bishop 1997, p. iv). Companies such as CBS, Turner Broadcasting, and Disney are spending billions of dollars on the development of new products called "edutainment," which are a blend of education and entertainment. In 1992, Lewis Pearlman, author of *School's Out*, wrote,

> We have the technology today to enable virtually anyone who is not severely handicapped to learn anything, at a 'grade A' level, anywhere, anytime. . . .[T]he status quo is on the rout, the unthinkable has become the commonplace, and the fabric of whole societies is being rewoven. As every major social structure in these lands is reappraised and redesigned or replaced, the most conservative social glue — educa-

tion — inevitably will be reinvented as well. (pp. 23, 340)

Today, increasing numbers of people agree with Pearlman. Snider (1996) predicts that as the transformation from the Industrial Age to the Information Age progresses, most educators will lose money, status, and power. Snider identifies five economic trends leading to this transformation. These economic trends are the movements: (1) from a labor-intensive industry to a capital-intensive industry where education resources are delivered via the information superhighway; (2) from locally delivered education to worldwide virtual courses, classrooms, and schools; (3) from small-scale to large-scale instruction, which could mean replacement of the 40,000 Algebra I teachers currently employed with a few "star" teachers; (4) from small-scale to large-scale evaluation of students and courses, and (5) from the monopoly of a local, public school district to the competition of choice. Snider likens the coming changes to the shift from 1800 when 90 percent of the workforce was engaged in agriculture to today when less than 3 percent of the population is so employed. He labels the period ahead as Education Wars and predicts that opposition to technological changes will come from unions, education schools, and legislators.

Software

The current trend in computer software is toward more interactivity. Effective interactive software provides students with immediate responses and nonsequential access, adapts to student needs and requests, and allows students to present information, and interrupt or initiate actions (Borsook and Higginbotham-Wheat 1991). The benefits of this type of software include increased student interest, higher cognitive processing, curriculum integration, application of higher level thinking skills, and increased teacher-student collaboration (Baker-Albaugh 1993). A variety of instructional strategies can be used to promote interactivity in computer-based instruction, including queries, notetaking, hypertext, and cooperative dialogue (Hannafin 1989).

In a 1996 position paper, the National Association for the Education of Young Children stated that, when used appropriately, technology enhances children's cognitive and social abilities (see Clements 1994, Haugland and Slade 1994). It is used best as one of a variety of options to support children's learning. Care should be taken to ensure equitable access to technology by students and their families and programs should be reviewed to ensure elimination of stereotyping and exposure to violence and the incorporation of problem-solving skills.

Multimedia and the Internet

The use of multimedia and the Internet in curriculum planning and instructional delivery is increasing.

Multimedia. Multimedia presentations pull together audio, text, and pictures to enable students with a variety of learning styles to gain knowledge and apply it to solving problems. Multimedia provides students with a variety of choices through their ability to navigate, access, and manipulate information. "Without multimedia, instructional problem-solving systems would not be feasible, nor would we be able to enrich the problem-solving facilities within schools at a fraction of the cost of physical laboratories" (Hirschbuhl and Bishop 1997, p. 118). Technology-rich classrooms are becoming known as "smart" classrooms.

Internet. The effect the Internet will have on education is as yet unknown. Without a doubt it provides easy access to an unlimited knowledge base. Chat rooms are created to discuss world events as they are happening; students frequently seek help with homework assignments using the World Wide Web; electronic field trips take students to the remotest regions of the world via satellite dishes and computers; classrooms on opposite sides of the globe are now electronically linked; and cultural, race, distance, and ethnic barriers are overcome as people communicate through words and pictures.

Technology Standards for Educators

The ratio of computers to students has increased dramatically over the past 10 years. In 1985 the ratio was one computer for 50 students; by 1990 the ratio had dropped to one computer for 20 students. In 1997, it is estimated that there is one computer available for each nine students (NCATE 1997). NCATE plans to set accreditation standards that will force teacher training institutions to integrate instruction in effective uses of technology into their teacher training programs. In addition, NCATE intends to use technology to improve the existing accreditation process, and to improve its

own operations.

Current NCATE (1997) technology standards for teacher training institutions include:

- Completion of a sequence of courses and/or experiences leading to technological competence;
- Experience with educational technology in the planning of instruction, assessment, and professional productivity;
- Assurance that faculty are knowledgeable about current technological practice and that faculty have been trained in technological applications; and
- Assurance that sufficient budgetary resources are available to support these activities.

School leaders face a perplexing array of technology-related questions about issues such as the kind of equipment that should be purchased, what professional development should be provided, the best way to evaluate the effectiveness of technology-based instruction, how to best deal with the equity issues related to student access to equipment, which administrative functions should be computerized, the role of the Internet in providing access to knowledge, the kind of maintenance program that will be required, and the best way to provide upgrades and technical support for school technology. Standards being developed for school leaders state that they should have "the ability to use Web pages and the Internet to communicate with staff and their communities; know how to use technology to enhance administration of business and support systems; and be able to apply technology in creating and managing instructional programs" (Trotter 1997, p. 31).

Experts advise school leaders to:
- Set goals, then consider what hardware/software is required to achieve the goals;
- Incorporate the technology plan into the overall district strategic plan;
- Connect instructional technology and administrative technology to maximize the effectiveness of each;
- Connect people at all levels in the organization through the use of e-mail, databases, and telephones;
- Seek input from all stakeholders, including teachers, parents, and business and community leaders, when making technology-related decisions; and
- Become avid users of technology.

Conclusion

Public education in the 21st century will be characterized by a different curriculum and instructional delivery system than is in use today. From here forward, more attention will have to be paid to the individual learning needs of children and youth; teachers will have to learn to accept and rely on data-driven decision making that keeps them informed about the link between their instructional practices and student achievement; greater attention will be devoted to higher-order thinking skills both in the planning of instruction and the assessment of what students learn; and all programs will be assessed for their effectiveness with both formative and summative measures.

Perhaps the greatest unknown about the future of public education is the effect technology will have on teachers' work and student learning. We suspect that classroom practices as we know them today will become obsolete, disappear, and be replaced with learning environments that truly enable all children to learn at high levels. Curriculum planning and development will remain at the center of the transformation of schools, and visionary school leaders must guide the transformation.

Use the following Skill Accomplishment Checklist to assess your skill level on each of the important topics discussed in this chapter.

Skill Accomplish Checklist for Chapter 5

Skills	Readings and Activities for Skill Mastery
Develop curriculum design and delivery systems for diverse school communities.	**Readings:** Choate et. al (1995), Hildebrand et al. (1996), Ramsey (1987) **Activities:** 1. Develop a plan for the revision of the curriculum in one content area that provides for instructional differences for diverse populations. 2. Develop and deliver a professional inservice to provide awareness of how diverse populations commonly learn best.
Create developmentally appropriate curriculum and instructional practice.	**Readings:** Saravia-Shore and Garcia (1995), Zeichner (1992) **Activities:** 1. Design a curriculum monitoring system to determine to what extent teachers are using diverse teaching strategies. 2. Develop a questionnaire to assess teachers' beliefs about student learning. 3. Review your present district curriculum to assess whether it focuses on higher-order thinking and problem solving.
Assess students' present and future learning needs.	**Readings:** Choate et al. (1995), English (1992), Pratt (1994), Steffy (1995), **Activities:** 1. Describe a plan for involving specialists, clients, and gatekeepers in the curriculum development process. 2. Create a validation matrix for the development of a new mathematics curriculum. 3. Develop a student assessment plan for your school.
Demonstrate an understanding of curricular alignment to ensure improved student performance and higher-order thinking.	**Readings:** Darling-Hammond (1997), English (1992), English and Larson (1996),Gardner (1991) **Activities:** 1. Plan and deliver an inservice dealing with key concepts related to curriculum alignment. 2. Develop a procedure to determine the degree of articulation and coordination of curriculum in your district's science curriculum. 3. Develop an assessment plan to determine the extent to which students are learning for understanding.

Skill Accomplish Checklist for Chapter 5—continued

Skills	Readings and Activities for Skill Mastery
Design, evaluate, and refine curricular, co-curricular, and extracurricular programs.	**Readings:** Herman, Morris, and Fitz-Gibbon (1990); Kauffman, Herman, and Watters (1996); Steffy and English (1997) **Activities:** 1. Develop a formative program evaluation design for a newly implemented program in your district. 2. Detail the steps you would take in the redesign of the district's social studies program.
Create curricula based on research, applied theory, informed practice, recommendations of learned societies, and state and federal policies and mandates.	**Readings:** Elmore and Sykes (1992), Venezky (1992) **Activities:** 1. Select a curriculum topic of interest to your district and prepare an annotated bibliography of pertinent research. 2. Prepare a synthesis of the research on textbook selection procedures 3. Develop and submit a request to present at the American Educational Research Association's annual conference.
Use technology, telecommunications, and information systems to enrich curriculum development and delivery.	**Readings:** Hirschbuhl and Bishop (1997), NCATE (1997), Pearlman (1992), Snider (1996), Trotter (1997) **Activities:** 1. Develop a district technology plan that can be integrated into a district's strategic plan. 2. Develop an attitude inventory regarding teacher use of technology. 3. Develop a technology staff development plan.

Resources

Apple, M.W. (1979). *Ideology and Curriculum.* London: Routledge & Kegan Paul.

Atkins, J. M., and E. House. (1981). "The Federal Role in Curriculum Development." *Educational Evaluation and Policy Analysis* 3, 5: 5-36.

Baker-Albaugh, P. R. (1993). "Definitions of Interactive Learning: What We See Is Not What We Get." *Journal of Instructional Delivery Systems* 7, 3: 36-39.

Barrow, R. (1988). "Over the Top: A Misuse of Philosophical Techniques?" *Interchange* 19, 2: 59-63.

Bernstein, B. (1977). *Class, Codes, and Control. Volume 3: Towards a Theory of Cultural Transmissions,* 2nd Ed. London: Routledge & Kegan Paul.

Borsook, T.K., and N. Higginbotham-Wheat. (1991). "Interactivity: What Is it and What Can It Do for Computer-Based Instruction?" *Educational Technology,* 31, 10: 11-17.

Bransford, J. D., and B.S. Stein. (1993). *The Ideal Problem Solver: A Guide for Improving Thinking, Learning, and Creativity* (2nd Ed.). New York: Freeman.

Caine, R. N., and G. Caine. (1997). *Education on the Edge of Possibility.* Alexandria, Va.: Association for Supervision and Curriculum Development.

Choate, J., B. Enright, L. Miller, J. Poteet, and T. Rakes. (1995). *Curriculum-Based Assessment and Programming* (3rd Ed.). Boston: Allyn and Bacon.

Clements, D.H. (1994). "The Uniqueness of the Computer as a Learning Tool: Insights from Research and Practice." In *Young Children : Active Learners in a Technological Age,* edited by J. L. Wright and D. D. Slade Washington D.C.: NAEYC.

Cole, R., ed. (1995). *Educating Everybody's Children: Diverse Teaching Strategies for Diverse Learners.* Alexandria, Va.: Association for Supervision and Curriculum Development.

Darling-Hammond, L. (1997). *The Right To Learn: A Blueprint for Creating Schools that Work.* San Francisco: Jossey-Bass.

Derry, S. (1991). "Beyond Symbolic Processing: Expanding Horizons for Educational Psychology." *Journal of Educational Psychology* 84, 413-418.

Elmore, R., and G. Sykes. (1992). "Curriculum Policy." In *Handbook on Research on Curriculum,* edited by Phillip W. Jackson. New York: Macmillian Publishing Co.

English, F.W. (1992). *Deciding What To Teach and Test.* Newberry, Calif.: Corwin Press.

English, F. W., and R.L. Larson. (1996). *Curriculum Management for Educational and Social Service Organization.* Springfield, Ill.: Charles Thomas.

Gallini, J.K. (1991). "Schema-Based Strategies and Implications for Instructional Design in Strategy Training." In *Cognitive Strategies Research: From Basic Research to Educational Applications,* edited by C. McCormick, G. Miller, and M. Pressley. New York: Springer-Verlag.

Gardner, H. (1991). *The Unschooled Mind: How Children Think and How Schools Should Teach.* New York: Basic Books.

Gonzalez, R. D. (1990). "When Minority Becomes Majority: The Changing Face of English Classrooms." *English Journal* 79, 1: 16-23.

Hannafin, M.J. (1989). "Instruction Strategies and Emerging Instructional Technologies: Psychological Perspectives." *Canadian Journal of Educational Communication* 18:3, 99. 167-179.

Haugland, S. W., and D.D. Slade. (1994). "Software Evaluation for Young Children." In *Young Children: Active Learners in a Technological Age,* edited by. J. L. Wright and D. D. Slade. Washington D.C.: NAEYC.

Herman, J., L. Morris, and C. Fitz-Gibbon. (1990). *Evaluator's Handbook.* Newbury Park: Sage Publications.

Hildebrand, V., L. Phenice, M. Gray, and R. Himes. (1996). *Knowing and Serving Diverse Families.* Columbus, Ohio: Merrill.

Hirschbuhl, J. J., and D. Bishop. (1997). *Computers in Education* (8th Ed.). Guilford, Conn.: Dushkin/McGraw-Hill.

Hobbs, V., and J. Christianson. (1997). *Virtual Classrooms.* Lancaster, Pa.: Technomic Pub. Co., Inc.

Hu, A. (1988). "Asian Americans: A Model Minority or Double Minority." *Amerasia* 15, 1: 243-257.

Kauffman, R., J. Herman, and K. Watters. (1996). *Educational Planning: Strategic, Tactical, Operational.* Lancaster, Pa.: Technomic Pub. Co., Inc.

Kliebard, H.M. (1986). *The Struggle for the American Curriculum, 1893-1951.* Boston: Routledge & Kegan Paul.

Mayer, R.E. (1992). *Thinking, Problem Solving, Cognition* (2nd. Ed.). San Francisco: Freeman.

McNeal, J. (1996). *Curriculum: A Comprehensive Introduction.* New York: Harper Collins.

Mills, H., T. O'Keefe, and D. Stephens. (1992). *Looking Closely: Exploring the Role of Phonics in One Whole Language Classroom.* Urbana, Ill.: National Council of Teachers of English.

National Council for the Accreditation of Teacher Education. (1997). *Technology and the New Professional Teacher: Preparing for the 21st Century Classroom.* Washington D.C.: author.

Ogbu, J.U. (1987). "Variability in Minority School Performance: A Problem in Search of an Explanation." *Anthropology and Education Quarterly* 18, 4: 312-324.

O'Hare, W., and J. Felt. (February 1991). *Asian Americans: America's Fastest Growing Minority Group.* Washington, D.C.: Population Reference Bureau Inc.

Pearlman, L.J. (1992). *School's Out: Hyperlearning, the New Technology, and the End of Education.* New York: William Marrow and Company, Inc.

Perkinson, H. J. (1985). "American Textbooks and Educational Change." *In Early American Textbooks 1775-1900,* edited by D. Svobodny. Washington, D.C.: Government Printing Office.

Pratt, D. (1994). *Curriculum Planning: A Handbook for Professionals.* Fort Worth: Harcourt Brace College Publishers.

Ramsey, P. G., (1987). *Teaching and Learning in a Diverse World: Multicultural Education for Young Children.* New York: Teachers College Press.

Saravia-Shore, M, and E. Garcia. (1995). "Diverse Teaching Strategies for Diverse Learners." *In Educating Everybody's Children: Diverse Teaching Strategies for Diverse Learners,* edited by R. Cole. Alexandria, Va.: Association for Supervision and Curriculum Development.

Snider, J.H. (May/June 1996). "Education Wars: The Battle Over Information-Age Technology." *The Futurist* 24-28.

Steffy, B.E. and F.W. English. (1997). *Curriculum and Assessment for World-Class Schools.* Lancaster, Pa.: Technomic Pub. Co., Inc.

Stainback, S., and W. Stainback. (1992). "Schools as Inclusive Communities." In *Controversial Issues Confronting Special Education: Divergent Perspectives,* edited by S. Stainback and W. Stainback. Boston: Allyn and Bacon.

Steffy, B. (1995). *Authentic Assessment and Curriculum Alignment: Meeting the Challenge of National Standards.* Pro>Active Publications.

Steffy, B., and M. Wolfe. (1997). *The Life Cycle of the Career Teacher: Maintaining Excellence for a Lifetime.* West Lafayette, Ind.: Kappa Delta Pi.

Suarez, L.M. (1991). "Needs Assessment Studies." In *International Encyclopedia of Curriculum,* edited by A. Lewy. New York: Pergamon.

Trotter, A. (Nov. 10, 1997). "A Test of Leadership." *Education Week* 17, 11: 30-33.

Venezky, R.L. (1989). "Representation of the Content and Process of Science." Paper Presented at the Annual Meeting of the American Educational Research Association, May 27-31, San Francisco, Calif.

Venezky, R. L. (1992). "Textbooks in School and Society." In *Handbook on Research on Curriculum,* edited by Phillip W. Jackson.. New York: Macmillian Publishing Co.

Zeichner, K. (1992). *Educating Teachers for Cultural Diversity.* East Lancing, Mich.: National Center for Research on Teacher Learning.

chapter 6 | *Skills in Instructional Management*

To have all students learning at high levels is the worthy goal this country has set for the public school system. However, "schools that educate all their students to high levels of intellectual, practical, and social competence continue to be, in every sense of the word, exceptional" (Darling-Hammond 1997). But the number is growing day by day, year by year. Shining examples like International High School and Central Park East in New York City are testimony to the success that can be achieved through vision, dedicated effort, and a "can do" attitude. Achieving the goal of having all students learning at high levels will require U.S. educators to do two things they have never before been called upon to do: "To teach for understanding, that is, to teach all students, not just a few, to understand ideas deeply and perform proficiently," and "to teach for diversity, that is, to teach in ways that help different kinds of learners find productive paths to knowledge as they also learn to live constructively together" (Darling-Hammond 1997, p.5). Success in accomplishing these two goals may well determine the future of public education.

Successful school administrators put in place instructional systems that combine research findings about learning, curriculum, instructional strategies, and instructional time, as well as advanced electronic technologies and other resources to maximize student learning. To do this, school administrators must be able to describe and apply research and best practice related to curriculum, classroom management, multicultural sensitivity, and assessment.

This chapter details the skills successful 21st century school leaders must possess to:

- Develop, implement, and monitor change processes to improve student learning, adult development, and learning climates;
- Understand the role of motivation in the instructional process;
- Promote effective classroom management;
- Encourage total student development;
- Analyze and assign financial resources to enhance student learning;

- Apply instructional strategies that reflect sensitivity to multicultural issues and varied styles;
- Monitor and evaluate student achievement based on objectives and expected performance; and
- Establish a student achievement monitoring and reporting system based on disaggregated data.

Developing, Implementing, and Monitoring Change Processes To Improve Student Learning, Adult Development, and Learning Climates

Planned educational change has been part of the local, state, and national dialogue for the past 30 years. Still, schools and classrooms remain relatively unchanged because powerful systemic forces support the status quo. To change public education, the culture of schools must change. School leaders play a pivotal role in initiating, implementing, and sustaining that effort.

Moral Purpose and Change Agentry

In *Change Forces: Probing the Depths of Educational Reform*, Michael Fullan (1993) identifies moral purpose and change agentry as the key to educational reform and identifies four core capacities of change agentry — personal vision-building, inquiry, mastery, and collaboration. Each of these has an organizational counterpart — shared vision-building and organizational structures, norms and practices of inquiry, focus on organizational development and knowledge, and collaborative work cultures.

John Goodlad (1990) describes four moral imperatives that contribute to the concept of moral purpose for educators: facilitating critical inculturation, providing access to knowledge, building an effective teacher-student connection, and practicing good stewardship. Ken Sirotnik (1990) added a commitment to inquiry, knowledge, competence, caring, freedom, well-being, and social justice to the list.

Fullan (1993) argues that it is insufficient to apply the concept of moral purpose to teachers and classrooms alone; moral purpose must become part of the foundation of the entire educational reform effort to achieve sustained, systemic change. From the foundation of change agentry and moral purpose, Fullan (1993, pp. 21-22) identifies eight basic lessons about change:

- You can't mandate what matters.
- Change is a journey, not a blueprint.
- Problems are our friends.
- Vision and strategic planning come later.
- Individualism and collectivism must have equal power.
- Neither centralization nor decentralization works.
- Connection with the wider environment is critical for success.
- Every person is a change agent.

The Impact of Social Change

Educators face myriad social changes outside the school environment that affect their daily lives. A few of these are a changing economy, growing public dissatisfaction with schools, changing parenting roles and family make-up, demographic changes, and the impact of technology on our daily lives. For effective change to take place in public education, school leaders must acknowledge and find ways to ameliorate the impact of negative social changes on schools. Levin and Riffel (1997, pp. 161-5) offer five themes related to social changes and the schools:

- Social change is seen as having powerful and often negative effects on schools, the appropriate responses to which are not at all evident.
- School systems are not sufficiently oriented toward learning about the nature and implications of social change. When a learning stance is adopted, it seems due more to fortuitous circumstances than deliberate intentions.
- Strategies for responding to change seem limited and unimaginative.
- Learning and change in systems are different than learning and change in individual organizations. Learning processes in educational systems are seriously inhibited by the dominance of conventional wisdom about the nature and purposes of schooling.
- Some [social] problems are intractable, and many of the solutions are beyond the reach of schools

alone. Nevertheless, it seems reasonable to expect a more outward-looking stance and more innovation on the part of schools and school systems. Moving beyond inherited ideas about the nature of learning, teaching, and schooling will be a struggle. Still, we need to do better. People can achieve a lot more than they think, in much simpler ways than they believe.

A Model for Continuous Change

Perhaps the greatest challenge facing school leaders today is that there is too much change going on in schools rather than too little. "The greatest problem faced by school districts and schools is not resistance to innovation, but the fragmentation, overload, and incoherence resulting from the uncritical and uncoordinated acceptance of too many different innovations" (Fullan and Stiegelbauer 1991, p. 197).

Building on the work of Fullan and others, Betty Steffy developed a model for productive, continuous change. The model includes three major components: collaborative leadership, stakeholder focus and connectivity, and linkage to an outside support system. Figure 6.1 on page 87 depicts the relationship of the three components to the process of continuous change.

Collaborative leadership. The leadership for change in schools must come from a base, or leadership team, that includes school leaders, community leaders, and leaders representing the home. This team may include the president of the chamber of commerce, the PTA president, the leader of the school association, and board representation as well as school principals, central-office staff, and teachers. It is important that this team enable *all* the voices of important stakeholders to be heard. Each leader is a viable member of the collaborative leadership team and must function as an advocate for his or her constituency. This team must operate by consensus and be committed to continuous improvement in student achievement. Children and their welfare are the primary concern of the leadership collaborative.

Stakeholder focus and connectivity. This component of the model assumes that consensus established by the leadership collaborative gives stakeholders within the system a sense of focus and connectivity regarding the direction of the district and the activities to be undertaken to reach desired goals. To establish this focus and connectivity, leaders within the community must advocate for the direction the

Figure 6.1 **A Model For Productive, Continuous Change**

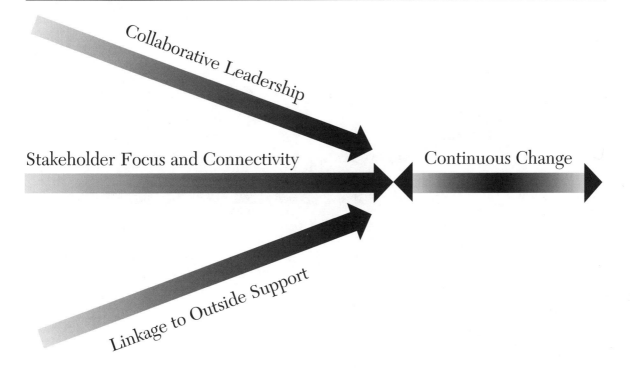

Collaborative Leadership

Stakeholder Focus and Connectivity

Continuous Change

Linkage to Outside Support

district is headed within their respective stakeholder groups. They can do this by periodically holding meetings, focus groups, and individual conferences to provide opportunities for stakeholder groups to meet, talk, and reach consensus about the value of the schools' direction. For the school association leader, this could take the form of small-group meetings with a variety of K-12 content area teachers. Business leaders, parents, and other community leaders can also engage in such conversations. The purpose of this effort is to establish a community consensus for change. Otherwise, subgroups often form within the community and oppose district or school change.

Linkage to outside support. Sustaining change over the two to five years required to institutionalize most efforts can be greatly assisted by linking into a national effort. This often comes in the form of grants to support the initiatives included in the change. Such a linkage not only puts local "movers and shakers" in touch with others across the nation, but can lead to a clarification of ideas.

Grant writing requires putting thoughts to paper and being clear about the objectives to be reached. It forces multiyear planning and the development of timelines for the implementation of activ-

ities. The going is rough at times with any new initiative. Most grants require the filing of periodic reports, including documentation of the activities put into place and the results achieved. As positive results begin to accrue, the national network can provide recognition of the district's accomplishments.

Administrators leading a change effort should carefully build these three components of the continuous change process. Without them, the change may be short lived.

Administrators' Power and Authority

Another key variable for guiding change within a system is the use of administrator power and authority to support change. Sergiovanni (1992) identifies five sources of administrative authority: moral, technical-rational, professional, bureaucratic, and personal (psychological) authority. Sergiovanni took the position that moral leadership was the most important characteristic for a school leader to exhibit when leading a change effort, but he maintained that all five forms of leadership are required to effect change. Figure 6.2 displays the relationship among these five sources of power in guiding effective change.

Figure 6.2 **Use of Power To Support Change**

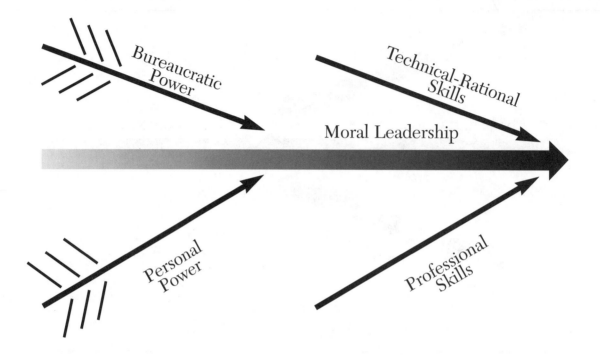

The shaft of the arrow represents an educator's moral leadership. This is the most important source of power; it enables the system to be transformed into an educational environment where all children learn at high levels. The point of the arrow is made up of the professional and technical-rational skills of the leader. This provides the direction and expertise to lead the change. The end of the arrow is made up of the leader's bureaucratic and personal power, which allow the arrow to fly straight and true. School leaders must have and use all five sources of power to bring about positive, lasting change.

Understanding the Role of Motivation in the Instructional Process

In the classroom, student motivation "is used to explain the degree to which students invest attention and effort in various pursuits, which may or may not be the ones desired by their teachers" (Brophy 1998, p. 3). For most educators, the motivated learner is the ideal student: one who shows initiative, is goal directed and persistent, and sustains focused effort over time. With motivated stu-

dents, teaching is fun and exciting, classrooms are energized, students are engaged, and the environment is filled with the electricity of learning.

Human motivation, however, is a complex issue. Generally, theorists have categorized motivation as either extrinsic or intrinsic (Spaulding 1992). Four major kinds of motivation theory have dominated the literature in the last half of the 20th century: behavior reinforcement theories, need theories, goal theories, and intrinsic motivation theories.

Behavior Reinforcement

Behavior reinforcement theories are commonly practiced in schools today in the form of grades, gold stars, honor rolls, awards ceremonies, and positive written and verbal comments by teachers. This type of motivation is external to the student and relies heavily on the student's response to cues. External reinforcers are considered good if they increase the desired behavior of the student. While external reinforcers are still prevalent in U.S. education, current behavioral approaches to motivation include increased attention to the learner's internal state of mind.

Need Theories

Probably the best-known need theory is Abraham Maslow's (1962) hierarchy of human needs (see Figure 1.2). Maslow's linear model suggests that a student experiencing psychological needs such as sleep, hunger, or thirst cannot focus attention on higher-order needs such as mastery of new skills and creative self-expression. This view is manifest in school breakfast and lunch programs, which rest on the belief that before students can be receptive to learning, they must be fed. Thus, need theories tend to be internally focused.

Goal Theories

Goal theories represent a shift from thinking about motivation as a reaction to either internal or external pressures to conceiving motivation as a result of goal-directed activity. Goal theory calls for educators to be both reactive and proactive in satisfying students' needs and desires. Classroom applications focus on classroom climate, safety, student engagement, interpersonal relationships, mastery of tasks, and demonstration of skills (Ford 1992).

As the area of motivational goal theories has expanded, studies have focused on the concepts of self-efficacy perceptions, performance outcomes, success or failure motivators, and cognitive and affective classroom experiences. Understanding how the external characteristics of the classroom environment affect students' internal capacity and desire to learn is the primary objective of goal theory studies.

Intrinsic Motivation Theories

The move to intrinsic motivation theories represents a shift that emphasizes the internal, self-directed nature of the learner more than the external environment. These motivational theories are most clearly linked to constructivist learning theory. According to internal motivation theorists, the learning environment must enable students to make choices about what to do and how to do it. Two examples of intrinsic motivation theories are self-determination theory (Deci and Ryan 1985) and flow (Csikszentmihalyi 1993).

Brophy (1998, p. 14) explains the expectancy x value model in *Motivating Students to Learn*. "The expectancy x value model of motivation holds that the effort that people are willing to expend on a task is the product of (1) the degree to which they expect to be able to perform the task successfully if they apply themselves (and thus the degree to which they expect to get whatever rewards that successful task performance will bring), and (2) the degree to which they value those rewards as well as the opportunity to engage in the processes involved in performing the task itself."

Motivation and Student Success

Other research indicates additional factors related to the level of motivation a student may exhibit in learning situations. Effort-outcome covariation refers to the connection a student makes between the level of effort required to succeed in a task and the level of mastery they are trying to achieve. Students are most highly motivated when they believe they can achieve the level of mastery required. When the task is too easy, they are disinterested; when it is too hard, they reject involvement (Cooper 1979).

Additionally, when students believe they control success in the learning situation — internal locus of control — rather than perceiving that control comes from external factors, they are more likely to be motivated to complete the task (Stipek and Weisz 1981). Related to the concept of internal locus of control is the concept of self as origin rather than pawn (deCharms 1976). Students who believe they are in charge of their learning are more highly motivated than students who view themselves as pawns.

The concepts of learned helplessness and resilience have come out of the field of developmental psychopathology (Wang, Haertel, and Walberg 1996). Learned helplessness describes the behavior of students who withdraw from learning situations. These students have low self-esteem and expect to fail. Resilience refers to students' ability to sustain focus and goal-directed behavior, even though their social and family backgrounds suggest that they are prone to becoming "at risk." Resilient students (Benard 1991) have high expectations, believe that life has meaning, are goal directed, have good problem-solving and interpersonal skills, are flexible, and maintain a sense of personal urgency.

Joyce Epstein (1989) identified six classroom dimensions that affect student motivation: task and work structures, authority and management structures, recognition and reward structures, grouping practices, evaluation practices, and time use. Pintrich and Schunk (1996) add two more: norms, values, and shared beliefs and climate.

Because all these dimensions affect student motivation, school leaders must pay attention to each. A synthesis of the wide-ranging research suggests that to promote student motivation, school leaders should:

• Engage faculty in the development of common school norms, values, and shared beliefs;
• Develop a school climate with strong, collegial relations among staff, parents, and the community;
• Help teachers design task and work structures to foster engagement;
• Design opportunities for all students to be recognized and rewarded;
• Encourage grouping practices that promote student interaction and dialogue;
• Develop building-wide student evaluation procedures that focus on documenting student progress and improvement; and
• Develop plans that provide for the flexible use of student and teacher time to support growth and change. (See Chapter 1 for more on motivation.)

Promoting Effective Classroom Management

Classroom management is seen by parents, teachers, and the public as the foundation for building a learner-centered classroom environment. Discipline was rated #1 16 of the first 18 years that the Gallup Poll assessed the public's perception of school problems. It ranked second the other two years. The school leader's ability to ensure that every teacher has good classroom management skills is critical to effective school management.

While a plethora of books provide teachers with numerous suggestions for dealing with disruptive students, no single list works with every student and every teacher every time. Effective classroom management is situational. Doyle (1983) pointed to six classroom characteristics that affect classroom management.

• *Multidimensionality.* Classrooms are multidimensional insofar as a variety of different activities go on at any one time, students are at a variety of learning levels, and the students learn in a variety of ways.
• *Simultaneity.* Simultaneity exists in that many activities are going on at any one time. Even if the teacher is in front of the class, students may be engaged in many different responses to instruction.
• *Immediacy.* A sense of immediacy exists in that action is taking place every minute through teacher talk and behavior.
• *Unpredictability.* Events in a classroom are unpredictable. Though the teacher may have a well-devised plan, events take place every day that disrupt the plan.
• *Observability.* Classrooms are public places, and whatever action takes place is generally observable by everyone in the class.
• *History.* Classrooms and classroom teachers have histories and these histories tend to follow teachers and students over time.

Classroom Management and Time on Task

The goal of classroom management systems is to increase the amount of time for learning to take place, to provide students with access to learning or the opportunity to learn, and to enable students to become better managers of their own learning (Woolfolk 1998). Numerous studies have codified the difference between time allotted for learning and the time students spend engaged in academic learning (Rosenshine 1979, Doyle 1983). Allotted learning time refers to the state-mandated hours that school is in session. Engaged learning time refers to the time when students are actively involved and learning is taking place. Rough estimates indicate that during only approximately one-third of the allotted time are students engaged and actually learning (Weinstein and Mignano 1997).

Getting Off to a Good Start

School leaders can help ensure positive classroom management practices by encouraging teachers to do the following things during the first few weeks of school:
• Classroom procedures should be in place and clearly followed by students. These should include procedures for administrative routines, student movement, accomplishing lessons, talk among students, and interactions between students and the teacher (Weinstein 1996, Weinstein and Mignano 1997).
• Rules detailing what is acceptable and what is not should be clearly stated and followed. Often, teachers write them down and post them in the classroom.

• Consequences for violating the rules should be specified and consistently enforced. The importance of consistency cannot be overstated. When students clearly understand the procedures, rules, and consequences established for the classroom and know that these are consistently enforced, classroom management problems decrease substantially.

Class Size

Classroom teachers frequently call for reduced class sizes. The basic assumption is that student achievement would increase in smaller classes because there would be more time for student-teacher interactions and an improvement in classroom atmosphere. Achilles (1997) determined, however, that in order for classroom achievement to increase significantly, the average class size would have to be reduced to 15 or fewer students per teacher, which is unrealistic in most current school arrangements.

Research points to several cost-effective alternatives to reduced class size for producing increased student achievement (Haynes and Chalker 1997). These include lengthening the school day and the use of instructional technology to provide individualized instruction. Employing classroom tutors and instructional assistants has also raised student achievement.

Class size and student-teacher ratios in the United States are among the lowest in the world (Haynes and Chalker 1997) . Classes in the Republic of Korea typically number 55-60 students with only one instructor. The lowest class size ratios are reported by Germany (15:1), Canada (17.5:1), and the United States (18.6:1). But issues of class size cannot be divorced from an analysis of the role and responsibilities of classroom teachers in the United States. McAdams (1993) studied school systems around the world and found that the demands placed on U.S. teachers made them work harder than their counterparts. Teachers in the United States routinely:

• Complete more paperwork;
• Work a longer day with fewer breaks or opportunities to meet with colleagues;
• Are required to more closely monitor student behavior;
• Contend with student concerns about grades and demands for higher grades than the student earned;

• Have a heavier class load; and
• Have less assistance from instructional aides.

School leaders concerned about class size should explore the possibility of reducing the classroom teacher's functions by using instructional technology and adding classroom assistants before recommending class size reductions. Some school systems are experimenting with assigning all certified staff to classrooms. In recent years the number of certified support staff has increased. When these teachers are given regular classroom assignments, the student-teacher ratios dramatically decline. But future research is needed to determine whether students achieve at higher levels in these classrooms than students in classrooms with high student-teacher ratios and teaching assistants.

Cooperative Learning

John Dewey advocated cooperative learning in the early 1900s. He believed that competition among students should be diminished and students should learn to work together in democratic learning communities. Since the 1960s, a resurgence of interest in fostering collaborative learning communities in schools has occurred. This movement is in keeping with the constructivist view that learning experiences should replicate real-life learning environments in which solving complex problems requires concentrated social interaction.

The five elements of true cooperative learning groups are: face-to-face interaction, positive interdependence, individual accountability, collaborative skills, and group processing (Johnson and Johnson 1994). In effective cooperative learning groups, student group interaction leads to heightened motivation, higher levels of inquiry, constructive argumentation, and more thoughtful explanation, elaboration, and interpretation (Webb and Palincsar 1996).

Teachers serve as facilitators and guides for cooperative groups. The groups are generally small, ranging in size from two to five students, and students are typically grouped heterogeneously. Group members perform specific roles, which can include any of the following, depending on the task to be accomplished: encourager, cheerleader, gatekeeper, coach, question commander, checker, taskmaster, recorder, reflector, quiet captain, or materials monitor (Kagan 1994).

Three popular formats for cooperative learning groups are Jigsaw, reciprocal questioning, and scripted cooperation. Jigsaw involves giving each group member a separate portion of the learning materials. Each member is charged with learning the material and then teaching it to the total group.

In reciprocal questioning, students work in groups of two or three and ask each other questions about material they have learned. To guide the questioning, teachers provide students with question stems such as, "Describe . . . in your own words" or "Why is . . . important?" Students are also encouraged to make connections with question stems such as, "How are . . . and . . . similar or different?" or "How does . . . tie in with . . . that we studied last week?" (King 1994, Woolfolk 1998).

Scripted cooperation (Dansereau 1985, O'Donnell and O'Kelly 1994) is a technique wherein two students work together to read, discuss, and analyze information. Both members of the group read the material, then one explains the material to the other. The member listening then asks questions and summarizes the material. Afterward, both members discuss the material and try to increase their levels of understanding.

Problem-Based Learning

When students are actively engaged, classroom management problems are less likely to arise. One way to promote student engagement is through problem-based learning. Problem-based learning involves four basic steps. First, students form a hypothesis when presented with a problem to solve or an event to explain. Next, students collect information to test the hypothesis. Then students draw conclusions based on the information reviewed. Finally, time is provided for reflection regarding the problem and the process used to draw the conclusions (Woolfolk 1998). This problem-solving model calls upon students' skills in analysis, comparison, induction, and deduction (Quellmalz and Hoskyn 1997) and the higher-order thinking skills (analysis, synthesis, and evaluation) found in Bloom's (1971) taxonomy.

Resnick and Klopfer (1989) designed what they referred to as the thinking curriculum, which is based on reasoning and problem-solving skills. Quellmalz (1987, 1991) developed a reasoning strategies framework based on (a) the cognitive strategies of analysis, comparison, inference and interpretation, application, and evaluation and (b) the metacognitive strategies of planning, drafting, monitoring and revising, and evaluation and reflection. Problem-based learning will continue becom-

ing more prevalent as classroom instruction moves more toward authentic instructional applications.

Encouraging Total Student Development

Total student development involves not only students' physical development but their personal, social, emotional, and cognitive and linguistic growth as well. Development in each of these areas occurs at different rates for individuals, is relatively orderly , and takes place gradually (Woolfolk 1998)

Physical Development

During the preschool years (ages 2-5), children develop their gross motor skills, and about 85 percent of children begin to show a preference for using their right hand. At this stage, identification of children with special needs is an important step in providing proper interventions.

During the elementary years (ages 6-11), physical development moves at a steady pace. Children become taller, leaner, and stronger, and fine and gross motor skills improve. There is a great deal of variation among students in terms of height, weight, and fine and gross motor abilities, and it is common for girls to be taller and to weigh more than boys.

During adolescence (ages 12-18), puberty begins and boys and girls experience growth spurts and other physical changes as sexual maturity evolves. These physical changes may significantly affect students' psychological well-being. Mood swings are common and peer groups become increasingly important.

Personal, Social, and Emotional Development

In 1963, Eric Erikson's influential book, *Children and Society*, was published. In it, Erickson offered a basic framework for understanding the psychosocial development of children. Erikson was interested in the relationship between the emotional needs of children and the social context in which they lived. His framework is developmental in that the stages are interdependent; what happens at an earlier level affects what happens at a later stage.

At each stage in the model, the individual faces what Erikson refers to as a developmental crisis. How the individual resolves this crisis affects the individual's self-concept and view of society. Erikson's developmental stages are shown in Figure 6.3.

Kohlberg (1963, 1975, 1981) divided moral reasoning into three levels. They are: (1) preconventional, when personal needs dominate; (2) conventional, when the views of society and laws are taken into account, and (3) postconventional, when the first two blend. Kohlberg then defined stages within each level. This model has been criticized, however, because the stages cannot be separated and apply differently depending on the situation an individual faces (Eisenberg et al. 1987, Sobesky 1983). The other criticism directed toward Kohlberg is that his model is based on Western male values and emphasizes individualism.

Carol Gilligan (1982) proposes an "ethic of care" as an alternative sequence for moral development. Gilligan suggests that "individuals move from a focus on self-interests to moral reasoning based on a commitment to specific individuals and relationships, and then to the highest level of morality, which is based on the principles of responsibility and care for all people" (Woolfolk 1998, p. 84).

The truth is that many factors affect how we behave. Two of the most significant are internalization and modeling. Children tend to internalize and model the moral behavior of adults who are significant to them. Educators thus have a duty to model appropriate moral behaviors for their students (Lipscomb, MacAllister, and Bregman 1985).

Cognitive and Linguistic Development

Jean Piaget. Piaget (Piaget, 1954, 1963, 1970a, b) asserted that thinking processes continue to change from childhood to adulthood as individuals respond and try to make sense of their world. Piaget's four stages of cognitive development have become well known to educators.

Stage	Age	Key Behaviors
Sensorimotor	0-2 years	Imitation, Thought Object memory Goal behavior
Preoperational	2-7	Language Logic
Concrete operational	7-11 years	Solves concrete problems Classification
Formal operational	11-adult	Solves abstract problems Concerned about social issues Concerned about identity

Lev Vygotsky. Educators have showed renewed interest in Lev Vygotsky's (1978, 1993) sociocultural theory because of its premise that

Figure 6.3 Erikson's Developmental Stages

Stage	Age	Important Event
Basic trust versus mistrust	Age 12-18 months	Feeding
Autonomy versus shame/doubt	Age 18 months to 3 years	Toilet training
Initiative versus guilt	Age 3 to 6 years	Independence
Industry versus inferiority	Age 6 to 12 years	School
Identity versus role confusion	Adolescence	Peer relations
Intimacy versus isolation	Young adulthood	Love relationships
Generativity versus stagnation	Middle adulthood	Parenting/ mentoring
Ego integrity versus despair	Late adulthood	Reflection on and acceptance of one's life

(Erikson 1993, 1968, 1980)

cognitive development is tied to culture. Vygotsky asserts that cognitive development is dependent on a child's interactions with others and the tools available in the child's world. He believes that the tools of the culture, such as computers and language, play an important role in cognitive development. According to Vygotsky, language is the most important cultural tool and children develop cognitively through a form of private speech (talking to themselves).

During the preschool years, children progress from saying their first words (9 to 18 months) to first sentences (about 18 months) to learning grammar and vocabulary (3-5 years). At the age of 20 months, the vocabulary of a child may include about 50 words (Nelson 1981). Between the ages of 2 and 6, the child is adding 6 to 10 words a day. Most six-year-olds have acquired a vocabulary of from 8,000 to 14,000 words. A child's fluency with language is intricately linked to cognitive development.

Analyzing and Assigning Financial Resources To Enhance Student Learning

Instructional management is related to budget development. The challenge is to continuously improve the productivity of our schools using the resources available to the system (Poston, Stone, and Muther 1992). "If your school organization establishes a solid relationship between what it does and how well it does it, and then uses that link to shape what it does next," the organization will improve in "its use of resources, reduce wasteful activity, terminate ineffective programs, and generally get better . . . over time" (p. 156).

The district budget development process must reflect the connection among goals, priorities, dollars, and evaluation results and ensure that key stakeholders in the system are involved in decisions. However, finding the balance between effective involvement and system accountability and cohesiveness is not always easy. The goal is to develop a network to track costs related to results, provide budgetary control, and create a database for policy and operational decisions.

Seven components of a curriculum-driven budget are rated in curriculum management audits. These components provide a guide for ensuring that resources are assigned in a cost-effective man-

ner that enhances student achievement. The six components are:

- Tangible, demonstrable connections between assessments of operational curriculum effectiveness and allocations of resources;
- Rank ordering of program components to permit flexibility in budget expansion, reduction, or stabilization based on changing priorities;
- Delineation of component cost benefits in curriculum programming for budget decision making;
- Budget request and submittal that permit evaluation of consequences of funding in terms of performance or results;
- Competition between budget requests for funding based upon evaluation of need and relationship to achievement of curriculum effectiveness;
- Involvement of key educational staff in decision making about setting priorities in the budget process; and
- Incorporation of suggestions for budget priorities into the decision-making process.

(Frase, English, and Poston 1995, p. 222)

Applying Instructional Strategies that Reflect Sensitivity to Multicultural Issues and Varied Styles

Today's classrooms are multicultural. James Banks (1997) predicts that by the year 2020, approximately 54 percent of all students will be white and the rest will be students of color, many the children of new immigrants. Cultural background is important, but it is not the sole predictor of academic success. Banks (1994 pp. 13-14) warns,

> although membership in a gender, racial, ethnic, social-class, or religious group can provide us with important clues about an individual's behavior, it cannot enable us to predict behavior . . . . Membership in a particular group does not determine behavior but makes certain types of behavior more probable.

Banks (1994) developed a five-dimensional model for multicultural education. The model focuses on: content integration, the knowledge construction process, prejudice reduction, equity pedagogy, and an empowering school culture and social structure. *Content integration* refers to using examples and content from a variety of cultures to teach key concepts and skills in content areas. The *knowledge construction* component calls for teachers to be knowledgeable about cultural assumptions that may affect a content area. *Prejudice reduction* requires teachers to have the skills necessary to enable students to confront and modify their own prejudices. *Equity pedagogy* refers to matching teaching styles to students' learning styles. Finally, the *empowering component* calls for the examination of labeling practices that bar some students from full participation in the learning community.

Cognitive Styles

Cognitive styles refers to the way people perceive and organize information, not their level of intelligence. These styles deal with "characteristic modes of perceiving, remembering, thinking, problem solving, and decision making reflective of information-processing regularities that develop around underlying personality trends" (Messick 1994, p. 122).

One cognitive style distinction is made between field dependent and field independent learners. Field dependent learners tend to view things globally, whereas field independent learners tend to look at independent parts of the whole. Field independent learners are not as attuned to social relationships but tend to do well in math and science.

Another cognitive style distinction is made between impulsive and reflective students. Impulsive students tend to make decisions quickly and consequently make more mistakes. Reflective student are more contemplative, slower to reach conclusions, and tend to ponder information (Woolfolk 1998).

Learning Styles

In the past 25 years there has been a great deal written about learning styles, and instruments have been developed to help teachers better assess students' preferred styles. A few of the most common instruments are *The Learning Style Inventory* (Renzulli and Smith 1978), *The Learning Style Inventory* (Dunn, Dunn, and Price 1984), and the *Learning Style Profile* (Keefe and Monk 1986). These instruments have been criticized for lack of reliability and validity, but the simple fact remains

that students learn differently and teachers need to be more sensitive to those differences in planning instruction.

(See Chapter 5 for more information about culturally sensitive teaching strategies.)

Monitoring and Evaluating Student Achievement Based on Objectives and Expected Student Performance

Student assessment strategies are evolving from traditional measures such as norm-referenced tests, criterion-referenced test, multiple choice, and completion tests to more authentic measures such as portfolios, exhibitions, performance events, and open-ended response items (Steffy 1995, Steffy and English 1997). These new assessments ask students to perform, create, produce, or do something and tend to require higher-order thinking and problem-solving skills. The assessment tasks are related to real-life applications and represent meaningful instructional activities with multiple right answers for each problem presented. Collectively, these new assessments require teachers to assume new instructional and assessment roles (Herman, Aschbacher, and Winters 1992).

Currently, a growing population of educators believes that assessment needs to be a part of the ongoing instructional process, not a series of one-shot events. For example, the National Council of Teachers of Mathematics' (NCTM 1995) standards on learning call for assessment tasks to be embedded within the curriculum. Stiggins (1988) observed that teachers spend approximately 20 to 30 percent of their professional time involved with student assessment issues, but the quality of the assessments used is low. According to Stiggins, the use of low-quality assessments deprives students from feeling the joy of applying reasoning and critical thinking skills to solving difficult problems.

Common Types of Authentic Assessment

Three types of authentic assessment commonly used today are open-ended response items, portfolios, and performance events and exhibitions.

Open-ended response items are problem-based and usually require a short essay response. Typical items may call for a student to identify the advantages and disadvantages of some action, take a position and defend it, predict an outcome, identify pros and cons of some action, or design a product. Open-ended response items are scored using a scoring rubric, which enables reviewers to grade multiple responses in a consistent manner even though no one right answer exists for these items. Scoring rubrics can include an assessment of the student's logic, the number and sophistication of details presented, and the strength of the position taken. These items are being integrated into tests such as the National Assessment of Educational Progress, the ACT, the SAT, and the International Baccalaureate.

Portfolios are collections of student work taking many forms that document progress over time. They provide a mechanism for students to evaluate their own and their peers' skills and to develop self-esteem, while offering insight into students' maturity and a vehicle to document students' writing skills (Knight 1992). Portfolios promote student ownership and can be applied to any content area. Reviewing portfolios allows parents, students, teachers, and the community to celebrate accomplishment. Portfolios are perhaps our best form of authentic assessment because they:

- Help students learn to evaluate their own work,
- Emphasize content and performance,
- Integrate reading and writing,
- Promote critical thinking,
- Support student ownership,
- Build on a student's background,
- Promote awareness of student achievement,
- Provide for ongoing assessment,
- Promote student-teacher interaction, and
- Meet accountability needs.

Performance events and exhibitions are individual or group activities often used as culminating events to measure student progress over time. When used with a group, they can measure the group's ability to work together to complete a task, design a product, or solve a problem. The variety and quality of individual's work can also be assessed. These assessments are product oriented and usually enable the group or individual to display creativity and logic.

All of these authentic assessments have limitations. Problems of reliability and validity have caused states such as Kentucky to eliminate performance events from their assessment systems. Authentic assessments take time to complete and

assess, and educators often debate whether the time spent on assessment is worth the lost instructional time. Alternative assessments are also costly and difficult to develop. However, the benefits of the authentic assessments discussed here (and others) far outweigh the disadvantages. The most prudent approach is a balanced assessment system using both traditional and authentic measures.

The Role of Standards

Nearly every state is working on a set of standards linked to state assessment programs. The American Federation of Teachers (AFT 1996) reviewed the status of these efforts and reported the following major findings:

- The commitment to standards-based reform remains strong; 48 states are developing common standards.
- States are using the core content areas as the organizer for the standards, but vague language is being used to describe the standards.
- Many states recognize the need for internationally competitive standards but few have been able to establish them.
- Most states have strong standards in one or more content areas, but the overall quality of the standards is mixed across content areas.
- Setting standards for English and social studies is problematic for states.
- All but a few states will eventually develop assessments to measure student achievement of the standards, but the standards are not stated clearly enough to provide a strong foundation for the development of such assessments.
- Less than half the states plan to develop penalties for students who do not meet the standards.
- Only 10 states require and fund intervention programs for low-achieving students
- In states with graduation exams, a clear trend toward increased rigor and alignment with state standards is apparent.
- Eight states plan to offer "differentiated diplomas" as a means of motivating students to achieve high standards.

Not all Americans endorse the standards movement. Lynne Cheney (1995, p. 26) commented that "the national history standards developed at the University of California at Los Angeles and released in the fall of 1994 are the most egregious example to date of encouraging students to take a benign view of . . . or totally overlook . . . the failing of other cultures while being hypercritical of the one in which they live." However, as time passes there appears to be a growing emphasis on setting standards as a means of promoting high expectations for what students should know and be able to do. The results remain to be seen.

Establishing a Student Achievement Monitoring and Reporting System Based on Disaggregated Data

Systemic change is required so that school leaders can develop a comprehensive system for monitoring student achievement at the classroom, school, and district level. This change involves:

- Strengthening leadership and breaking through bureaucratic cultures;
- Creating high expectations for adults and students;
- Making sure all professionals assume responsibility for change;
- Coordinating change efforts both vertically and horizontally within the system;
- Clarifying responsibility for student learning so that all classroom teachers accept responsibility for high standards for all students;
- Involving all key stakeholders, including parents, students, and the community;
- Building consensus and resolving conflict as the process continues;
- Minimizing the mobility of teachers and students if possible;
- Reallocating resources, particularly time;
- Emphasizing professional development;
- Using outside change facilitators skilled in equity work; and
- Monitoring the success of the initiative with comprehensive disaggregated data.

(Johnson 1996, pp. 11-15)

Disaggregated Data

Student achievement data disaggregated by gender, ethnicity, and socioeconomic status must be examined when trying to improve student achievement (Leithwood and Aitken 1995). Dealing only with district, school, and classroom averages does not promote development of the kind of focused

intervention necessary to ameliorate low student performance. A school community must be dissatisfied with the status quo before significant change will take place. If data indicate that, on average, students are doing average, nothing may be done. However, if disaggregated data show that 60 percent of African-American males are achieving in the lowest quartile, a district or school might be propelled to action to correct the problem.

Ruth Johnson (1996), in *Setting Our Sights, Measuring Equity in School Change*, provides many examples of how to display classroom, school, and district disaggregated data. Johnson urges school leaders to become data users, noting that most school staffs do truly want students to perform at high levels. "They work hard, become excited about implementing changes, and are disappointed when the changes do not result in tremendous improvements in education" (p. 11).

Grades are the most common feedback given to students and parents. Before grades can be used as a point of comparison, administrators must be sure that everyone is using the same definition of what each letter grade means. It is possible to compare classroom grades across time and classes only when common standards are used for content and performance. This, however, is difficult to ensure.

Grades can be used to track student achievement from one grade to another by following the same group of students over time, from one department to another, within a department, and by teacher. A simple display of the data will often generate a multitude of questions about whether all teachers use the same criteria for issuing grades, whether the school is satisfied with the distribution, what other information is needed, possible contributors to the results, and the kind of improvements that should be implemented. Within a department, it may be useful to look at the percentage of As and Fs given by gender or ethnicity or the difference in As and Fs from fall to spring given by the same teachers. Such an examination leads to worthwhile questions about why some teachers are failing students at much higher rates than others, what type of assistance students receive, and whether variations in grades are related to varying instructional strategies and content rigor.

Disaggregation of data by grade point average is also useful. Add to this a display by ethnicity and a more revealing picture is presented. While the achievement gap between Asian-American, African-American, Latino, and white students has narrowed, it is still significant.

At the building level, data showing course enrollment across departments and within departments is important. For example, displays of 8th grade enrollment in algebra by ethnicity often show a discrepancy between the percentage of students in each ethnic group taking such a course. Enrollment in high school college-preparatory or honors courses is also useful, as is looking at data by gender in higher level mathematics courses. Such data analysis provides insight into the opportunities afforded and taken advantage of by different segments of the school population.

Another valuable use of disaggregated data is to analyze students' access to college by counselor, across time, by type of institution attended, and by race and ethnicity. Disaggregated data are also useful for analyzing graduates' freshman success and college graduation rates.

Conclusion

In this chapter we have described the skills school administrators need to be successful instructional leaders. These skills are at the very heart of school leaders' work because they affect what happens to students at the point of instruction. They include being able to manage change, motivate students and faculty, and effectively create and manage a productive classroom environment where the needs of an increasingly diverse student population are served and where improvements are made based on a careful analysis of data.

As the late Ernest Boyer (1997) said, "Children are our most precious resource. In the end, they're all we have. And if we as a nation cannot help the coming generation, if we cannot prepare all children for learning and for life, then just what will bring America together?" Meeting this challenge brings with it vast rewards for school leaders because "life's greatest gift is the opportunity to throw oneself into a job that puts meaning and hope into the lives of other people. Seizing this opportunity is the surest way to put meaning and hope into one's own life" (Haberman 1995).

Use the following Skill Accomplishment Checklist to assess your skill level on each of the important topics discussed in this chapter.

Skill Accomplish Checklist for Chapter 6

Skills	Readings and Activities for Skill Mastery
Develop, implement, and monitor change processes to improve student learning, adult development, and learning climates.	**Readings:** Fullan (1993), Fullan and Stiegelbauer (1991), Goodlad (1990), Levin and Riffel (1997), Sergiovanni (1992), Sirotnik (1990) **Activities:** 1. Conduct an inservice session for district leaders about Fullan's basic lessons. 2. Identify district leaders and organize a series of meetings to plan change initiatives. 3. Develop a plan to ensure stakeholder focus and connectivity regarding district change initiatives.
Understand the role of motivation in the instructional process.	**Readings:** Brophy (1998), Epstein (1989), Maslow (1962),Wang, Haertel, and Walberg (1996) **Activities:** 1. Develop a survey to assess the motivation level of students within the district. 2. Create a task force to review the results of the survey and develop a plan to improve student motivation. 3. Create a series of inservice sessions for classroom teachers dealing with student motivation.
Promote effective classroom management.	**Readings:** Haynes and Chalker (1997), Johnson and Johnson (1994), Weinstein (1996), Weinstein and Mignano (1997) **Activities:** 1. Conduct a districtwide study of class size. 2. Develop a survey to identify teachers' perceptions about classroom management. 3. Review a sample of classroom lesson plans to determine the type of instructional strategies being used in classrooms.

Skill Accomplish Checklist for Chapter 6—continued

Skills	Readings and Activities for Skill Mastery
Encourage total student development.	**Readings:** Erickson (1963), Kohlberg (1963, 1975, 1981), Piaget (1954, 1963, 1970a, b), Vygotsky (1993), Woolfolk (1998) **Activities:** 1. Develop a staff inservice session about Vygotsky's work and engage staff in dialogue regarding the significance for classroom instruction.
Analyze and assign financial resources to enhance student learning.	**Readings:** Frase et al. (1995), Poston et al. (1992) **Activities:** 1. Develop a plan to link resources to curriculum initiatives. 2. Conduct a cost-benefit analysis of a new district program implemented in the past two years.
Apply instructional strategies that reflect sensitivity to multicultural issues and varied styles.	**Readings:** Banks (1993, 1994), Bennett (1995), Messick (1994) **Activities:** 1. Analyze projected student population trends in the district by ethnicity for the next 10 years. Develop recommendations based on the data. 2. Organize professional development sessions for classroom teachers dealing with the sociocultural characteristics of various ethnic groups.
Monitor and evaluate student achievement based on objectives and expected performance.	**Readings:** AFT (1996), Phye (1997), Steffy (1995) **Activities:** 1. Form a task force to develop a district student assessment plan made up of traditional and authentic assessment measures. 2. Designate teachers to develop a compendium of alternative assessments to be shared with all teachers.
Establish a student achievement monitoring and reporting system based on disaggregated data.	**Readings:** Johnson (1996), Leithwood and Aitken (1995) **Activities:** 1. Design a system for reporting student achievement results by class, building, and district with disaggregated data by gender, SES, and race. 2. Prepare a board policy requiring yearly reporting of disaggregated student achievement data by building and district.

Resources

Achilles, C.M. (October 1997). "Small Classes, Big Possibilities." *The School Administrator* 9, 54: 6-15.

American Federation of Teachers. (1996). *Making Standards Matter 1996: An Annual Fifty-State Report on Efforts to Raise Academic Standards.* Washington, D.C.: author.

Banks, J. A. (1997). *Teaching Strategies for Ethnic Studies* (6th Ed.). Boston: Allyn & Bacon.

Banks, J. A. (1994). *Multiethnic Education: Theory and Practice.* Boston: Allyn & Bacon.

Beck, L. (1997). *Child Development.* (4th Ed.). Boston: Allyn & Bacon.

Benard, B. (August, 1991). *Fostering Resiliency in Kids: Protective Factors in the Family, School and Community.* Portland, Ore.: Northwest Regional Educational Laboratory.

Bennett, C. I. (1995) *Comprehensive Multicultural Education: Theory and Practice* (3rd Ed.) Boston: Allyn & Bacon.

Bloom, B. (1971). *Taxonomy of Educational Objectives Handbook: Cognitive Domain.* New York: McGraw-Hill.

Boyer, E. (1997). *Selected Speeches.* New Jersey: The Carnegie Foundation for the Advancement of Teaching.

Brophy, J. (1998). *Motivating Students to Learn.* Boston: McGraw-Hill.

Buenning, M., and N. Tollefson. (1987). "The Cultural Gap Hypothesis as an Explanation for the Achievement Patterns of Mexican-American Students." *Psychology in the Schools* 14: 264-271.

Cheney, L. (1995). *Telling the Truth: Why Our Culture and Our Country Have Stopped Making Sense — And What We Can Do about It.* New York: Touchstone.

Cooper, H. (1979). "Pygmalion Grows Up: A Model for Teacher Expectation Communication and Performance Influence." *Review of Educational Research* 49: 389-410.

Csikszentmihalyi, M. (1993). *The Evolving Self: A Psychology for the Third Millennium.* New York: Harper Collins.

Dansereau, D. (1985). "Learning Strategy Research." In *Thinking and Learning Skills. (Vol. 1) Relating Instruction to Research,* edited by J. Segal, S. Chipman, and R. Glaser. Hillsdale, N.J.: Erlbaum.

Darling-Hammond, L. (1997). *The Right to Learn: A Blueprint for Creating Schools that Work.* San Francisco: Jossey-Bass.

Das, J. P. (1995). "Some Thought on Two Aspects of Vygotsky's Work." *Educational Psychologist,* 30: 93-97.

DeCharms, R. (1976). *Enhancing Motivation: Change in the Classroom.* New York: Irvington.

Deci, E., and R. Ryan. (1985). *Intrinsic Motivation and Self-Determination in Human Behavior.* New York: Plenum.

Doyle, W. (1983). "Academic Work." *Review of Educational Research* 53: 159-200.

Dunn, R., K. Dunn, and G.E. Price. (1984). *The Learning Styles Inventory.* Lawrence, Kan.: Price Systems.

Eisenberg, N., R. Shell, J. Pasernack, R. Lennon, R. Beller, and R.M. Marty. (1987). "Prosocial Development in Middle Childhood: A Longitudinal Study." *Developmental Psychology,* 23, 712-718.

Ennis, R. (1987). "A Taxonomy of Critical Thinking Disposition and Abilities." In *Teaching Thinking Skills: Theory and Practice,* edited by J. B. Baron and R. J. Sternberg. New York: Freeman.

Epstein, J. (1989). "Family Structures and Student Motivation: A Developmental Perspective." In *Research on Motivation in Education (Vol. 3),* edited by C. Ames and R. Ames. San Diego: Academic Press.

Erikson, E. (1980). *Identity and the Life Cycle* (2nd Ed.). New York: Norton.

Erikson, E. (1968). *Identity, Youth, and Crisis*. New York: Norton.

Erikson, E. (1963). *Childhood and Society* (2nd Ed.). New York: Norton.

Frase, L., F. English, and W. Poston Jr. (1995). *The Curriculum Management Audit: Improving School Quality*. Lancaster, Pa.: Technomic Publishing Co. Inc.

Ford, M. (1992). *Motivating Humans: Goals, Emotions, and Personal Agency Beliefs*. Newbury Park, Calif.: Sage.

Fullan, M. (1993). *Change Forces: Probing the Depths of Educational Reform*. New York: The Falmer Press.

Fullan, M., and S. Stiegelbauer. (1991). *The Meaning of Educational Change*. Ontario: OISE Press.

Garcia, E. E. (1992). "Hispanic Children: Theoretical, Empirical, and Related Policy Issues." *Educational Psychology Review* 4: 69-94.

Gilligan, C. (1982). *In a Different Voice: Psychological Theory and Women's Development*. Cambridge, Mass.: Harvard University Press.

Goodlad, J. (1990). "Studying the Education of Educators: From Conception to Findings." *Phi Delta Kappa* 71, 9: 698-701.

Gordon, E. W. (1991). "Human Diversity and Pluralism." *Educational Psychologist* 26: 99-108.

Haberman, M. (1995). *Star Teachers of Children in Poverty*. West Lafayette, Ind.: Kappa Delta Pi.

Hale-Benson, J. E. (1986). *Black Children: Their Roots, Culture, and Learning Styles* (Rev. ed.). Baltimore: Johns Hopkins University Press.

Haynes, R., and D Chalker. (1997). *World Class Elementary Schools: Agenda for Action*. Lancaster, Pa.: Technomic Pub. Co., Inc.

Herman, J., P. Aschbacher, and L. Winters. (1992). *A Practical Guide to Alternative Assessment*. Alexandra, Va.: Association for Supervision and Curriculum Development.

Johnson, R. S. (1996). *Setting Our Sights: Measuring Equity in School Change*. Los Angeles, Calif.: The Achievement Council.

Johnson, D., and R. Johnson. (1994). *Learning Together and Alone: Cooperation, Competition, and Individualization*. (4th Ed.) Boston: Allyn & Bacon.

Kagan, S. (1994). *Cooperative Learning*. San Juan Capistrano, Calif.: Kagan Cooperative Learning.

Keefe, J. W., and J.S. Monk. (1986). *Learning Style Profile Examiner's Manual*. Reston, Va.: National Association of Secondary School Principals.

King, A. (1994). "Guiding Knowledge Construction in the Classroom: Effects of Teaching Children How to Question and How to Explain." *American Educational Research Journal* 31: 338-368.

King, J., E. Hollins, and W. Hayman. (1997). *Preparing Teachers for Cultural Diversity*. New York: Teachers College Press.

Knight, P. (1992). "How I Use Portfolios in Mathematics." *Educational Leadership*. 49, 8: 71-72.

Kohlberg, L. (1963). "The Development of Children's Orientations Toward Moral Order: Sequence in the Development of Moral Thought." *Vita Humana* 6: 11-33.

Kohlberg, L. (1975). "The Cognitive-Developmental Approach to Moral Education." *Phi Delta Kappan* 56: 670-677.

Kohlberg, L (1981). *The Philosophy of Moral Development*. New York: Harper & Row.
Kozulin, A., and B. Presseisen. (1995). "Mediated Learning Experience and Psychological Tools: Vygotsky's and Feuerstein's Perspectives in the Study of Student Learning." *Educational Psychologist* 30: 67-75.

Leithwood, K., and R. Aitken. (1995). *Making Schools Smarter: A System for Monitoring School and District Progress*. Newbury Park, Calif.: Corwin Press.

Levin, B., and A .Riffel. (1997). *Schools and the Changing World: Struggling Toward the Future.* New York: The Falmer Press.

Lipscomb, T. J., H.A. MacAllister, and N.J. Bregman. (1985). "A Developmental Inquiry into the Effects of Multiple Models on Children's Generosity." *Merrill-Palmer Quarterly* 31: 335-344.

Manning, M. L., and L.G. Baruth. (1996). *Multicultural Education of Children and Adolescents* (2nd Ed.). Boston: Allyn & Bacon.

Marsh, H. W., and R. Shavelson. (1985). "Self-Concept: Its Multifaceted, Hierarchical Structure. *Educational Psychologist* 20: 107-123.

Maslow, A. (1962). *Toward a Psychology of Being.* Princeton, N.J.: Van Nostrand.

McAdams, R. (1993). *Lessons from Abroad.* Lancaster, Pa.: Technomic Pub. Co., Inc.

Messick, S. (1994). "The Matter of Style: Manifestations of Personality in Cognition, Learning, and Teaching." *Educational Psychology* 29: 121-136.

National Council of Teachers of Mathematics. (1995). *Assessment Standards for School Mathematics.* Reston, Va.: author.

Nelson, K. (1981). "Individual Differences in Language Development: Implications for Development and Language."*Developmental Psychology* 17: 170-187.

O'Donnell, A., and J. O'Kelly. (1994). "Learning from Peers: Beyond the Rhetoric of Positive Results." *Educational Psychology Review* 6: 321-350.

Phye, G., ed.. (1997). *Handbook of Classroom Assessment: Learning, Adjustment and Achievement.* San Diego: Academic Press.

Piaget, J. (1954). *The Construction of Reality in the Child* (translated by M. Cook). New York: Basic Books.

Piaget, J. (1963). *Origins of Intelligence in Children.* New York: Norton.

Piaget, J. (1970a). "Piaget's Theory." In *Handbook on Child Psychology* (3rd Ed.), edited by P. Mussen. New York: Wiley.

Piaget, J. (1970b). *The Science of Education and the Psychology of the Child.* New York: Orion Press.

Pintrich, P., and B. Schrauben. (1992). "Students' Motivational Beliefs and Their Cognitive Engagement in Academic Tasks." In *Students' Perceptions in the Classroom: Causes and Consequences*, edited by D. Schunk and J. Meece. Hillsdale, N.J.: Erlbaum.

Pintrich, P., and D. Schunk. (1996). *Motivation in Education: Theory, Research, and Applications.* Englewood Cliffs, N.J.: Prentice-Hall.

Poston, W. Jr., P. Stone, and C. Muther. (1992). "Making Schools Work: Practical Management of Support Operations." In *Successful Schools: Guidebooks to Effective Educational Leadership*, edited by F. English. Newbury Park, Calif.: Corwin Press.

Quellmalz. E. S. (1991). "Developing Criteria for Performance Assessments. The Missing Link." *Applied Measurement in Education* 4, 4: 319-332.

Quellmalz, E. S. (1987). "Developing Reasoning Skills." In *Teaching Thinking Skills: Theory and Practice*, edited by J R. Baron and R. I. Sternberg. New York: Freeman.

Quellmalz, E.S., and J. Hoskyn. (1997). "Classroom Assessment of Reasoning Strategies." In *Handbook of Classroom Assessment*, edited by G. Phye. San Diego, Calif.: Academic Press.

Quellmalz, E. S., and J. Hoskyn. (April 1988). "Making a Difference in Arkansas: The Multicultural Reading and Thinking Project." *Educational Leadership* 45, 51-55.

Renzulli, J. S., and L.H. Smith. (1978). *The Learning Styles Inventory: A Measure of Student Preferences for Instructional Techniques.* Mansfield Center, Conn.: Creative Learning Press..

Resnick, L. B., and L.E. Klopfer. (1989) *Toward the Thinking Curriculum. Overview.* Arlington, Va.: Association for Supervision and Curriculum Development.

Rosenshine, B. (1979). "Content Time, and Direct Instruction." In *Research on Teaching: Concepts, Findings, and Implications*, edited by P. Peterson and H. Walberg. Berkeley, Calif.: McCutchan.

Sergiovanni, T. (1992). *Moral Leadership: Getting to the Heart of School Improvement.* San Francisco: Jossey-Bass.

Sirotnik, K. (1990). "Society, Schooling, Teaching, and Preparing to Teach." In *The Moral Dimension of Teaching*, edited by J. Goodlad, R. Soder, and K. Sirotnik. San Francisco: Jossey-Bass.

Snow R.E., L. Corno, and D. Jackson. (1996). "Individual Differences in Affective and Cognitive Functions." In *Handbook of Educational Psychology*, edited by D. Berliner and R. Calfee. New York: MacMillan.

Sobesky, W. E. (1983). "The Effects of Situational Factors on Moral Judgment." *Child Development* 54: 575-584.

Spaulding, C. (1992). *Motivation in the Classroom.* New York: McGraw-Hill.

Steffy, B. (1995). *Authentic Assessment and Curriculum Alignment: Meeting the Challenge of National Standards.* Lancaster, Pa.: Technomic Pub. Co., Inc.

Steffy, B., and F. English. (1997). *Curriculum and Assessment for World-Class Schools.* Lancaster, Pa.: Technomic Pub. Co., Inc.

Stiggins, R. J. (1988). "Revitalizing Classroom Assessment: The Highest Instructional Priority." *Phi Delta Kappan* 69: 363-368.

Stipek, D. (1988). *Motivation to Learn: From Theory to Practice.* Englewood Cliffs, N.J.: Prentice-Hall.

Stipek, D., and J. Weisz. (1981). "Perceived Personal Control and Academic Achievement." *Review of Educational Research* 51: 101-137.

Vygotsky, L. S. (1993). *The Collected Works of L. S. Vygotsky: Vol 2.* (Translated by J. Knox and C. Stevens.). New York: Plenum.

Vygotsky, L. S. (1978). *Mind in Society: The Development of Higher Mental Process.* Cambridge, Mass.: Harvard University Press.

Wadsworth, B. J. (1989). *Piaget's Theory of Cognitive Development: An Introduction for Students of Psychology and Education* (4th Ed.). New York: Longman.

Wang, M., G. Haertel, and H. Walberg. (1996). "Educational Resilience in Inner Cities." In *Strategies for Improving Education in Urban Communities*, edited by M. Wang and H. Walberg. Philadelphia: Temple Center for Research in Human Development and Education.

Webb, N., and A. Palincsar. (1996). "Group Processes in the Classroom." In *Handbook of Educational Psychology*, edited by D.C. Berliner and R.C. Calfee. New York: MacMillan.

Weinstein, C. (1996). *Secondary Classroom Management: Lessons from Research and Practice.* New York: McGraw-Hill.

Weinstein, C., and A. Mignano Jr. (1997). *Elementary Classroom Management: Lessons from Research and Practice* (2nd Ed.). New York: McGraw-Hill.

Woolfolk, A. (1998). *Educational Psychology* (7th Ed.) Boston: Allyn and Bacon.

chapter 7 | *Skills in Staff Evaluation and Personnel Management*

taff evaluation is a mixture of art and science. While there are basic skills in staff evaluation that can be taught and practiced, thoughts about which evaluation tools to use under different teaching or management conditions remain speculative. However, using the right assessment tool at the right time to catch and measure a specific staff member's performance is worth the time and energy involved. Effective staff evaluation is one key to improving teacher and administrator performance.

Staff evaluation processes and personnel management systems stand at a crossroads. One road leads to a system created by legislators and special interest groups who push for competitive, test score-driven merit pay and other incentive-pay alternatives to the single salary scale. The other road leads to a system created by educational practitioners and researchers working with state and national professional associations and state education department personnel to improve teacher, administrator, and student performance through evaluation systems that are less competitive and punitive and more team oriented.

A staff evaluation model based on the values of trust, honesty, and collaboration among teachers, administrators, parents, and the school board can help create the kind of learning communities futurists dream about. Though no single evaluation system fits the needs of all school districts or schools, the Teacher Evaluation for Continuous Improvement (TECI) and the Administrator Evaluation for Continuous Improvement (AECI) are vehicles that help school leaders reach higher levels of performance appraisal and team building.

As a new century approaches, U.S. schools face potential shortages of qualified educational personnel. School leaders must create and skillfully manage a personnel system that recruits America's finest young leaders, evaluates them effectively, and supports their professional growth. They will have to create coalitions across government, business, and other agencies to communicate the need for attracting and keeping the best and brightest in the education profession.

This chapter details the skills successful 21st century school leaders must possess to:

• Apply effective staff evaluation models and processes to assess teacher and administrator performance;
• Develop personnel recruitment, selection, development, and promotion procedures;
• Understand legal issues related to personnel administration; and
• Conduct a district or school human resources audit.

Applying Effective Staff Evaluation Models and Processes

Few educators question the need for appraising individual performance. In fact, most are committed to an equitable and educationally sound evaluation process. Such a process should make it clear to everyone:

• What the standards of the evaluation are;
• How the evaluation results will be used;
• Who will do the evaluation;
• What types of instruments and methods will be used;
• How many times they will be evaluated;
• Whether high evaluation scores truly reflect their competence as educators; and
• What the appeal procedures are if they disagree with the evaluation results.

Teachers and administrators are vitally interested in improving the quality of education and in the improvement of student achievement, but it is difficult to develop and improve appraisal procedures and to create greater understanding of the purposes and limitations of such procedures. Evaluations should be conducted by competent professionals employing thorough and open methods. Such evaluations promote ongoing communication and mutual support, which, in turn, create a climate of trust.

Evaluating Teacher Performance

School leaders, especially principals, are under great pressure to ensure high levels of teacher performance. Catherine Jones Brooks, an elementary principal in Houston, Texas, knows about the pressure all too well. Brooks' school was rated by the Texas Education Agency as "low performing," a label that is like an albatross. Knowing her job was in jeopardy, Brooks fought to turn the school around and lived through many anxious days. But after several staff changes and instructional improvements through targeted staff development, higher test scores and student attendance rates resulted in a 1997 rating of "acceptable." Brooks stated, "Accountability tied to your future is serious. That's the kind of pressure I felt" (Markley 1997, p. 37A).

Teachers also feel extreme pressure from administrators and the public to improve student test scores, but they are often skeptical about the methods administrators use to evaluate and help them improve classroom performance. Shafer (1990, pp. 340-342) believes that teachers find little help in most routine appraisals. She writes: "Routine appraisals aren't very telling because they generally just provide an opportunity for the administrator to say something nice about the teacher's work." Shafer continues, "Once in a while a principal will deliver an unpopular message and ruffle feathers for a while, but usually everything will get back to normal by the start of the next year." Shafer does believe, however, that ". . . if an administrator has a good grasp of communications, he or she ought to be able to tell whether the teacher and students are connecting." She contends that if administrators use the best teacher appraisal practices, do less office work, and conduct frequent drop-ins and walk throughs, they can help teachers become more effective.

Teacher evaluation models are available, but they work if, and only if, teachers and evaluators view them as a positive process for achieving the intrinsic rewards of professional growth. True professionals need open, threat-free workplaces that nurture self-expression and respect. Open, team-oriented performance assessments will not only improve professional practice; they can attract new leaders to the teaching force in the 21st century.

The Need for More Qualified Teachers

Governors, legislators, and state boards of education express deep concern about the prospect of having fewer and less qualified teaching candidates in universities and the shortage of teachers in some specialty areas — especially math and special education. President Clinton's Secretary of Education Richard Riley reported that the number of school children attending America's schools reached a record 52.2 million in September 1997. He estimated at the time that 6,000 additional schools would be needed and 2 million more teachers would have to be hired over the following 10 years to meet the rapid growth in student enrollment. Riley also expressed concern about the shortage of qualified teachers in some subject areas, stating, "We can't expect to raise the academic standards while lowering teacher standards just so we can put an adult in front of every classroom" (Abu-Nasr 1997).

According to Joanna Pasternak, vice president of the Houston Federation of Teachers, the Houston Independent School District is often forced to hire uncertified substitutes rather than certified teachers to fill openings. This hiring practice is causing observers of teacher supply to wave a red flag. Bright young people who see personnel administrators hiring uncertified teachers and state agencies requiring meaningless tests and unreliable performance measures back away from teaching and seek professions that command greater respect from the public and higher salaries.

Despite these concerns, there is reason to believe that many dedicated, bright young people will enter teaching and stay. National polls about the most respected people in society include teachers in the top 10, even though teachers' salaries do not reflect the high ranking. When people are asked who was most influential in their lives, teachers frequently appear as one of the top three responses. And during the late 1990s a renewed sense of service to others occurred among America's youth, inspiring the "Teach for America" program in urban school districts and leading a growing number of the "best and brightest" university students to select education as a major and enter teaching.

Ironically, personnel evaluation systems work better with brighter, more dedicated personnel. A bright, enthusiastic teacher is more enjoyable to evaluate than one having serious problems. While some legislators and administrators see the purpose of evaluation as a means of firing incompetent teachers and rewarding outstanding ones, most educational leaders realize that teacher evaluation has a much greater value as a tool for improving performance. The challenge facing school leaders is how to use teacher evaluation to improve teaching and student performance and to attract the "best and brightest" to the teaching profession.

Indicators of Good Teaching

Research shows that students are more attentive in intellectually challenging, businesslike, threat-free, task-oriented classrooms where they receive immediate feedback. A key to a businesslike classroom is not time-on-task alone but "academic learning time" (ALT). ALT is the amount of time students actually spend on an appropriate learning activity in which they are achieving a high rate of success. Researchers have found that in effective classrooms, teachers waste less time in starting and ending instructional activities and spend more time with curricular materials that match students' interests and abilities. Effective teachers also build high expectations for students and themselves and keep in close contact with students' parents. Therefore, any teacher evaluation form should include the following indicators:

- ✔ Motivates students to achieve
- ✔ Uses academic learning time effectively
- ✔ Demonstrates command of the language or languages
- ✔ Promotes students' academic and social growth
- ✔ Establishes clear learning objectives
- ✔ Employs a variety of teaching strategies (e.g., problem-based learning, computer games, group projects, and individual research)
- ✔ Aligns learning objectives with assessment strategies
- ✔ Keeps parents informed about each student's progress
- ✔ Works well with other teachers to the benefit of all students and the school
- ✔ Treats each child or youth with respect and dignity
- ✔ Involves parents and community members in students' learning activities

Obviously, other important observable and nonobservable behaviors contribute to any overall evaluation of a teacher's performance. However, if the above indicators are not measured or present, other factors indicate little about a teacher's ability.

Tying Teacher Evaluation to Student Performance

The most controversial element of any teacher evaluation system is the linking of a teacher's performance to student achievement. Many teachers believe it is completely unfair to judge their effectiveness on how well their students do on a standardized or state-designed test. Teachers worry that testing seems to be the only purpose of education and that the excessive amount of time devoted to "teaching to the test" stifles creative teaching and learning. Texas is attempting to strike a balance in this controversy by holding both the teacher and the school accountable for student performance.

Texas' Professional Development and Appraisal System (PDAS) for Texas Teachers, which

One Trend in Teacher Evaluation

Danielson (1996) has constructed a research-based framework for teacher evaluation based on 4 domains and 22 components. The four domains are: planning and preparation, classroom environment, instruction, and professional responsibilities. The fourth domain of Danielson's framework, professional responsibilities, is somewhat unique to teacher evaluation systems, which typically focus inside the classroom. This domain focuses primarily on activities that take place outside the classroom. The components of this domain include reflecting on teaching, maintaining accurate records, communicating with families, contributing to the school and district, growing and developing professionally, and showing professionalism. Within each component area, teachers are identified as unsatisfactory, basic, proficient, or distinguished. For example, in the category of relationships with colleagues, an unsatisfactory rating would be given if the "teacher's relationships with colleagues are negative or self-serving," basic if the "teacher maintains cordial relationships with colleagues to fulfill the duties that the school or district requires," proficient if "support and cooperation characterize the teacher's relationships with colleagues," and distinguished if the "teacher takes initiative in assuming leadership among the faculty" (p. 114). It is expected that this trend toward including activities outside the classroom as part of teacher appraisal systems will continue.

was developed with input from teachers and other professionals, aims to develop:

• A fair and practical appraisal process that builds upon and makes improvements in the current Texas Teacher Appraisal System;
• A system that acknowledges and reinforces what research shows to be good teaching practices; and
• A system that promotes and supports high-quality professional development among teachers.

The PDAS includes evaluation criteria organized in eight domains. These criteria are based on input from over 10,000 teachers and are more inclusive of individual teaching styles and less directive than the old Texas Teacher Appraisal System criteria. The eight domains are:

Domain I: Active, Successful Student Participation in the Learning Process

Domain II: Learner-Centered Instruction

Domain III: Evaluation and Feedback on Student Progress

Domain IV: Management of Student Discipline, Instructional Strategies, and Materials

Domain V: Professional Communication

Domain VI: Professional Development

Domain VII: Compliance with Policies, Operating Procedures, and Requirements

Domain VIII: Improvement of Academic Performance of All Students on the Campus

Domain VIII constitutes the student performance link. This domain includes 10 criteria. Five of the criteria relate to teacher planning, analysis, and instructional delivery. One relates to the teacher's continuing efforts to monitor student attendance and work to improve any attendance problems. Four focus on the teacher's efforts to help identify and work with at-risk students.

The PDAS scores teachers on 52 criteria in these 8 categories, including school campus ratings. Teachers are observed by an evaluator at least once a year for at least 45 minutes, with additional walk-throughs as necessary. Currently, observations may be scheduled or unscheduled at the discretion of the district. Teachers receive a written observation summary and appraisal report annually. The schools are rated as exemplary, recognized, or low performing, based largely on the Texas Assessment of Academic Achievement (TAAS) scores, but also according to school dropout rates and attendance records.

When the PDAS system is fully in place, teachers will be evaluated on how well their school is doing in the state accountability system; thus each teacher's ratings will reflect the state's rating for the school as a whole. Even though each teacher will be independently evaluated by the principal or a designee, the main emphasis of the state accountability system is on team or school success.

Proponents of PDAS claim that it will not be punitive to teachers and will encourage teamwork and the sharing of ideas to help individual students and the entire school perform at higher levels. Critics of the plan include John O'Sullivan of the 26,000-member Texas Federation of Teachers, who claims it is "half-baked and about as fair as teachers assigning a student a grade based on the performance of the class as a whole. It just doesn't make sense" (Walt 1997).

A field test of the PDAS plan was conducted in the 1996-97 school year before its statewide 1997-98 implementation. Reviews of the field test were mixed; some claim that PDAS will build stronger team effort, while others see no change from the old system (Texas Education Agency 1996).

The PDAS or any other approach to teacher evaluation is only as effective as the administrators and teachers involved. If administrators are protecting images of total authority over "their" teachers, then the best evaluation models and instruments are useless. Likewise, if teachers feel they do not need supervision, choose to ignore school policy, and view the principal, supervisors, and peers as the enemy, then any system, regardless of its claims of a "mutual-benefit" or team approach, will do little to improve teaching and learning.

Some observers of the Mutual-Benefit model (see discussion later in chapter) and other team models are skeptical because of the mixed signals the models send about who is actually accountable — the individual teacher or all teachers in the school.

The Flaws in Teacher Evaluation

Why have many teacher evaluation plans been faulty? The answers to this question remain unchanged since McLaughlin (1982) reported in a RAND Corporation study that teacher evaluation was an idea not clearly thought through and underdeveloped and that very few school systems had a true evaluation system. Some of the problems that have plagued teacher appraisal for years include:

• Principals' attitudes and competence due to their conflicting roles as colleagues and evaluators;
• Perceptions of teacher evaluation as an added chore;
• Teacher apathy and resistance; and
• A lack of uniformity and consistency among school buildings that leaves too much room for a principal's disposition or bias to enter into rankings.

In response to these four problems, Darling-Hammond (1990) writes,

Quite often, school districts take as given that any evaluation method can be made to suit any purpose; that school principals will "find" time for whatever evaluation requirements are enacted; that all evaluators will be equally competent; that the nature and level of evaluation needs will not vary from teacher to teacher or from school to school; and that the results of the evaluation will be used,. . . [which] lessens the credibility of evaluation, making the activity susceptible to shirking, avoidance, pro forma compliance, and dissension, [which are] sometimes more damaging than helpful to teaching, teacher morale, and the organizational cohesion necessary for improvement (p. 161).

Lewis (1982) believes that teacher evaluation could be a useful tool for teacher improvement if the process could strike a careful balance between standardized, centrally administered criteria and teacher-specific approaches to evaluation and professional development. Lewis and others agree that the central-office staff, building principals, and teachers must work out a delicate balance between common, centrally administered performance criteria and criteria specific to each building, content area, classroom, and group of students.

According to Stiggins and Bridgeford (1984), administrators in four Pacific Northwest school districts had mixed feelings about their teacher evaluation systems. In two districts, administrators were generally satisfied with the evaluation process, but they were concerned about the time necessary to conduct the classroom observations.

In the two other districts, administrators were dissatisfied with their systems of evaluation. They found that teachers did not trust the process, the evaluation criteria were unclear, and the focus was on meeting state accountability guidelines rather than promoting lasting improvements in the teaching-learning process. When asked how evaluation could be more directly related to the improvement of teaching, administrators in the four districts recommended (Stiggins and Bridgeford 1984, p. 21):

• Changes in system management, including increased staff involvement in goal setting and emphasis on improvement as a district priority;
• Improved methods of conducting observations;
• Allowing more time for evaluation and observations;
• Development of evaluators' skills;
• A stronger link between evaluation and staff development; and
• Accountability for all principals conducting evaluations.

These suggestions mirror those made by other school leaders across the nation. Most agree that evaluation could be much more effective in diagnosing teachers' needs, improving their skills, and improving student learning if the process included more teacher involvement, clearer criteria, more time for observations, and a stronger link to staff development (Hoyle 1990). Moreover, state and locally developed evaluation systems must link teacher performance to student achievement. After looking at hundreds of teacher evaluation systems, Shinkfield and Stufflebeam (1995) concur that the systems are not grounded in clear rationale and policy, focused on defensible criteria, reliable, credible, sensitive to particular teaching settings, or influential. Instead, they found them to be biased, superficial, and demoralizing.

Despite these many flaws, the public and state legislators demand some form of evaluation of teachers. Political figures and school boards continue to push for merit pay or career ladder systems to reward master teachers or weed out those found incompetent and to provide financial incentives to encourage more young people to enter teaching.

Where We Have Been in Administrator Evaluation

According to Brown and Irby (1997a, p. 3), "Administrator appraisal has historically been approached from basically two procedural vantage points: (1) informal, inconsistent evaluation, and (2) formal checklists on observable management functions." The informal models continue in numerous school districts today, especially in rural schools, but hold little promise for continuous improvement in the practice of administrators or the district or school. The formal checklist method holds more promise in that checklists frequently reflect the current skills and standards developed by professional associations at the state or national levels.

Management by Objective

Checklists have been a key part of the Management by Objective (MBO) model, which calls for the superintendent to begin each year in conference with the school board or its evaluation committee, setting performance goals for the school year. Then in early spring the superintendent and the board decide how many of the goals on the checklist have been met. The board bases its judgment about the superintendent's position and contract on this list of accomplishments. The superintendent follows the same process with all office and building administrators to determine their yearly progress.

This process is the same as the Leadership by Objectives and Results (LBO/R) model included in the last edition of this book (Hoyle, English, and Steffy 1994). LBO/R included feedback from superiors, subordinates, and peers, but did not involve

The North Carolina State Department of Public Instruction (1986) studied the time required for evaluation. If, for example, a preobservation conference requires 30 minutes, an observation requires 60 minutes, a post-observation conference requires 45 minutes with an additional 45 minutes for the data analysis, and the actual evaluation requires 60 minutes, the time would add up to 570 minutes per teacher. In a school with 50 teachers, the principal would spend approximately 60 8-hour days doing nothing but teacher evaluation.

teachers, other staff members, and parents as the 360 Degree Feedback model does.

During the past five years the pressure for accountability of schools and administrators has increased along with greater emphasis on site-based decision making. These factors require the new and more team-oriented administrator evaluation models.

Assessment Centers

Assessment centers have been a part of personnel assessment, selection, and development in business and industry for over 50 years. Each center has a group of highly trained assessors, who observe and evaluate candidates in various exercises and simulations. Participants are evaluated on 12 skill dimensions: problem analysis, judgment, organizational ability, decisiveness, leadership, sensitivity, stress tolerance, oral and written communication, personal motivation, and educational values. NASSP created one of the most comprehensive assessment centers, which is still active. Research into the NASSP assessment effort (Schmitt and Cohen 1990) shows that assessment centers help identify promising candidates for the position of principal because the overall ratings received by those assessed are valid, reliable, and related to the real day-to-day job of a principal.

Additional assessment centers have been created in Kentucky, Texas, and other states with the support of AASA and state agencies. While data to support the success of these efforts are not widely available, reports provide promising signs about their ability to assist agencies and administrators in continuous improvement efforts.

The major problems and questions raised about assessment centers are that they are very labor intensive in terms of the time it takes to assess each individual; the process is expensive, $400 - $1,000 per individual; and the skills (standards) created by national professional groups (and featured in this book) have not been consistently tested in the centers. Perhaps in time a more economical, less time-consuming assessment center model will emerge based on the new standards for administrator evaluation, including those from AASA, ISLLC, NCATE, NASSP, and NAESP.

Evaluating Administrator Performance

In many school districts, the evaluation of building-level administrators and superintendents is carried out in a highly professional way, while in other districts it is an annual exercise that must be done and makes little difference to the daily operation of the system.

What is Good Administrator Performance?

Principals are praised when a school is rated as high performing and condemned when a school is rated as a low performer. The literature on the principalship concludes that "you can't have a great school without a great principal." Put yourself in the chair of a principal who has completed her first year in a new school. Her previous school was a perpetual high-flying, award-winning experience. She won a "principal of the year award" and her success led a superintendent in a neighboring state to recruit her at a substantial increase in salary to take over a suburban secondary school that had fallen from grace in the community because of low tests scores, increasing dropouts, and low teacher morale.

The end-of-year test scores, dropout numbers, and teacher morale measures remained dismal in spite of the efforts of this new principal. She had done all of the things that had made her suc-

cessful before but made little apparent headway — at least on paper. The superintendent and the director of secondary schools called her in and wanted to know why she could show no signs of turning the school around after a full year. They concluded that the principal's performance was subpar and required her to agree to a clearly specified professional growth plan, which called for higher test scores, fewer dropouts, and higher teacher morale. The evaluators told the principal that they would reevaluate her performance within the next year and make a personnel decision at that time.

• • •

A superintendent in a medium-sized school district in the upper Midwest fought for four years to move his district off dead center by strengthening the high school curriculum and leading the entire community through a vision-building process and designing a state-of-the art strategic plan for the coming five years. The community and the school board were proud of their dynamic superintendent, who had received the highest possible evaluations for the past three years . A multi-million dollar bond

---

Merit Pay and Other Alternative Compensation Efforts

According to Martin, Schoeder, and Nelson (1997, p. 146),

the subject of alternative compensation is one of the most controversial and complex issues in private, public, and educational organizations. Throughout the nation, citizens, business leaders, and legislators are calling for alternative compensation programs in order to address some of the perceived problems, including inadequate pupil performance, the lack of incentives for high-performing educators, failure to dismiss incompetent educators, and a rising concern over education's cost-effectiveness at local and state levels.

Merit pay is a compensation plan that allows those whose performance is judged as superior to earn more than those whose work is judged as average or below average. Alternative compensation plans like merit pay have been created by policymakers and community members who question the standard teacher salary schedule. The single salary schedule, claim the critics, is unfair to high-performing teachers who make the same money as average or below average teachers. Advocates of merit pay believe extra money will motivate teachers to teach better, which, in turn, will push students to higher levels of performance. Despite numerous efforts to introduce merit pay plans into school districts around the nation, very few have worked successfully over a period of time.

Another alternative compensation plan is a "group incentive plan" (Martin et al. 1997). Used in Douglas County, Colo., the group incentive plan defines a group as teachers within a school or other teachers, district specialists, or coordinators assigned to specific schools. Groups are rewarded for meeting specified goals. A Group Incentive Board reviews proposals, which meet the following criteria:
• Goals are teacher designed and linked to school or district objectives that reflect the district's core values.
• Goals are valuable to the school and community and will benefit students.
• Goals are clearly communicated to and supported by the community, administration, state, and the Group Incentive Board.
• Goals are stated in specific, measurable terms with clearly stated responsibilities and timelines.
• Goals are designed to improve student performance "above the local standard" (pp. 150-151).

issue was passed for a new school and repairs on other facilities. The future for the school district and the superintendent were bright and exciting. But, as John Lennon once wrote, "Life is what happens while you are busy making other plans."

The local high school football team was poised to win another district championship to add to three others and to one state title. The coaches and the community were full of anticipation to see "their boys do it again." But there was a problem: As a result of the stiffer requirements in math and English for high school graduation, three of the team's stars had failed both classes in the summer and were therefore ineligible to play that fall. When the school board met about the situation, they decided to ask the superintendent to use the "grandfather clause" and return to the old graduation requirements for these players, which would allow them to play football. The superintendent told the board that they could not change the requirements for these athletes without changing them for all students; otherwise they would be breaking the law. The board left the room angry at the superintendent and told all who would listen that the superintendent was antiathletics and did not care about the three kids. The team did not win the district title. The superintendent's evaluation was the lowest in his tenure, and he resigned at the end of the year.

Aspiring and practicing administrators should keep these cases in mind as we briefly review the trends, struggles, and successes of evaluation.

Paper-and-Pencil Teacher and Administrator Assessment Instruments

The search for the best teacher and administrator evaluation processes has eluded the best detectives. In a definitive book, *Assessment of Teaching* (Mitchell, Wise, and Plake 1990), James Popham, Edward Haertel, Donald Medley, William Merhrens, Linda Darling-Hammond, Richard Stiggins, and George Madaus contribute the best thinking on the state-of-the art in teacher assessment. They express concerns about the validity of paper-pencil assessment instruments and the need to reexamine the complex issues surrounding teacher testing for licensure and certification and the improvement of the profession.

All paper-pencil examinations of educator performance, including the National Teachers Examination (NTE), face a perceived legitimacy problem. When human beings, however expert in

performance appraisal, examine the validity of test items to assess the skills of other professionals, many questions arise. With regard to educator evaluation, these questions include: Should the tests examine an educator's general knowledge, pedagogy, classroom management, and knowledge in English, chemistry, math, and so on? Should the test for the licensure of principals and superintendents include test items drawn from the knowledge base of educational administration? How many of the items should be content specific and how many should be practice based? What, if any, are the relationships between a paper-pencil assessment instrument and the skills to be successful in teaching, in the principalship, or in the superintendency? These questions continue to press researchers and practicing school leaders.

Whether a test is intended for entry-level licensure, to confer a permanent license after a period of provisional service, or for a career ladder incentive system, test items need to be carefully designed and field tested to overcome perceived legitimacy problems. If better methods of professional performance evaluation are not found soon, external groups and agencies will exert their power and impose other ways of evaluating teachers and administrators.

Even though merit pay systems may look promising on the surface, many have led to charges of unfairness and caused divisiveness, which, in turn, may produce low morale and an unhealthy, competitive school climate. Those who argue against merit pay plans believe that individuals who choose teaching for a career are intrinsically motivated because they are molding lives and trying to build a better society.

Recent school reform efforts, however, have stressed the need to make the practice of teaching fully "professional." This includes holding professional educators to the highest standards of performance as well as insisting on customer satisfaction. When professionals feel pressured by arbitrary and external rules, they will not take personal responsibility for their performance (Sagor 1996). Therefore, educational leaders must identify the goals of evaluation and explore the types of systems that support improved teacher and student performance. Good systems of evaluation are necessary to guide school reform efforts, which depend on improving the results of teaching.

Personnel Evaluation Standards

Daniel Stufflebeam (1988) and a joint committee of 13 professional education societies developed professional standards for planning, operating, assessing, and validating educational personnel evaluation systems. According to the committee, the purpose of educational personnel evaluation is to "promote sound education principles, fulfillment of institutional missions, and effective performance of job responsibilities so that the educational needs of students, community, and society are met" (p. 21). The committee supported the idea that all educator evaluation systems should have four basic attributes: propriety, utility, feasibility, and accuracy. These four attributes help ensure that educational professionals strive for continuous improvement and possess a willingness to share growth experiences with their peers (Krovetz and Cohick 1993).

Approaches to Evaluation

In 1980, Don Haefele summarized 12 approaches to teacher evaluation and concluded that a mutual benefit/goal-setting approach that includes growth plans, though demanding, is best because it is based on mutual trust and the overall vision, mission, and goals of the district or school. While new, more participatory and peer-oriented evaluations, including the use of portfolios, have been developed, the mutual benefit/goal-setting approach continues to dominate teacher evaluation.

Mutual Benefit/Goal-Setting Evaluation. The Mutual-Benefit/Goal-Setting Model of evaluation posits that teachers should have input into selecting criteria for their evaluation and for their own professional development. Under the model, ". . . each teacher selects developmental goals and identifies strategies for achieving them. These strategies might include observing other teachers, coursework, workshop attendance, or readings" (Seyfarth 1996, p. 157). Locke and Latham (1990) believe that goal theory has produced positive results because specific and difficult goals produce higher levels of performance than vague, nonquantitative goals; difficult goals, if accepted, result in higher levels of performance; and goals are strong motivators regardless of whether they are self-selected, jointly chosen, or assigned by others.

Pioneering work by Richard Manatt and colleagues (1976), George Redfern (1980), and Dale Bolton (1980) has influenced the widespread use of goal-setting models. Variations of the models used throughout the United States and Canada are characterized not only by mutual goal setting by teachers and administrators and teacher involvement in the evaluation process, but also by a balance between centralized and local school site teaching standards.

Portfolios. The major addition to the improvement of the goal-setting approach has been the growing use of portfolios. According to Seyfarth (1996, p. 158), "Teachers prepare a portfolio by assembling a variety of information pertaining to their teaching and presenting it to an evaluator." Brown and Irby (1997b, p. 4) describe a portfolio as a ". . . purposeful, self-selected collection of artifacts and reflective entries that represent a [teacher's or] administrator's growth."

Most critical observers agree that the portfolio holds promise for strengthening teacher and administrator appraisal. According to Bird (1990, pp. 241-256) and Turk and colleagues (1994, pp. 3-5), the teacher portfolio should include the following:

- Goals — to allow teachers to document and monitor their progress.
- Student and parent evaluations — related to a teacher's instructional ability, communication, classroom management, and respect for individuals.
- Classroom videotapes — to give teachers a visual reality check of their classroom behaviors and instructional processes.
- Student work samples — student homework or other material selected over a period of time on a random or regular basis.
- Peer coaching data — data gleaned from colleagues observing a peer over a sustained period of time.
- Parent communication — summaries of telephone calls and conferences with parents; successful and unsuccessful interactions.
- Instructional materials samples — a sampling of instructional materials over a semester or year, both those that have been successful and those that have not.
- Professional development activities — a teaching license or certificate and other samples of professional development accomplishments.
- Nonclassroom professional duties — a list of noninstructional tasks and responsibilities (e.g., club sponsor, student activity coordinator, curriculum committee member, site-based team member).

The use of portfolios to evaluate administrators is far from common in the United States. In a study of Texas administrator appraisal systems, Brown and Irby (1997) found that most administrators (68%) had suggestions for improving their current evaluation system, but only 10 percent of the respondents suggested the inclusion of portfolios. However, when asked if portfolios should be included in their evaluations, 63 percent of the administrators surveyed agreed that portfolio evaluation would be valuable.

Based on a review of the current literature, Brown and Irby conclude,

> The use of the evaluation portfolio, as a component of an evaluation system, overcomes many of the deficiencies of current evaluation systems, which: (a) do not promote professional growth, (b) are not perceived to result in school improvement, (c) do not evaluate the substantive aspects of the administrators' work, (d) do not address the complexity of the job, (e) are not authentic — do not afford the opportunity to present concrete evidence of success, (f) do not address the contingent and situational aspects of leadership, (g) do not address the moral dimensions of leadership, (h) do not promote collaborative relationships, and (I) do not promote ongoing dialogue among administrators (p.8).

In a follow-up to the Texas study, Brown and Irby (1997) provided administrators training in the use of portfolios. Some of the study participants felt "overwhelmed" with the detail and the time required in the process but afterwards were positive. The participants suggested that the process could be improved by:

- Keeping the system nonthreatening during the pilot year;
- Helping principals focus on their goals.
- Never overlooking the importance of mentors to the system.
- Developing an artifacts file on diskette and updating it throughout the year to address the critical issues of time.
- Ensuring that from the beginning all participants understand that portfolios are being used to keep everyone focused on accountability and growth.

Due to ongoing flaws in the conduct of informal and checklist approaches to administrator evaluation, portfolios are becoming more visible and gaining praise from those learning to use them. Though portfolio contents range widely, the following items are a minimum for an administrator evaluation portfolio (Brown and Irby 1997, p. 15):

- Academic credentials and licenses;
- Samples of administrative initiatives created in the past year and written or taped assessments of the success or failure of past initiatives;
- Professional and personal goals for the coming year and personal reflections on successes or problems reaching last year's goals;
- Plans for professional development activities for the coming year with written reflections on which activities were most helpful in the accomplishment of last year's goals;
- Parent, community agency, and business contact plans for the coming year and a self-assessment of the success of last year's plans;
- A plan for monitoring student test scores, attendance records, and incidents of student behavior problems; and
- A record of the dates and amount of time spent observing and conferencing with teachers and other staff members during performance evaluations.

Portfolios hold much promise for promoting self-assessment, team accountability, unity among all levels of staff, and team efforts and mentoring (Damon, Schory, and Martin 1993). They also promote reflective thinking that can bring about needed changes and improved leadership for school districts and schools.

Portfolios will be a key part of assessing superintendents in AASA's Leadership Institute for School Administrators (LISA) program. Each superintendent who chooses to work toward national certification will complete a portfolio, based in part on standards discussed in this text. National and state examinations for principals and other administrators being created by state departments of education, ISLLC, and other professional groups are also considering the use of portfolios as part of the exam process.

The use of portfolios for self- and peer assessment and by supervisors to evaluate educators is gaining headway to help improve classroom teaching, team solidarity, and school accountability (Glatthorn 1997). One middle school principal (Cummins 1997) praises the use of portfolios, saying: "I read all 60 of my teachers' portfolios and I learned more about the talents, interests, activities, and successes of each teacher than I ever knew before. Portfolios are great. In time we will grow in our understanding of how best to use them to improve teaching effectiveness." The systematic development and testing of the portfolio model is one solution to the problems found in traditional evaluation systems.

The 360 Degree Feedback Model. The 360 Degree Feedback Evaluation model has been in place in industry and the military for several years. It is a reworking of the management-by-objectives and mutual benefit models that dominated personnel appraisal in the 1960s but with several promising additions. The model uses multiple data sets for employees doing different jobs in the school and school district. According to Manatt (1997, p. 9), "The data sets include feedback from principals, peers, parents, and students, as well as self-reflection and student achievement gains."

Like the Texas PDAS model, the 360 Degree Feedback model is designed to be nonpunitive and to encourage the entire school to be responsible for student achievement rather than pointing accusing fingers at individual teachers. Manatt (1997, p. 9) reports that while using the 360 degree plan over a 5-year period, "the Hot Springs County School district in Thermopolis, Wyo., had a 15 percent increase in achievement across all subjects measured by the SRA standardized tests."

The Teacher Evaluation for Continuous Improvement Model. The Teacher Evaluation for Continuous Improvement (TECI) model is based on the mutual benefit/goal-setting approach to evaluation. The model incorporates the ideas of Redfern, Locke and Latham, and Bolton along with the 360 Feedback model. Additionally, because portfolios are added to the goal-setting process, the TECI model should prove to be the most effective model to date (Glatthorn 1997, Brown and Irby 1997, Turk et al. 1994). TECI stresses team accountability while providing individual data for continuous professional improvement.

TECI is based on the following six assumptions, which apply to evaluating teachers and administrators:

- Teachers and administrators are goal oriented and want to improve their professional skills and to help students reach their highest levels of achievement.
- Teachers will teach more and students will learn more if administrators promote a positive, team- and performance-centered program based on goal theory.
- Teachers need a good idea of what is expected from them as individuals and as members of a learning community.
- General job responsibilities should be stated in writing and include a clear explanation of where

(to whom) teachers and administrators should look for guidance and supervision.
- General performance objectives that incorporate both the district and school vision, mission, and goals should be clearly written, and performance results should be monitored and evaluated systematically by each individual, peers, supervisors, and selected parents.
- The school board, superintendent, central-office and building administrators, teaching staff, and community must support the program if it is to succeed.

The following steps are involved in creating TECI teacher evaluation forms and procedures. The same steps should be followed when existing forms need to be refined.

Step 1. A committee composed of eight or nine elected teachers from elementary, middle, and high schools; an administrator from each level; the director of personnel; representatives from parent, business, and community groups; and a consultant meets in a retreat setting to develop or revise the evaluation model, procedures, instruments, and supporting rationale. The committee facilitator should stress the importance of creating a districtwide model, but each division or school has the freedom to make the model fit its special needs or differences.

Step 2. The committee studies research and information about teacher evaluation and examples of evaluation models, processes, and instruments.

Step 3. The committee develops evaluation instruments that include three parts:
- Part I should include the evaluation of those "best practice professional skills and activities that are observable in the classroom." Examples include artifacts collected by teachers and added to their portfolios, which represent best practice teaching skills, classroom management and activities.
- Part II should include other teacher responsibilities on which the principal and other evaluators will make summary judgments before making overall recommendations about the teacher's progress and future employment. Sample activities include student advising, club sponsorship, team teaching and planning activities, and professional development activities.
- Part III should provide a format to record growth targets and specific action to be taken by the evaluators and the teacher to reach the targets. Examples include curriculum development and instructional

Figure 7.1 **Teacher Evaluation for Continuous Improvement Model (TECI)**

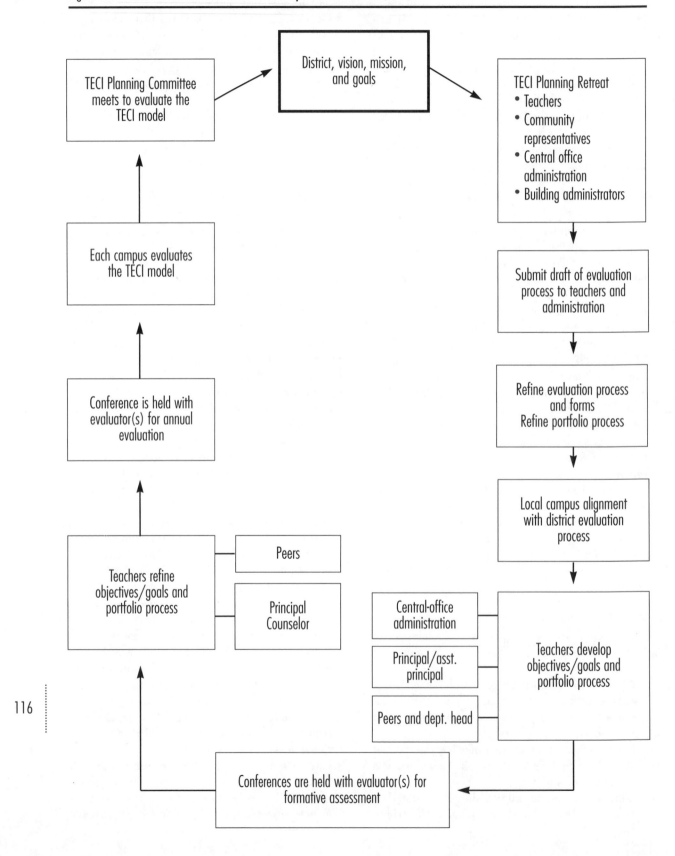

strategies adopted to improve curriculum proficiencies and student achievement and teaching processes adopted to reach growth targets.

Step 4. The committee writes a rationale statement to explain its reasons for including each part of the instrument.

Step 5. The committee submits the three instruments and the rationale to teachers and administrators in the district for their suggestions or additions.

Step 6. The committee evaluates and incorporates the suggestions and returns the revised instruments to any contributor who wishes to review the changes.

Step 7. The committee provides a copy of the final forms along with the rationale and TECI cycle information to each teacher and administrator.

Step 8. The TECI cycle begins.

Step 9. The committee reviews the TECI cycle after the first year.

The TECI model is far less subjective than most other checklist evaluation models and instruments. It provides a variety of specific data for professional development for all staff members. Properly employed, the TECI model:

- Establishes clear, value-based goals for the district and each school;
- Improves performance by improving supervision;
- Inspires self-evaluation and continuous improvement by helping individual educators develop a growth plan and build a portfolio;
- Provides plans for individual growth and development;
- Enhances greater collaboration among the entire school district and within each school to improve performance;
- Provides information to assist in improving the performance of individuals and teams;
- Identifies individuals' special talents, interests, and skills; and
- Provides a means of protecting both individual and school district rights in selecting personnel for advancement and for determining dismissals due to substandard performance.

Each year at least two observers visit each teacher at least three times for 30-minute periods. During the first two years of the TECI process, the primary observer is the principal or a designee; a secondary observer could be a department head, instructional supervisor, associate superintendent,

or assistant principal. As each teacher and principal is trained and becomes more familiar with the use of the portfolio and peer assessment, the pool of evaluators should expand to includes master teachers. Each evaluator must be trained to:

- Identify the teacher's strengths and weaknesses and provide assistance.
- Recognize best practice in teaching performance.
- Identify whether the teacher is stressing the national and state standards for each curriculum area.
- Use the vocabulary of staff evaluation and instructional management.
- Use motivational skill to inspire teachers to do their best (see Chapter 1 of this book for more about motivation).

The Administrator Evaluation for Continuous Improvement Model (AECI). Like the TECI, the AECI model is a combination of the best thinking from the mutual-benefit/goal-setting models, the 360 Degree Feedback model, and the portfolio process.

The AECI model calls for the superintendent, board, administrators, teachers, and community to move to value-based education and to systemically change the way things have been done in the past. According to Patterson (1997, p.4), "Real systemic change is achieved only when school leaders and other educators examine and alter beliefs, norms, and power relationships within a school district." Patterson adds "The power to make the most difference in the lives of children generally rests with those closest to the students. Leaders become more powerful by giving up control that they never had in the first place and taking responsibility for providing others access to the support, information, and resources needed to make things happen" (p. 30).

The AECI model is based on trust, risk-taking, and doing what is best for every child and youth in the district and school. With the proper shared values and a commitment to improve the system to maximize human potential, this model produces positive results. The following steps are involved in the AECI model. (See Figure 7.2 on page 119)The first step assumes that the district vision, mission, and goal statements are in place and supported by the board, the central-office staff, building administrators, site-based teams, and the community.

Step 1. The superintendent and a planning committee composed of school board members, administrators at all levels (including department

117

heads), and representatives from the district site-based team plan a retreat to establish the AECI cycle.

• Each administrator should review the district or their school vision, mission, and goal statements a few days before the retreat.
• Administrators and board members should bring to the retreat five or six objectives, not necessarily in behavioral form, that relate directly to the district's vision, mission, and goal statements and a list of activities that will have to be carried out to accomplish each goal. In addition, three or four other goals and objectives should be prepared that relate to each person's specific job description or role and lead to personal and professional improvement. These goals and objectives should be drawn or adapted from the standards and skills included in this book, which are adaptable to all administrative levels.
• All of the individuals invited to the retreat should attend the opening session to learn the details and rationale for the system, and should be encouraged to stay for the entire retreat to ensure that the model is clearly understood and supported.

Step 2. The superintendent, director of personnel, or a consultant delivers the opening address about school improvement and the value of shared power and trust in the assessment process. The intent of the address is to stress the point that administrator evaluation is "not to prove but to improve" the performance of the entire school district for children and youth. Continuous improvement in an environment of trust and risk-taking must be stressed over and over.

Step 3. All administrators present their goals and objectives to their supervisors at the retreat and to their subordinates. The individuals most closely affected by the goals discuss the value of the goals and the processes to be used to accomplish them. Once the goals and objectives are discussed and approved by the small group, members agree on the best way to monitor the data from evaluation observations and conferences. At this point the use of portfolios becomes a major part of the discussion.

Step 4. Staff members who report directly to the superintendent discuss their written goals with the superintendent and others representing the entire district and community. The superintendent also presents his or her goals to a diverse group who bring a wider perspective about the goals and the activities to carry them out.

Step 5. The retreat should end with remarks from the superintendent and board president reas-suring participants that evaluations will be done "with" and not "to" administrators. It should be made clear when the evaluations will occur, who will evaluate whom, and what steps will be taken after each evaluation.

For every administrator, copies of the goals/objectives and the related activities should be prepared in triplicate — one copy for the central personnel file, one for the key evaluator, and one for the administrator. Each administrator will prepare a portfolio as supporting data for the evaluation.

Step 6. A representative of each group at the retreat should be selected to oversee the AECI process and to begin making plans for the next retreat — a time for reflection on the success of the AECI and any needed adjustments.

Developing Personnel Recruitment, Selection , Development, and Promotion Procedures

Personnel recruitment, selection, appointment, development, and promotion is a vital part of school leadership. The staff "makes or breaks" the system. The superintendent, personnel administrator, and building administrators are all part of the district's personnel management system. The school leadership team must constantly evaluate the personnel needs of the district and each school by watching the demographics of both the district and staff and forecasting needed future staff replacements and additions.

Recruitment

Winning teams and "good reputations" attract outstanding recruits to universities. Notre Dame in football and North Carolina in basketball are marquee names that attract the best student athletes in the nation. The renown gained by winning makes it very difficult for other Division I teams without well-established winning traditions to compete in the recruiting wars.

Unfortunately, recruiting outstanding staff for school districts has many parallels with the recruitment of athletes. Young college graduates or others looking to move from one district to another are attracted to districts and schools with "good reputations" and "winning records" — high graduation rates, strong SAT scores, low dropout rates, strong community support, and school pride. These districts and schools are also usually at the top of the

Figure 7.2 **Administrator Evaluation for Continuous Improvement Model (AECI)**

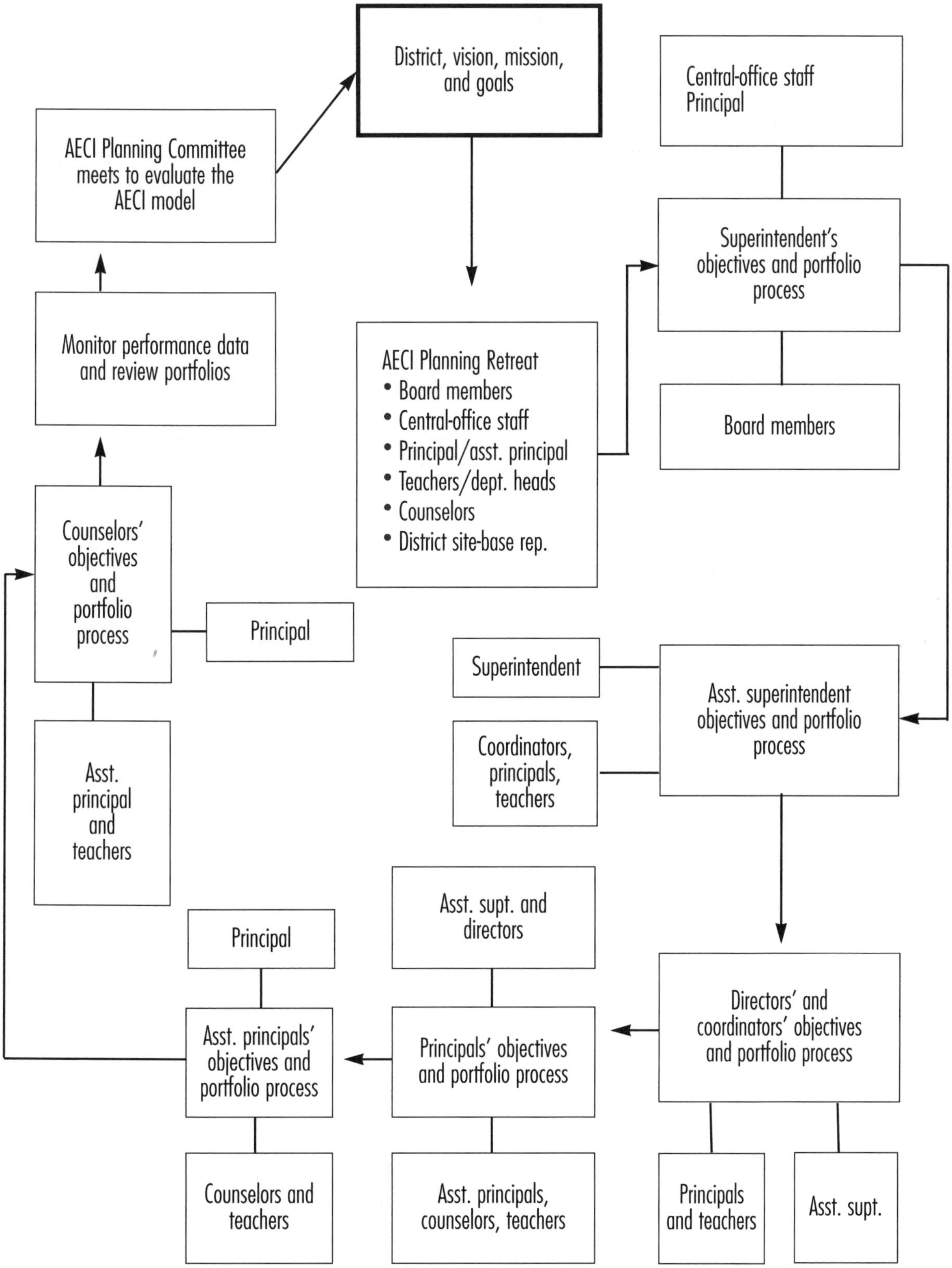

pay scale. It is no surprise that these districts have far more applicants than positions, making recruitment easier than for less desirable districts.

In the "good reputation" districts there are far fewer noncertified or unqualified teachers and administrators. Districts in major urban areas struggle with the perception and fact of higher poverty, dropout figures, and teacher turnover; minimal community support; higher levels of vandalism and other forms of crime and violence; and lower SAT scores and performance in general. Recruiting good teachers and administrators for schools in these areas is a difficult task for the best school leader.

The facts of economic life and the personnel needs of a school district are closely linked. However, a well-designed strategic personnel plan embedded in the overall district plan offers a solid first step in creating a human resource process that will guide strong recruitment efforts for the district and each school. Personnel recruiting in the "good reputation" districts and schools should be as determined and systematically planned as in less desirable schools. If personnel administrators in either situation become complacent, especially those in less desirable locations, the children will suffer educationally and their communities will not become better places to live and work.

Concerns about preparing and attracting greater numbers of teachers to urban and rural schools grow each year. Colleges of education continue to be overlooked at budget time by upper university administration and state legislators who fail to grasp the importance of maintaining a strong pool of teachers. The rhetoric is there but the financial resources are not. Some legislators and policymakers forget that their success is largely due to the teachers and administrators who guided them. Education deans and faculty are stretching their energies and limited resources to recruit young people. As mentioned, each year growing numbers of service-oriented students lean toward teaching as a career. However, unless salaries and working conditions improve, more and more talented young teachers will become disillusioned with the profession and leave.

The number of future teacher organizations is growing in the middle and junior high schools, each seeking to plant the "teaching seed" early in the minds of talented and caring young people. Universities near urban centers are creating partnerships with school districts to train future teachers on site in urban classrooms. Also, in collaboration with university faculty, school districts, inter-

mediate units, and education service centers have created alternative certification programs. These positive efforts to expand the teacher pool are helping to close part of the teacher shortage gap, but they are far from enough. Teacher supply and demand could become a national crisis unless substantial financial resources are directed to university preparatory programs.

Unless this crisis is averted, personnel recruiters will find it more difficult to locate and hire well-qualified staff. The best way to prepare for this potential crisis is by creating a well-planned personnel program. Castetter (1996, p. 91) describes the following premises upon which good recruiting programs rest.

- Recruitment is viewed as a carefully planned, organized, directed, controlled, and ongoing process.
- Staff participation is encouraged in formulating and implementing recruitment plans.
- The board of education is the prime mover in recruitment planning. The board develops employment conditions calculated to attract and retain qualified personnel.
- The board of education delegates responsibility for implementing its recruitment policy to its executive officer, the superintendent.
- The superintendent's specific duties in recruitment include determination of immediate and long-term qualification standards for all personnel, preparation of current and long-term budgetary plans that embrace provisions calculated to satisfy personnel needs, development of a systematic plan to locate and attract qualified persons, and later appraisal of the effectiveness of recruitment plans.
- The use of computer technology contributes significantly to improved recruitment. This includes collection of internal data on the quantity and quality of personnel needed, particular types of skills and backgrounds required, and matching position requirements with applicant characteristics and capabilities.

Site-based decision-making teams are vital cogs in the recruitment machine. In some districts, members of these teams are sent to universities and teacher job fairs to help recruit outstanding individuals who have the skills and attitude to be members of a particular school. Locating individuals compatible with the vision and "personality" of a faculty makes good sense for both the faculty and students and the potential employee. Happy people in the right teaching slot tend to stay long enough to establish roots, grow professionally, and find job satisfaction.

After the central-office personnel staff conduct thorough reference and character checks, the site-based team and other staff members interview candidates and make recommendations to the central office. This sharing of responsibility among central office and each school site for recruiting and selecting personnel leads to higher morale and stronger team efforts to improve schools.

Recruiting Administrators

Finding and hiring individuals who will set the tone for a winning climate and high performance is equally important in recruiting. Potential administrators for the superintendency, central office roles, and building administrator positions can found both inside and outside the system. According to Lundenburg (1996, p. 499), "There are some advantages to using internal recruitment. First, it allows administrators to observe an employee over a period of time and to evaluate that person's potential and job behavior. . . . Second, when employees see that competence is rewarded with promotion, their morale and performance will likely be enhanced." Recruiting administrators from within is well established in many school systems across the country. As a result, in-house leadership preparation academies have been created to provide continuous training for the pool of potential school leaders.

External recruiting of administrators also has benefits. Newcomers usually bring in new ideas to add to the local planning "stew" and carry little political baggage associated with close friends or the "good old boy or girl" connections that are usually part of an internal candidate's package. External recruiting, claims Lundenburg (1996, p. 503), ". . . infuses the organization with 'new blood,' which may broaden present ideas and knowledge and question traditional ways of doing things."

When looking for a superintendent, most medium-sized to large school districts employ a consultant or head hunter. These consultants assist the board in establishing a timeline to locate and hire a superintendent, help advertise the opening in a variety of places(e.g., AASA's *Leadership News, Education Week*, state administrator publications, and on the Internet). The consultant, in collaboration with the school board, screens the applicant list

to select 5-10 candidates whose credentials fit the needs of the district. The consultant and board then schedule interviews with the board for each candidate. After the board interviews and ranks the candidates, the consultant advises these candidates on the salary package, benefits, job description, and other details. Each district that employs a consultant uses some variation of this recruitment and employment process. Small, usually rural, districts, may rely on another superintendent or university faculty members to make recommendations for a vacant position and then conduct the recruitment and hiring process on their own.

The level of competition for the position of superintendent is more intense in some districts than in others. The attractiveness of the community, high salary, and the freedom to lead given by the school board to the superintendent are some of the inducements used to attract candidates.

Central-office and building administrators are also recruited from internal and external personnel pools. Suburban and urban districts tend to have a mix from both pools because of a large number of vacancies due to retirements and resignations. Candidates are recruited through formal announcements, acquaintances, graduate programs, and other sources. Personnel administrators screen the applications for proper credentials and present the personnel folders to the superintendent or members of his or her staff to narrow the list down to the most qualified candidates. An interview team at the central office and at the building level has become an important element in selecting two or three finalists and recommending them to the superintendent or a designee, who usually has the final say in the process.

Maintaining an active file of individuals who have expressed interest in an administrative position is important. Likewise, contacts with university professors and placement centers provide information about talented individuals "in the pipeline."

Understanding Legal Issues Related to Personnel Administration

The best bet against being found guilty of violating the rights of individuals during hiring is to be well informed about statute and case law governing personnel administration. When advertising, recruiting, sending application forms, conducting interviews, and building files on individuals, a school leader must be careful not to violate any individual's legal rights. The job announcement, for example, must clearly state that all individuals with the proper credentials are invited to apply for the position.

The following federal statutes relate to discrimination in employer/employee relations:

- The Civil Rights Act of 1964 prohibits discrimination with respect to compensation and terms, conditions, or privileges of employment on the basis of race, color, national origin, sex, or religion. The legislation also prohibits segregating or classifying employees in any way that deprives an individual of employment opportunities or otherwise adversely affects his or her status as an employee.
- The Age Discrimination in Employment Act of 1967, amended in 1986, bans discrimination against individuals above the age of 40 in hiring, promotion, and in the terms and conditions of employment.
- The Equal Pay Act of 1963 was passed to stop employers from paying higher wages or salaries to one sex than the other. The courts have held that even though the jobs of one sex may appear to be more complex or of greater risk, the pay for similar positions must be equal.
- The Rehabilitation Act of 1973 and the Americans with Disabilities Act of 1990 are directed at employment decisions regarding qualified individuals who have some disability. An individual who is able to perform the "essential functions" in a teaching, administrative, or other staff position may not be refused employment solely on the basis of the disability (see Rebore 1987, Seyfarth 1996).

Other related legal issues (e.g., sexual harassment, which is a form of sex discrimination and illegal, and affirmative action, both of which fall under Title VII of the Civil Rights Act) must be closely monitored to ensure the constitutional rights of every individual in the school district and school.

Two excellent sources for greater detail on the legal issues in personnel management are *The Human Resource Function in Educational Administration*, 6th ed. (1996) by William B. Castetter, and *Personnel Management for Effective Schools*, 2nd ed. (1996) by John T. Seyfarth.

Conducting a District or School Human Resources Audit

The steps of the personnel management process, which are affected by legislative constraints and, in many states, union demands, must be frequently audited by school leaders to ensure compliance with the law and to maintain a thorough knowledge of the process. According to Lundenburg (1996), there are six key human resource functions that must be monitored on a regular basis: planning, recruitment, selection, training and development, personnel appraisal, and compensation.

Tracey (1994) provides an outline for auditing a human resources program. The audit is designed to help school leaders review the functions and interrelationships of human resource activities and provides information that can lead to adjustments in the process and improved results. The following is an adaptation of the steps of Tracey's personnel audit.

Step 1. Determine the overall purpose and extent of the audit and link it to predetermined district and divisional goals.

Step 2. Select or appoint and sufficiently train an audit team and provide members with a general direction and purpose for the audit.

Step 3. Determine the inputs, including budget for resources, materials, instruments, software, surveys, and staff time.

Step 4. Use a variety of data-gathering strategies, including interviews, written materials about the program, surveys, and participant observations.

Step 5. Compare the personnel program with a list of standards or criteria from similar systems, national and state personnel agencies, and the literature (e.g.,the *American Association of School Personnel Administrators' Standards for School Personnel Administration* 1988).

Step 6. Present preliminary findings, conclusions, and recommendations to the superintendent or a designee and invite suggestions and additions to the first draft.

Step 7. Present copies of the final audit report to the superintendent and executive team for their review before wider distribution.

Step 8. Give an oral overview of the findings, conclusions, and recommendations to appropriate audiences and entertain questions.

Step 9. Begin implementing the strategies and activities called for in the recommendations on a priority basis and continue an ongoing audit.

(The CIPP model presented in chapter 9 is an excellent guide for the formative audit process.)

Personnel records and files should be carefully monitored to protect individual privacy and human dignity. Four key points found in the Privacy Protection Act of 1974 are helpful to school leaders who wish to maintain the integrity of personnel records. They are (Walker 1993):

- Collect and store only data relevant to district operations.
- Allow employees to review their records and correct inaccuracies in them.
- Allow disclosure of information from personnel files only to those with the right and need to receive the information.
- Do not allow data collected for one purpose to be used for other purposes.

Personnel files should not be a hiding place for secret materials or reports about teachers, administrators, and other staff members. All employees should be encouraged to review their folders at least once each year to add new documents and to study the accumulated materials. Where an open invitation for employees to review their personnel files exists, trust and support prevail, rather than fear and distrust.

Conclusion

This chapter has presented a review of the major trends and ideas about educator assessment, including the latest research and best practice. The appraisal models for teachers and administrators discussed here include assessment centers, portfolios, and collaborative assessment models and processes. The closing section on personnel management contains information about the foundation of performance assessment programs that promote continuous improvement. The authors have not attempted to review all of the research and writings on human resource management; instead, we attempted to select the most important issues and topics that challenge practicing school leaders daily and to provide the most relevant ideas and recent research to assist graduate students and practicing administrators with these issues.

Use the following Skill Accomplishment Checklist to assess your skill level on each of the important topics discussed in this chapter.

Skill Accomplish Checklist for Chapter 7

Skills	Readings and Activities for Skill Mastery
Apply effective staff evaluation models and processes for teacher and administrator evaluation.	**Readings:** Brown and Irby (1997), Castetter (1996), Manatt (1996), and Seyfarth (1996) **Activities:** 1. Review current district or school evaluation models and processes and compare them with the TECI and AECI models. 2. Survey teachers and others about the current evaluation model in your district or school.
Develop a personnel recruitment, selection, development, and promotion procedure.	**Readings:** Castetter (1996), Lundenburg (1996), Seyfarth (1996) **Activities:** 1.Compare recommended personnel management systems in two schools. 2. Design a teacher recruitment plan for a district with 25,000 students in a rapidly growing community.
Understand legal issues related to personnel administration.	**Readings:** McCarthy and Cambron-McCabe(1987), Seyfarth (1996) **Activity:** 1. Review a district's personnel policies for the proper legal language about equity and privacy of school records.
Conduct a district or school human resources audit.	**Readings:** American Association of School Personnel Administrators (1988), Tracey (1994) **Activity:** 1. Using Tracey's guidelines, conduct an audit of a district personnel program.

Resources

Abu-Nasr, D. (August 22, 1997). "School Enrollment Jumps in U.S., Spurring Fear of Crowding Crisis." *Houston Chronicle* 5A.

American Association of School Personnel Administrators. (1988). *Standards for School Personnel Administration.* author.

Bird, T. (1990). "The School Teacher's Portfolio: An Essay on Possibilities." In *The New Handbook of Teacher Evaluation,* edited by J. Millman and L. Darling-Hammond. Newbury Park, Calif.: Sage. (241-256).

Bolton, D. (1980). *Evaluating Administrative Personnel in School Systems.* New York: Teachers College Press.

Bratcher, R. (1998). "Teacher Portfolios: The Impact on Teaching Performance and Student Achievement as Perceived by Selected Teachers in the Conroe Independent School District." Unpublished doctoral dissertation. College Station, Texas: Texas A&M University.

Brown, G., and B. Irby. (1997a). "A New Construct for Administrator Evaluation." *In School Administration: The New Knowledge Base. The Fifth Yearbook of the National Council of Professors of Educational Administration*, edited by L. Wildman. Lancaster, Pa.: Technomic Pub. Co., Inc.

Brown, G., and B. Irby. (August 1997c). "Administrative Appraisal System." Paper presented at the Annual Meeting of the National Council of Professors of Educational Administration in Vail, Colo.

Brown, G., and B. Irby. (1997b). *The Principal Portfolio.* Thousand Oaks, Calif.: Corwin Press.

Castetter, W. B. (1996). *The Human Resource Function in Educational Administration.* (6th Edition.) Englewood Cliffs, N.J.: Merrill.

Cummins, D. (September 2, 1997). Personal communication.

Damon, D., W. Schory, and M. Martin. (February 1993). "A Portfolio Approach to Administrative Appraisal in the Boulder Valley School District." Paper Presented at The National Conference on Education©, American Association of School Administrators Conference-Within-A-Conference in Orlando, Fla.

Danielson, C. (1996). *Enhancing Professional Practice: A Framework for Teaching.* Alexandria, Va.: Association for Supervision and Curriculum Development.

Darling-Hammond, L. (1990). "Teacher Evaluation in an Organizational Context." In *Assessment of Teaching*, edited by J. Mitchell, S. Wise, and B. Plake. Hillsdale, N.J.: Lawrence Erlbaum.

English, F. (1985). "Still Searching for Excellence: A Preliminary Report from the ASCD Task Force on Merit Pay and Career Ladders." *Educational Leadership* 42: 34-35.

Glatthorn, A. (1997). *The Teacher's Portfolio: Fostering and Documenting Professional Development.* Rockport, Maine: Pro>Active Publication.

Haefele, D. (1980). "How To Evaluate Thee, Teacher — Let Me Count the Ways." *Phi Delta Kappan* 61, 5: 349-352.

Hoyle, J. (1995). *Leadership and Futuring: Making Visions Happen.* Thousand Oaks, Calif.: Corwin.

Hoyle, J. (1990). "Teaching Assessment: The Administrators' Perspective." In *Assessment of Teaching*, edited by J. Mitchell, S. Wise, and B. Plake. Hillsdale, N.J.: Lawrence Erlbaum.

Hoyle, J., F. English, and B. Steffy. (1994). *Skills for Successful School Leaders.* 2nd ed. Arlington, Va.: American Association of School Administrators.

Krovetz, M., and D. Cohick. (1993). "Professional Collegiality Can Lead to School Change." *Phi Delta Kappan* 75: 331-333.

Lewis, A. C. (1982). *Evaluating Educational Personnel*. Arlington, Va.: American Association of School Administrators.

Locke, E.A., and G.P. Latham. (1990). *A Theory of Goal-Setting and Task Performance*. Englewood Cliffs, N.J.: Prentice-Hall.

Lundenburg, F.C. (1996). *Educational Administration: Concepts and Practice* (2nd Edition). New York: Wadsworth Publishing Co.

Manatt, R. (1997). "Feedback from 360 Degrees: Client-Driven Evaluation of School Personnel." *The School Administrator* 3, 54: 8-13.

Manatt, R., K. Palmer, and E. Hidlebaugh. (1976). "Evaluating Teacher Performance with Improved Reading Scales." *NASSP Bulletin* 60: 40.

Markley, M. (August 10, 1997). "TAAS Touted as a Benefit to Education." *Houston Chronicle* 37A.

Martin, M., A. Schoeder, and R. Nelson. (1997). "Examining the Research on Pay for Performance: Lessons and Recommendations for Policy Makers." In *School Administration: The New Knowledge Base. The Fifth Yearbook of the National Council of Professor of Educational Administration*, edited by L. Wildman. Lancaster, Pa.: Technomic Pub. Co., Inc.

McCarthy, M., and N. Cambron-McCabe. (1987). *Public School Law: Teachers' and Students' Rights*. Boston, Mass.: Allyn & Bacon.

McLaughlin, M. W. (1982). *A Preliminary Investigation of Teacher Evaluation Practice*. RAND Corporation.

Mitchell, J., S. Wise, and B. Plake. (1990). *Assessment of Teaching*. Hillsdale, N.J.: Lawrence Erlbaum.

North Carolina State Department of Public Instruction. (1986). *Teacher Performance Appraisal System Training: A Report of Outcomes*. Raleigh, N.C.:Author.

Patterson, J. (1997). *Coming Clean About Organizational Change*. Arlington, Va.: American Association of School Administrators.

Rebore, R. (1987). *Personnel Administration in Education*. (2nd Ed.) Englewood Cliffs, N.J.: Prentice-Hall.

Redfern, G. B. (1980). *Evaluating Teachers and Administrators: A Performance Objective Approach*. Boulder, Colo.: Westview Press.

Sagor, R. (1996). *Local Control and Accountability: How To Get It, Keep It, and Improve School Performance*. Thousand Oaks, Calif.: Corwin Press.

Schmitt, N., and S. Cohen. (1990). *Criterion-Related and Content Validity of the NASSP Assessment Center*. Reston, Va.: National Association of Secondary School Principals.

Seyfarth, J. T. (1996). *Personnel Management for Effective Schools*. (2nd Edition). Boston, Mass.: Allyn and Bacon.

Shafer, P. (1990). "Appraisal: The Teacher's Perspective." In *Assessment of Teaching*, edited by J. Mitchel, S. Wise, and B. Plake. Hillsdale, N.J.: Lawrence Erlbaum Associates.

Shinkfield, A., and D. Stufflebeam, D. (1995). *Teacher Evaluation: Guide to Effective Practice*. Boston, Mass.: Kluwer Academic Publishers.

Short, P., and J. Greer. (1997). *Leadership in Empowered Schools*. Columbus, Ohio: Merrill-Prentice Hall.

Stiggins, R.J., and N.J. Bridgeford. (1984). *Performance Assessment for Teacher Development*. Washington, D.C.: ERIC Clearinghouse on Teacher Education. (Eric Document Reproduction Service No. Ed 244-717).

Stufflebeam, D., ed. (1988). *The Personnel Evaluation Standards: How to Assess Systems for Evaluating Educators*. Report of the Joint Committee on Standards for Educational Evaluation. Newbury Park, Calif.: Sage.

Texas Education Agency. (1996). *Professional Development and Appraisal System: Executive Summary*. Austin, Texas: The Texas Education Agency, Division of Educator Appraisal.

Tracey, W.R. (1994). *Human Resources Management and Development Handbook*. (2nd Ed.). New York: Amacom.

Turk, R., P. Anderson, L. Sanchez, and J. Morris. (February 1994). "Teacher Self-Assessment: A Portfolio Process." Paper presented at The National Conference on Education, American Association of School Administrators Conference-Within-a Conference in San Diego, Calif.

Walker, A. (1993). *Handbook of Human Resource Information Systems: Reshaping the Human Resource Function with Technology*. New York: McGraw-Hill.

Walt, K. (January 30, 1997). "TAAS Scores to Help Grade the Teachers." *Houston Chronicle* 5A.

chapter 8 | *Skills in Staff Development*

A famous football coach once said: "If my life depended on chopping down a tree in one hour, I'd spend the first 30 minutes sharpening my ax." Effective staff development should be the whetstone for sharpening professional educators' skills. Such staff development merges the personal growth needs of individuals in the organization and the institutional needs of the system (Getzels 1958). Without this linkage, systemwide organizational improvement does not take place. But through systematic application of the Teacher Evaluation for Continuous Improvement (TECI) Model and the Administrator Evaluation for Continuous Improvement (AECI) Model (see Chapter 7), staff development is a powerful school improvement tool.

Given that no school can be better than the people responsible for ensuring student success, all staff development programs must be designed to promote the self-improvement of every member of the school district. Programs must not be confined to one or two inservice days when the faculty listens to a motivating speaker, attends a show-and-tell workshop, and chats with co-workers over coffee and danishes. Staff development that promotes true school improvement demands thoughtful, long-term planning; a commitment to specific goals; and the same tender nurturing required in guiding students to reach their individual potential.

This chapter details the skills successful 21st century school leaders must posses to:

• Develop a plan to identify areas for concentrated staff development;
• Evaluate the effectiveness of comprehensive staff development programming;
• Implement future-focused personnel management strategies;
• Assess individual and institutional sources of stress and develop methods for reducing distress;
• Demonstrate knowledge of pupil personnel services and categorical programs;
• Improve organizational health and morale; and
• Train staff in teamwork skills.

Developing a Plan To Identify Areas for Concentrated Staff Development

Well-designed staff evaluation processes help systematically define staff development needs so that teacher and administrator training can be targeted to promote individual and group self-improvement. A needs assessment is essentially an assessment of the difference between what is and what should be. Such assessment can focus on needs within the system or external to the system, identify needed organizational efforts and results, or specify societal goals and objectives. A needs assessment, whether simplistic or comprehensive, is the basic problem-solving tool for any organization or institution.

School leaders should take the following steps to determine teachers' and administrators' staff development needs, design programming to meet those needs, and monitor how well the programming is accomplishing its goals:

(1) Analyze student performance data (i.e., test scores, classroom behaviors, attendance, motivation levels, etc.).
(2) Analyze staff evaluation data to determine staff members' areas of strength and weakness.
(3) Distribute a questionnaire to all staff members to gather suggestions for staff development programming.
(4) Develop a master staff development plan for the district or school.
(5) Have district and school-based teams conduct a review of the staff development program plan to pinpoint necessary additions or possible deletions.
(6) Revise the plan based on stakeholder input and established priorities.
(7) Allocate resources to support the staff development program.
(8) Initiate staff development programming.
(9) Regularly evaluate the program so it can be altered and updated to meet changing needs in the district and each school.

Adult Learners

Just as children do not learn in the same way and on the same day, the professional development needs of educators, as adult learners, vary according to factors such as the life cycle of the teacher (Steffy 1989, Steffy and Wolfe 1997), the content to be learned, the context of the application, and the status of the organization. A comprehensive needs assessment takes all of these into consideration to determine the most effective staff development plan.

Houle (1961) is credited with the identification of three main groups of learners in terms of motivation to learn: the goal-oriented learner, who learns for a specific purpose; the activity-oriented learner, who uses each learning experience as an opportunity to socialize and values the activity itself; and the learning-oriented learner, who learns for the sake of learning. Through the years, this typology has been illuminated, but not challenged.

Most educators tend to be goal-oriented in their learning, responding to job-related pressures to improve and update their skills or to prepare for a better job. Glatthorn's (1990, p. 143) synthesis of the research on how adults learn should be considered by anyone undertaking a staff development needs assessment. According to Glatthorn, staff development designers must address the following four areas in order to create meaningful programming for busy school personnel.

The **Structure of Learning Experiences**, which should

- Take into account teacher time pressures and provide flexibility.
- Promote choice of pace and learning experiences for self-identified needs.
- Emphasize live, face-to-face learning experiences as opposed to videos.
- Use heterogeneous groups so participants can share their different points of view.

The **Learning Climate**, which should

- Promote peer support, trust, and acceptance of differences.
- Provide opportunities for participants to express their views.
- Take learner expectations into consideration.

The **Focus on Learning**, which should

- Promote reflection and thoughtful analysis of experience.

- Help participants create personal meaning.
- Provide practical, "how-to" experiences.

The **Teaching/Learning Strategies and Media**, which should

- Value problem-solving and cooperative learning.
- Promote active participation and constructive feedback.
- Avoid long lectures.

A focus on these elements helps staff development designers ensure that individual and group self-improvement occurs.

The Life Cycle of the Career Teacher

"Teachers are complex individuals, moving in different ways through certain phases and stages of development, finding themselves at varying stages of career progression, and preferring to learn in rather special ways" (Glatthorn 1990, p. 144). Steffy and Wolfe (1997) have identified six phases in the life cycle of the career teacher. Teachers' staff development needs are different in each phase.

- The *novice* phase occurs during preservice training. At this phase the teacher is just beginning to make visitations to classrooms and is still learning about instructional theories and practices.
- The *apprentice* phase begins during student teaching when the candidate assumes responsibility for the planning and instruction of an entire class. This phase continues through the induction period after the first job is attained. During this phase the teacher still thinks in categories such as classroom management, opening exercises, and specific instructional strategies.
- By the time teachers enter the *professional* phase, they are able to integrate the activities of the classroom into a whole. At this point, there is a sense of unity in the class, pacing is appropriate, and transitions are smooth. Currently, the majority of classroom teachers are in the professional phase of their careers.
- The *expert* teacher is a master. Teachers at this phase are recognized by their colleagues, the parent community, and students as accomplished professionals. They are self-confident and they self-actualize through the act of teaching. Expert teachers are adept at meeting the individual needs of most of their children, and because of their skills, disruptions rarely occur in their classrooms.
- *Distinguished* teachers are those professionals

who exceed our highest expectations. They create the new knowledge base for our field through their experimentation because they are always pressing the envelope of the craft. These teachers are truly gifted.

- The last phase in this model is reserved for teachers who are officially *retired* but who continue to be involved through political advocacy, volunteerism, and mentoring. These teachers are wise in the ways of the classroom and want to continue to be connected to the field.

In order to maintain excellence throughout each phase of their career, all teachers must go through a cycle of reflection, renewal, and growth (Valli 1997). Through reflection, practitioners develop a greater level of self-awareness about how their performance affects children. Osterman and Kottkamp (1993, pp. 46-47) have proposed a credo of reflective practice. It includes six basic beliefs:

- Teachers need professional growth opportunities.
- All teachers want to improve.
- All teachers, just like children, can learn at high levels.
- Teachers are capable of assuming responsibility for their own growth and development.
- Teachers need and want feedback about their performance.
- Reflection, collaboratively done, enriches professional development.

Unless this reflection, renewal, growth cycle takes place, teachers tend to backslide into a spiral of withdrawal. Initial withdrawal takes place when the teacher begins to stop growing, and can continue into persistent and deep withdrawal. Part of the purpose of staff development is to prevent this downward cycle. School administrators preparing a needs assessment for professional development should take into consideration the life cycle phases of the teachers who will be involved in the activities. Targeted, relevant staff development can inspire those who have lost their zeal for teaching .

Content and Context Analysis

Recent literature on training needs assessment has focused on a levels-of-analysis approach. Goldstein and associates (1989) present a model with three categories. The first category deals with content. A determination must be made about whether the content should focus on an organiza-tion (the entire system), a task (formal work groups such as department chairs or principals), or a person (an individual in the task group). The next category in this model is levels. Will staff development be delivered to the entire organization, to a subunit within the organization, or to individuals within a unit? The third category deals with application of the new learning. Is the staff development aimed at conceptual, operational, or interpretational objectives. Making decisions about each of these categories helps school leaders design appropriate needs assessments for effective staff development.

Evaluating the Effectiveness of Comprehensive Staff Development Programming

Effective staff development programming can take many forms, including clinical supervision, learning-centered supervision, and differentiated supervision. The ultimate goal of all of these efforts is improved student achievement.

Clinical Supervision

Clinical supervision is "that aspect of instructional supervision that draws upon data from first-hand observation of actual teaching, counseling, or administering and involves face-to-face and other associated interactions between the observer(s) and the person(s) observed in the course of analyzing the observed professional behaviors and activities and seeking to define and/or develop next steps toward improved performance" (Goldhammer, Anderson, and Krajewski 1993, p. 4). Most of the current clinical supervision models have been derived from the work of Morris Cogan (1973). Like the mutual benefit model described in Chapter 2, clinical supervision focuses on collegiality, which makes it a mechanism of collaborative growth. The TECI model (see Chapter 7) also stresses clinical supervision.

The following nine characteristics have been associated with the clinical supervision model (Cogan 1973, p. 52).

- It is a technology for improving instruction;
- It is a deliberate intervention into the instructional process;
- It is goal-oriented, combining the school needs with the personal growth needs of those who work within the school;

129

- It assumes a professional working relationship between teacher(s) and supervisor(s);
- It requires a high degree of mutual trust, as reflected in understanding, support, and commitment to growth;
- It is systematic, although it requires a flexible and continuously changing methodology;
- It creates productive (i.e., healthy) tension for bridging the gap between the real and the ideal;
- It assumes that the supervisor knows a great deal about the analysis of instruction and learning and also about productive human interaction; and
- It requires both preservice training, especially in observation techniques, and continuous inservice reflection about effective approaches.

As originally conceived, the clinical supervision model is based on five stages.

Stage 1: Preobservation conference
Stage 2: Observation
Stage 3: Analysis and strategy
Stage 4: Supervision conference
Stage 5: Postconference analysis

In the preobservation conference the teacher and observer (typically a school leader) discuss the date and time for the upcoming observation, review the objectives of the lesson to be observed, and determine specific items or problems upon which the observation will focus. The techniques used to collect data are also discussed and agreed upon. This conference serves as a communication link and helps reduce the natural tension created by the observation process.

During observation, the observer views the lesson as planned in the preobservation conference.

During the analysis and strategy stage, the observer develops a plan for helping the teacher grow. The process includes reviewing the events of the lesson in terms of the teacher's intent and past history, the teaching techniques used, and the outcome. Because all school personnel are busy, the observer must review the teacher performance data and choose priority items to discuss during the conference. Determining what behavior a teacher can change requires knowledge of the areas of instruction and personal dynamics. It is one thing to suggest that a teacher may need to adopt a new instructional strategy, but quite another to assess whether the teacher has the competence and personal motivation necessary to make that happen. The success of the clinical supervision model depends on the observer's skills in this area more than any other.

The supervisory conference provides a time for the observer to give the teacher feedback. Again, the success of this conference depends on the observer, who is responsible for maintaining the pace of the conference, effectively communicating areas of success and weaknesses of the lesson, and making the conference a growth opportunity for the teacher. Conference time can be used most effectively to provide adult awards and satisfactions, define and authenticate issues in teaching, offer didactic help (if appropriate), train the teacher in techniques for self-supervision, and develop incentives for professional self-analysis (Goldhammer et al. 1993).

The postconference analysis stage offers the teacher and observer a chance to reflect on the effectiveness of the process. During postconference, teachers provide observers with feedback about their effectiveness in carrying out the democratic, humane objectives of this time-consuming, highly structured procedure. This feedback makes this stage the second most import in the process, preceded only by the analysis stage.

Few educators question the spirit of the clinical supervision model or its methodology. Unfortunately, it is not used effectively in many situations. The amount of time required to implement the process effectively is the most often raised concern.

Learning-Centered Supervision

Learning-centered supervision calls for an opening conference to establish rapport, a preobservational conference to discuss the observations, an unfocused observation, a focused observation, observational analysis, a feedback conference, and a formative assessment conference (Glatthorn 1984). Like pure clinical supervision, learning-centered supervision requires a great deal of time and may best be reserved for beginning teachers or those having problems.

Differentiated Supervision

Differentiated supervision is a method of professional development that provides teachers with options about the type of supervisory services they want (Glatthorn 1997). While many variations to this model have been developed by local school districts, it is used primarily to assist the development of newly hired, nontenured teachers and teachers experiencing difficulties. The model includes three developmental options — intensive development, cooperative development, and self-directed development — and two evaluative options — intensive evaluation and standard evaluation.

Intensive development involves a cycle of observation, analysis, conferencing, and coaching, which might be repeated as many as eight times during the school year. Because this model is so labor intensive, it is impossible for a supervisor to use it for all teachers.

Cooperative development involves small groups of teachers working together to help each other develop professionally. The teachers operate as a support team for one another, frequently working together to conduct action research and develop instructional materials. Group members observe, confer, and supply constructive criticism for one another.

Self-directed development allows teachers to work independently to improve their practice. Teachers employing this model typically set improvement goals, develop a plan to meet those goals, and periodically report on their progress.

Intensive evaluation is used to make high-stakes decisions, such as those related to tenure and promotions. "An intensive evaluation is based upon specific research-supported criteria; involves several observations and conferences; evaluates performance of the noninstructional functions; and is typically carried out by a school administrator" (Glatthorn 1997, p.7). Standard evaluation refers to the normal, contractual procedures applied to all teachers in the district.

Joyce and Showers' Model

Bruce Joyce and Beverly Showers (1983, p. 1) envisioned a need for "a major change in the ecology of professional life based on the development of a synergistic environment where collaborative enterprises are both normal and sustaining and where continuous training and study both of academic substance and the craft of teaching are woven into the fabric of the school and bring satisfaction by virtue of an increasing sense of growth and competence." Transfer, the foundation for their staff development program, assumes that, given intensive training, which may include identifying a new strategy, guided practice and feedback, plus a need for application of the strategy, most teachers can learn to become proficient with new procedures.

They propose a training program that includes:

- Learning the meaning of horizontal transfer of learning;
- Developing high degrees of skill before attempting classroom implementation;
- Knowing when to use a new skill;
- Providing coaching by peers through a peer support team; and
- Generating a "learning how to learn" effect.

According to Joyce and Showers, the coaching component is critical and should include development of coaching teams. In highly developed coaching environments, colleagues view one another as sources of companionship and technical feedback and as facilitators of application analysis and assistants in skill adoption. Joyce and Showers emphasize the importance of transfer in a staff development process because of the inevitable difference between being told about a technique and working out that technique in the classroom environment.

• • •

Evaluating the effectiveness of any of these approaches to staff development must focus on an analysis of results. United Way of America (1996) has published a practical, easy-to-follow program evaluation design entitled *Measuring Program Outcomes*. Developed by a task force representing a variety of public sector organizations, permission is granted to not-for-profit organizations to reproduce exhibits and worksheets from this publication for the purpose of planning and implementing a program outcome measurement system.

The basic premise of the United Way model is that inputs (resources) lead to activities (what the program does), which lead to outputs (products of program activities), which produce results. These results can take the form of new knowledge, increased skills, changed attitudes, modified behavior, improved conditions, or an altered state or condition (United Way 1996, p. 3). Inputs consist of money, staff and staff time, facilities, equipment, and supplies. Professional development resources may also include conference attendance, consultants, and training materials. The outputs of professional development, which are frequently tabulated, include the number of people who participated in an inservice, the number of sessions, the overall evaluation of the sessions, and the number of hours of inservice delivered.

131

Developing and implementing a plan to measuring program outcomes is a challenging task. The United Way process identifies eight steps in the process.

Step 1 — Get Ready

Everyone involved in measuring program outcomes must realize that four basic assumptions undergird the process. The first is that the organization is committed to conducting program evaluations. The second is that, while one person is in charge of the process, a work group of key stakeholders will be assembled and given the responsibility of monitoring and making decisions about each step in the process. The third is that the work group will seek input from others as deemed necessary. And the fourth assumption is that the primary purpose of the activity is to provide the necessary information to improve the program being evaluated.

The work group's nine major responsibilities are to (United Way 1996, p. 15):

- Decide which program(s) to start with,
- Develop a timeline,
- Identify outcomes to measure,
- Construct a program logic model,
- Identify outcome indicators,
- See that data-collection instruments are prepared, data-collection plans are developed, and all instruments and plans are pretested;
- Plan for and monitor a pilot process;
- Monitor data-analysis and report preparation; and
- Evaluate the results of the pilot and make necessary changes.

Step 2 — Choose the Outcomes You Want To Measure

It is neither prudent nor practical to evaluate all of a program's outcomes. Consequently, it is imperative to identify those outcomes that track the benefits of the program. These outcomes become the foundation for subsequent planning and implementation activities, so they must be selected with care. To accomplish this, the work group must gather ideas about what the critical program outcomes are from a variety of sources. For instance, group members can review written materials describing the program and talk with program staff and participants, interested parties from relevant committees, and current and past participants in the program.

The next task is to construct a logic model for the program. This is a description of how the program theoretically works. It can be organized using the categories of inputs, activities, outputs, and outcomes (initial, intermediate, and longer-term).

The third task is to select the most important outcomes to measure. Work group members must determine which outcomes are important to achieve if the program is to fulfill its mission or objectives, which clearly define the intended scope of the program's influence; and which are likely to be effective in communicating the benefits of the program to its respective publics.

The last task in this step is to get feedback on the logic model and the outcomes selected for measurement.

Step 3 — Specify Outcome Indicators

Making a determination about specifically what information will document the effectiveness of the program is critical. These indicators must be observable, measurable characteristics that represent attainment of the outcome, including specific statistics that will summarize the level of achievement. One or more indicators should be selected for each outcome.

Because not all staff development participants will achieve at the same level, it is necessary when evaluating staff development programs to determine the circumstances under which participants are successful and whether these are program specific or participant specific.

Step 4 — Prepare to Collect Data on the Indicators

This step includes three tasks: identifying data sources for the indicators, designing data-collection methods, and pretesting the data-collection instruments and procedures. Typical data sources include records, individuals, the general public, trained observers, and mechanical tests and measurements. In determining the data-collection methods to be used, consideration should be given to cost, the amount of training required by data collectors, the amount of time required to complete the data collection, and the anticipated response rate.

The final task for this step involves pretesting of the data-collection instruments.

Step 5 — Try Out the Outcome Measurement System

Tasks in this step include developing a trial strategy, preparing the data collectors, tracking and collecting outcome data, and monitoring the outcome measurement process. The trial can take place at one site or unit or with a small group. One person is assigned to monitor and track the data-collection process.

Step 6 — Analyze and Report Findings

The tasks in this step include entering the data and checking for errors, tabulating the data, analyzing data broken out by key characteristics, providing for explanatory information related to the findings, and formatting the data in a clear and understandable way.

Step 7 — Improve the Outcome Measurement System

During this step, work group members review the trial-run experience and make any necessary adjustments before full-scale implementation of the process. As the full implementation process continues, it is important to monitor and review the system periodically to identify and correct problems that did not surface during the pilot.

Step 8 — Use the Findings

Findings can be directed to both internal and external use. Internal uses include providing direction for staff, identifying program improvement needs, and outlining the need for additional support, budget, or additional programs. External uses include promotion of the program, enhancement of the program's image, and recruitment of more participants for the program.

Careful planing, implementation, and evaluation are the keys to staff development that helps educators and, in turn, students, reach their individual and collective potential.

Implementing Future-Focused Personnel Management Strategies

Many central offices have been downsized during the past 10 years. The goal has been to create flatter, leaner central administrations and to make schools the center for decision making so they can be more flexible and responsive. This downsizing, which is expected to continue in the future, has placed new demands on building-level administrators and teachers. These new demands can be frightening, but they are also sources of purpose, membership, and meaning.

Central-office downsizing has made it necessary for teachers and administrators to become more of a school management team. This is a dramatic change from when teachers were isolated in their classrooms and gave little thought to the management of the school. Boyett and Conn (1991)

describe this emerging work environment in *Workplace 2000*. This new environment will be characterized by a substantial increase in the type and amount of information available to classroom teachers and building administrators. It will no longer be necessary to wait for state test results to determine the effectiveness of the instructional program. Teachers will receive almost instantaneous information about student achievement and be required to routinely analyze the data and present recommendations regarding students. Administrators will be responsible for tracking the progress of individual students, classrooms, and the school as a whole.

As Boyett and Conn (1991, p. 4) point out, "In Workplace 2000, flexibility and creativity will be more important for success than endurance and loyalty." And because schoolwide accountability measures are likely to increase, peer pressure will become a powerful force compelling all teachers to put forth their best efforts. Pay will no longer be based primarily on longevity in the system. Rather, it is expected that rewards, recognition, and reinforcement will go to teams for team performance rather than to individuals for their performance. The end result will be a movement away from managerial control to self-control. Teamwork will become more highly valued and the most revered employees will be those who can wok collaboratively, generate creative ideas, and effectively help groups reach consensus.

Along with these changes will come an expectation that all workers keep current in their fields and that schools make routine and significant contributions to teachers' education and retraining. This retraining will be performance based and tied to continuing licensure. The days of the permanent certificate are gone. Continuous learning is becoming a common expectation for all employees.

These changes in the school environment are being prompted for several reasons. First, some believe that the expectations for student achievement and school employees' accountability for this achievement are too low. Second, many believe that national and state legislation will provide parents with more flexibility in choosing the type of learning environment best suited for their children. As a result, parents will become astute judges of school effectiveness and school comparison shopping will become common. Therefore, school leaders must implement personnel management strategies that take these trends into account to improve schools, help teachers and building-level administrators adapt to new roles, and ensure that educators earn the public's confidence.

Assessing Individual and Institutional Sources of Stress and Developing Methods for Reducing Distress

"Stress is a state of physical or mental tension resulting from factors that alter the body's equilibrium" (Berryman-Fink and Fink 1996, p. 287). Stress is real. Unaltered, it can become the path to grief, disease, and premature death. Stress of a positive nature can lead to happiness, health, and longevity (Morse and Furst 1979). Figure 8.1 compares positive stress, or eustress, with negative stress, or distress. School leaders need to maximize opportunities for staff, students, and peers to enjoy eustress and minimize the occasions when distress is produced by the work environment.

Figure 8.1 Factors Leading to Positive and Negative Stress

Eustress	Distress
Exercise	Being overly competitive
Self-fulfilling work	Repetitive work
Diversions	Rationalizations
Long-range planning	A propensity to worry
A positive outlook	Unrealistic goals
A belief in the "goodness of man"	Inappropriate amounts of sleep, relaxation, or inactivity
Proper diet and sleep	Improper diet
Spiritual commitment	Antisocial behavior
Maintaining appropriate weight	Being overweight or underweight
Positive family relationships	Dependence on drugs
Supportive friends	Solitude

Distress

[Editor's Note: Typically, when people refer to "stress" they are referring to "distress." Therefore, we will do so in the remainder of this section. The distinction between eustress and distress, however, is an important one in our daily lives.]

Certain occupations, including policeman, nurse, air traffic controller, and teacher, are noted for their stress-producing nature. The effects of individual and institutional stress can be costly for an organization. Stress can manifest itself in ailments such as cardiovascular disease, hypertension, ulcers, depression, and alcohol and drug dependency. Individuals experiencing stress are often irritable and prone to engage in conflicts with coworkers, friends, and family members.

Employees' stress may be personal, organizational, or environmental. Personal sources of stress include family and personal problems, such as financial and marital concerns, as well as personal relationships in the workplace. The basic structure and philosophy of an organization can also produce stress. An organization with a strict chain of command and cumbersome rules, policies, and procedures often produces a high level of stress for employees. Stress-provoking environmental conditions include noise, temperature, lighting, and crowding. Symptoms of stress include chronic anger, despair, anxiety, and depression. Stressed individuals have trouble dealing with small irritations that come from normal encounters with people and may also have trouble concentrating and becoming abusers of alcohol, caffeine, or other drugs.

Stress management programs provide individual and organizational stress reduction practices. Individual stress reduction strategies include (Berryman-Fink and Fink 1996, pp. 292-294):

- Recognizing stress by being attuned to attitudinal, behavioral, and physical indicators;
- Learning time management skills;
- Allowing time for leisure pursuits;
- Practicing relaxation techniques such as yoga, meditation, biofeedback, and progressive muscle relaxation;
- Developing and sticking to an exercise program;
- Practicing good nutrition by eating moderately and monitoring the intake of fat, sugar, salt, and calories;
- Socializing with people other than coworkers so that work demands do not spill over into leisure time;

- Developing a network of social support that can be depended upon for advice and comfort as needed; and
- Moderating life changes so stress-producing events can be somewhat controlled.

School leaders must be sensitive to and help staff members overcome stress-producing situations that affect work performance. The day-to-day factors that influence staff members' stress are not easily learned by school leaders, however, unless a firmly established relationship of mutual trust exists. Staff development begins with the cultivation of this kind of relationship.

Organizational stress reducers. Organizations can reduce employee stress by (Berryman- Fink and Fink, pp. 294-295):

- Providing stress management training that enables supervisors and managers to recognize the signs of stress in themselves and employees;
- Improving internal communication and encouraging employees to communicate with their superiors;
- Making sure employees know what is expected of them and receive periodic feedback;
- Clarifying role expectations and reporting relationships;
- Developing conflict-resolution procedures;
- Implementing an employee assistance program so employees can get assistance from professionals;
- Redesigning jobs when necessary to avoid overloading workers; and
- Providing a safe and comfortable working environment free from extreme noise, toxic substances, and safety hazards.

Demonstrating Knowledge of Pupil Personnel Services and Categorical Programs

Children differ in many respects. These differences manifest themselves in terms of intelligence, ability, creativity, cognitive and learning styles, and learning challenges. Seeing that differences are accommodated is the school leader's responsibility.

Approximately 12 percent of students are identified as exceptional. With each label comes both the protection provided by legislation and a stigma (Keogh and MacMillan 1996). In 1966, Congress made its first attempt to provide for

exceptional children in schools by adding a provision to the Elementary and Secondary Education Act. In 1973, Section 504 of the Rehabilitation Act was passed, and in 1975 Public Law 94-142, the Individuals with Disabilities Education Act, took effect. These laws help define the special provisions school must make to serve exceptional children.

Learning Disabled

The largest percentage of exceptional children fall into the learning disabilities category. Approximately two-thirds of exceptional children (8 percent of the total student population) are labeled as learning disabled. These children do not all exhibit the same disability. They may have problems with coordination or hyperactivity, problems organizing and interpreting information, thinking disorders, and/or difficulties making and keeping friends (Hallahan and Kauffman 1997). Most learning disabled students have difficulty reading (Stanovich 1991).

Gifted and Talented

Students labeled as gifted and talented also have special educational needs. There is growing recognition that gifted students are poorly served by our schools. In 1990, a national survey determined that more than half of the gifted students in the country were not achieving at their potential.

Currently, no consensus exists on a common definition of giftedness. Renzulli and Reis (1991) define giftedness as possessing above average general abilities, a high level of creativity, and a high level of task commitment or motivation to achieve in certain areas. The definition is traditionally based on intelligence, but one must remember that Gardner (1983) has identified seven kinds of intelligence and Guilford (1988) has identified 180.

The individual IQ test is still the single best predictor of academic giftedness (Woolfolk 1998) although many psychologists recommend a case study approach that includes gathering information from test scores, grades, work samples, projects, and portfolios. Teaching gifted students requires a focus on abstract thinking, problem solving, and critical thinking.

Other Special Needs Groups

Exceptional children also might have physical and sensory challenges, including seizure disorders

135

(epilepsy), cerebral palsy, hearing impairments, or visual impairments. Communication disorders include speech impairments, articulation disorders, and stuttering. Emotional or behavioral disorders, including hyperactivity and attention disorders, also affect students' ability to learn.

Other categories of children who need special services include those for whom English is a second language, children with AIDS, and children on medication (Johnson and Bauer 1992). Between 1 and 2 percent of the student population receives some type of medication on a daily basis (Barkley 1990).

It is up to school leaders to make sure that *all* students get the best possible education.

Improving Organizational Health and Morale

The organizational health and morale of a school is often referred to as organizational climate or culture. These concepts refer to a set of assumptions, beliefs, and behaviors held by employees. While the concepts are often used interchangeably, they have separate meanings, which are important to understand when attempting to determine a school's organizational health. They encompass how employees communicate, dress, think, behave, work, and make decisions.

Organizational climate has a powerful influence on the dynamics and interpersonal relationships within the organization. It can guide behavior, affect morale, and impact the organization's identity.

Organizational culture most generally refers to the character of institutional life or the basic feel or sense in an organization. This is not a new concept. In the 1930s and '40s researchers such as Mayo (1945) and Bernard (1938) discussed concepts such as norms, sentiments, and values and the impact these have on the informal organization. Ouchi (1981, p. 41) defines organizational culture as "systems, ceremonies, and myths that communicate the underlying values and beliefs of the organization to its employees." Mintzberg (1983, p.152) defines it as "a system of beliefs about the organization, shared by its members, that distinguishes it from other organizations." Schein's (1985, p. 6) definition refers to "the deeper level of basic assumptions and beliefs shared by members of an organization, which operate unconsciously and define in a basic 'taken-for granted' fashion an organization's view of itself and its environment." And finally, Robbins (1991, p. 572) defines culture as "a

common perception held by the organization's members; a system of shared meaning."

Fundamental to all of these definitions is the idea that organizational culture, while an abstract concept, is influenced by a set of shared values. From these shared values come organizational behavioral norms. The explicit manifestation of these norms is commonly referred to as the organizational climate.

According to Hoy and Tarter (1997, p. 9): "A healthy organization is one that not only survives in its environment, but continues to grow and prosper over the long term. An organization on any given day may be effective or ineffective, but healthy organizations avoid persistent ineffectiveness." A healthy organization has the ability to adapt to change, keep its eye on the attainment of long-range goals, and maintain cohesion. In healthy schools, the effectiveness of academic programs is of central concern and teachers are protected from undue pressure from the outside. Principals are respected and respectful, and a positive esprit de corp exists among faculty, staff, and students, which leads to harmonious interpersonal relationships throughout the organization.

(See Chapter 1 for information about school climate evaluation instruments and techniques.)

Training Staff in Teamwork Skills

Many jobs require the use of teams to solve problems, create new programs, and plan strategically for the future. Educating children is definitely such a job. By sharing knowledge and skills, a team can often complete a difficult task more quickly than an individual. Increasingly, teams are becoming relatively permanent work groups. Team building strives to increase the morale, trust, cohesiveness, communication, and productivity of such groups. Berryman-Fink and Fink (1996) have identified several key steps in team building.

Step 1 — Establishing Team Structure

Teams must be designed in such a way that they have enough structure to tackle and solve difficult problems and still exhibit creativity. This is not an easy balance to achieve. Well-facilitated meetings are a must. The leader should be trained in agenda development, keeping the pace of meetings moving, assigning necessary tasks, avoiding group-think, resolving conflicts, and enabling all members of a group to contribute (see Harrington-Mackin 1993).

Characteristics of High-Performance Teams (Hitchcock 1994)

With high-performing teams:

- Once the goals and objectives have been identified, all members are committed to accomplishing them.
- Team members trust one another and are open with each other.
- Team members participate freely within the team.
- Diverse experiences, ideas, and opinions are valued.
- Team members are continually learning and improving their skills.
- Roles and responsibilities are understood and members share their skills and knowledge.
- Consensus decision making is used.
- Team members communicate openly, listen to one another, and show respect for different opinions.
- Conflict is handled in an atmosphere that does not lead to resentment or hostility.
- Participative leadership is practiced.

Step 2 — Collecting Information

Team building can begin with a needs assessment activity aimed at finding out about the group's needs. Members can collect information about each other's attitudes, perceptions, and learning styles. This provides an opportunity for team members to get to know one another, builds a climate of trust and consensus decision making, and develops team members' knowledge of team goals.

Step 3 — Discussing Needs

With the results of the need assessment activity, team members can discuss the team's strengths and areas that need improvement. Through this activity, team members become sensitive toward each other and team cohesion develops. When this process is complete the team should feel confident in its ability to analyze problems and create solutions.

Step 4 — Developing Skills

The rest of the team-building process focuses on activities to develop team skills. Team skills include an awareness of group development, role clarification, problem solving, consensus decision making, conflict resolution, and results evaluation. [See Berryman-Fink and Fink (1996) for specific activities.]

Step 5 — Planning Goals and Setting Technical Targets

The team is now ready to set its goals and develop action plans to achieve them.

Conclusion

This chapter is closely linked to Chapter 7 because staff evaluation and staff development are complimentary parts of school improvement. In this chapter, we have dealt with the skills necessary to foster effective staff development activities in order to ensure that the school environment is responsive to the needs of children and provides teachers and administrators with the professional development necessary to support growth and renewal. We have addressed the topics of needs assessment, personnel management strategies, staff training, and organizational health and morale. School administrators leading today's educators must be proficient in all of these areas.

Use the following Skill Accomplishment Checklist to assess your skill level in each of the important topics discussed in this chapter.

Skill Accomplish Checklist for Chapter 8

Skills	Readings and Activities for Skill Mastery
Develop a plan to identify areas for concentrated staff development.	**Readings:** Kauffman (1988), Steffy (1989), Steffy and Wolfe (1997) **Activities:** 1. Design a needs assessment to assess teachers' staff development needs. 2. Prepare an inservice session to acquaint administrators and teachers with the teacher life cycle model. 3. Customize a staff development session to meet the needs of teachers at different points on the life cycle model.
Evaluate the effectiveness of comprehensive staff development programming.	**Readings:** Glatthorn (1997), Goldhammer et. al. (1993), United Way of America (1996) **Activities:** 1. Conduct five supervisory appraisals with five different teachers at various places on the life cycle using the clinical supervision model. 2. Design a staff development program evaluation using the steps outlined in this chapter.
Implement future-focused personnel management strategies.	**Readings:** Boyett and Conn (1991), Danielson (1996), Gretz and Drozdeck (1992) **Activities:** 1. Create a flatter organizational design that allows for broader input from stakeholders in a school's or district's decision-making of the organization. 2. Write a paper about the implications of *Workplace 2000* for school leaders. For teachers.
Assess individual and institutional sources of stress and develop methods for reducing distress.	**Readings:** Berryman-Fink and Fink (1996), Morse and Furst (1979) **Activities:** 1. Develop a process for assessing the degree of eustress and distress within your school or district. 2. Analyze your own activities to determine which lead to distress and which lead to eustress. Develop a plan to reduce the distress and maximize the eustress. 3. Study the current decision-making processes used in your district. Identify those practices that lead to the development of stress, both good and bad.
Demonstrate knowledge of pupil personnel services and categorical programs.	**Readings:** Keogh and MacMillan (1996), Woolfolk (1998) **Activities:** 1. Identify the special programs in your district designed to meet the needs of exceptional children. 2. Review your district's procedures for inclusion of special needs children and develop a plan to improve those services. Share your plan with the superintendent. 3. Develop a report for the board of education describing how the district provides services to children for whom English is a second language. Be sure to include how the program is evaluated to ensure that high-quality services are delivered.
Improve organizational health and morale.	**Readings:** Halpin and Croft (1962-63), Hoy et. al. (1991), Hoy and Tarter (1997), Miles (1965) **Activities:** 1. Administer the OCDQ and analyze the results (see Chapter 7). 2. Develop a plan to ameliorate the gaps between what is desired and the current situation.

Skill Accomplish Checklist for Chapter 8—continued

Skills	Readings and Activities for Skill Mastery
Train staff in teamwork skills.	**Readings:** Fink (1996), Hitchcock (1994) **Activities:** 1. Create and deliver an inservice session about the steps involved in team building. Train administrators and department chairs in the process. 2. Identify an area where you need to establish a team to complete a task. Outline the process to be used by the team. 3. Analyze the teams in your building relative to the criteria for high-performance teams. Develop a plan to enable the teams under your direction to operate at that level.

Resources

Barkley, R.A. (1990). *Attention Deficit Hyperactivity Disorder: A Handbook for Diagnosis and Treatment.* New York: Guilford.

Barnard, C. L. (1938). *Functions of the Executive.* Cambridge, Mass.: Harvard University Press.

Berryman-Fink, C., and C.B. Fink. (1996). *Manager's Desk Reference.* New York: American Management Association.

Boyett, J.H., and H.P. Conn. (1991). *Workplace 2000: The Revolution Reshaping American Business.* New York: Dutton.

Cogan, M. (1973). *Clinical Supervision.* Boston: Houghton Mifflin.

Danielson, C. (1996). *Enhancing Professional Practice: A Framework for Teaching.* Alexandria, Va.: Association for Supervision and Curriculum Development.

Getzels, J. (1958). "Administration as a Social Process." In *Administrative Theory in Education,* edited by A. Halpin. Chicago: Midwest Administration Center, University of Chicago.

Glatthorn, A. (1997). *Differentiated Supervision (2nd Ed.)* Alexandria, Va.: Association for Supervision and Curriculum Development.

Glatthorn, A. (1990). *Supervisory Leadership: Introduction to Instructional Supervision.* Glenview, Ill.: Scott, Foreman/Little, Brown Higher Education.

Goldhammer, R., R.H. Anderson, and R. J. Krajewski, R. (1993). *Clinical Supervision: Special Methods for the Supervision of Teachers.* Fort Worth, Texas: Harcourt Brace Jovanovich College Publishers.

Gretz, K.F., and S.R. Drozdeck. (1992). *Empowering Innovative People: How Managers Challenge, Channel and Control the Truly Creative and Talented.* Chicago: Probus Publishing Company.

Halpin, A.W., and D.B. Croft. (1962). *The Organizational Climate of Schools* (Research Project, Contract No. SAE 543-8639). Washington, D.C.: U.S. Office of Education.

Halpin, A.W., and D.B. Croft. (1963). *The Organizational Climate of Schools.* Chicago: Midwest Administration Center of the University of Chicago.

Harrington-Mackin, D. (1993). *The Team Building Tool Kit: Tips, Tactics, and Rules for Effective Workplace Teams.* New York: American Management Association.

Hitchcock, D. (1994). *The Work Redesign Team Handbook: A Step-by-step Guide to Creating Self-Directed Teams.* White Plains, N.Y.: Quality Resources.

Hoy, W.K., C.J. Tarter, and R.B. Kottkamp. (1991). *Open Schools/Healthy Schools: Measuring Organizational Climate.* Newbury Park, Calif.: Sage.

Hoy, W.K., and C.J. Tarter. (1997). *The Road to Open and Healthy Schools: A Handbook for Change.* Thousand Oaks, Calif.: Corwin Press.

Houle, C.O. (1961). *The Inquiring Mind.* Madison: University of Wisconsin Press.

Johnson, L.J., and A.M. Bauer. (1992). *Meeting the Needs of Special Students: Legal, Ethical, and Practical Ramification.* Newbury Park, Calif.: Corwin Press.

Joyce, B., and B. Showers. (1983). *Power in Staff Development Through Research on Training.* Alexandria, Va.: Association for Supervision and Curriculum Development.

Kauffman, R. (1988). *Planning Educational Systems: A Results Based Approach.* Lancaster, Pa.: Technomic Pub. Co., Inc.

Mayo, E. (1945). *The Social Problems of Industrial Civilization.* Boston: Graduate School of Business Administration, Harvard University.

Miles, M. (1965). "Planned Change Is Organizational Health: Figure and Ground." In *Organizations and Human Behavior*, edited by F. D. Carver and T. J Sergiovanni. New York: McGraw-Hill.

Mintzberg, H. (1983). *Power In and Around Organizations.* Englewood Cliffs, N.J.: Prentice Hill.

Mitchell, J., S. Wise, and B. Plake. (1990). *Assessment of Teaching.* Hillsdale, N.J.: Lawrence Erlbaum.

Osterman, K.F., and R.B. Kottkamp. (1993). *Reflective Practice for Educators: Improving Schooling Through Professional Development.* Newbury Park, Calif.: Corwin Press.

Ouchi, W. (1981). *Theory Z.* Reading, Mass.: Free Press.

Raudsepp, E., and J.C. Yeager. (1981). *How to Sell New Ideas: Your Company's and Your Own.* Englewood Cliffs, N.J.: Prentice Hall.

Robbins, S. P. (1991). *Organizational Behavior: Concepts, Controversies, and Applications.* Englewood Cliffs, N.J.: Prentice Hall.

Schein, E. H. (1990). "Organizational Culture." *American Psychologist,* 45: 109-119.

Steffy, B. E. (1989). *Career Stages of Classroom Teachers.* Lancaster, Pa.: Technomic Pub. Co., Inc.

Steffy, B.E., and M. Wolfe. (1997). *The Life Cycle of the Career Teacher: Maintaining Excellence for a Lifetime.* West Lafayette, Ind.: Kappa Delta Pi International.

United Way of America. (1996). *Measuring Program Outcomes: A Practical Approach.* Alexandria, Va.: United Way of America.

Valli, L., ed. (1997). *Reflective Teacher Education: Cases and Critiques.* Albany: State University of New York Press.

Woolfolk, A.E. (1998). *Educational Psychology (7th Ed).* Boston: Allyn and Bacon. RAND Corporation.

chapter 9 | *Skills in Educational Research, Evaluation, and Planning*

School leaders in the 21st century will need new skills in conducting research and using research findings to improve student performance. Systematic research is the foundation for program evaluation, long- and short-range planning, and school operations. Without a strong research base, school reform cannot be successful. As John Anderson (1997, p.48) states:

> . . . [G]overnance changes . . . will not succeed unless schools also introduce research-based improvements in teaching and learning, redefine key stakeholder roles, and redeploy resources to focus less on specialists outside the classroom and more on helping teachers play multiple roles inside and outside the classroom. The overarching goal must be the development of data-driven, results-focused, decentralized systems of schools.

In *Competitive Intelligence*, Kahaner (1996) states that we are no longer merely in the Information Age; we are living in an age of intelligence, and the two are different. Kahaner asserts that "Intelligence . . . is a collection of information pieces that have been filtered, distilled, and analyzed. . . . [and] turned into something that can be acted upon" (p. 21). School leaders must work smarter and faster with information (data) to facilitate the transformation of America's schools to prepare citizens for this Intelligence Age.

The press for accountability and quality control has prompted a much higher regard for educational research. Greater emphasis on research, evaluation, and planning is evident in most preparation and professional development programs today than a decade ago because school leaders and those who prepare them realize that the public is no longer satisfied with being told that the schools are "doing a good job." People want to know how good.

The push for national testing puts school leaders in a research "catch 22." Paul Houston, AASA's executive director, believes that administrators cannot appear to oppose national testing for fear of appearing to be hiding poor student performance. However, school administrators know that a student's test scores, family income, and parents' educational attainment are closely linked. Tests and test scores, therefore, reveal the accumulated learning experiences of children and youth, not just their school learning. Educational research focuses on testing and other measures of human performance and other areas of education to help frame and solve perplexing problems.

A recent book does an excellent job of helping school leaders deal with the question in its title: *What Do We Know About Declining (Or Rising) Student Achievement?* (Rothstein 1997). Research is the key to answering this question.

While not attempting to review the vast literature on research, evaluation, and planning, this chapter does stress the processes and strategies most useful to practitioners charged with solving school-related problems.

This chapter details the skills 21st century school leaders must possess to:

- Use various research designs and methods;
- Select the proper data-gathering, analysis, and interpretation methods;
- Use basic descriptive and inferential statistics;
- Use research-based models and standards for evaluation of educational programs; and
- Engage in strategic planning and futuring.

Research: Definition, Problems, and Value

Research is a systematic effort to investigate and solve problems. Applied research is usually directed at quick answers to solve immediate problems; basic research takes longer, tests for relationships and causality, and is usually generalizable to the larger population. Comparing two methods of

141

teaching mathematics to 6th grade students is an example of applied research. Developing ways to measure the degree of openness or efficacy in a school climate is basic research. Educational researchers try to find answers to such complex issues as the effect of administrative behavior on student performance; relationships between teacher behavior and student performance; and the impact of various levels of administrator and teacher job satisfaction on their performance.

State and national political leaders seek sound research findings to help them develop policy or push legislation that benefits schools. Policymakers often look for research evidence that "proves" the effectiveness of one type of school organization over another or determines the most effective teacher-supervisor ratios to improve student achievement. Research evidence, however, is not always enough to convince policymakers to change the ways of doing "education business." What is found to be statistically significant is not always found to be practically significant. As Charles M. Achilles (1997, p.6) points out, since the early 1980s, a large-scale project in Indiana, a major experiment in Tennessee, and numerous smaller studies and evaluations of projects that use low adult-to-student ratios have found that youngsters in small classes (1:15 or so) obtain higher test scores, participate more in school, and demonstrate improved behavior. Despite this overwhelming evidence, policymakers continue to support a ratio of 1:25 or 1:30 because it is more cost effective.

No Quick Answers

The fact is, quick answers to pressing educational problems are rarely available. No research method can ensure that an educational problem will be solved. Unfortunately, educational research is an inexact process sometimes conducted by people with agendas of their own.

"Quality Counts" (Olson 1997, p. 3), a national study of America's schools compiled by *Education Week*, concludes the following:

> As the new millennium approaches, there is growing concern that if public education doesn't soon improve, one of two outcomes is almost inevitable: Our democratic system and our economic strength, both of which depend on an educated citizenry, will steadily erode or alternative forms of education will emerge to replace public schools as we have known them.

Growing criticism of schools and colleges of education is forcing educational leaders to provide information for immediate solutions to school and classroom problems. But America's schools have been around for over 200 years, and old habits die hard. It is difficult to change a system that has served us well and is the primary reason for the nation's wealth and world leadership. Within the system are hundreds of schools that rank with the best in world, but far too many children and youth are caught in schools that offer a mediocre or poor education. Lynn Olson (1997, p.7) expresses her concerns about the critical importance of quality schools for all children for the nation's future with these words:

> No nation can rise above the level of its people's abilities very long. To solve the formidable problems the United States faces and to capitalize on the incredible opportunities the future holds, we need all the brainpower, talent, and energy we can muster.

Futurists are calling for much greater cooperation between the higher education system and the public schools. A transformation in the public school system must occur if American is to remain a world leader in the next millennium. Hoyle (1990) suggests that the two systems combine their resources and become one system to serve all children and youth beginning at age three through graduate school. To facilitate this transformation requires systematic research using the best methods. The time pressures for quick fix research have increased activity in applied research and downplayed the usefulness of basic research. The true value of research, however, is not in simply providing quick answers to practical problems. Rather, its value lies in developing sound answers that lead to problem solving and school improvement. Impatient to solve problems, many educators have adopted new programs that research later proved valueless or even detrimental to the education process. School leaders must not continue to make this mistake.

Using Various Research Designs and Methods

Research design and methods of data gathering are too complex for in-depth treatment here. Readers should consult a good basic research textbook to gain a stronger foundation in research (see

Borg and Gall 1983; Kerlinger 1986; Ary, Jacobs, and Razavich 1996; Erlandson, Harris, Skipper, Allen 1993; and Eisner 1998). However, it is important to highlight several key research areas and skills.

Designs and Methods

Different research methods and procedures enable researchers to look at data in different ways. For example, researchers interested in the relationship between a principal's use of supervision and teaching performance can take different approaches to analyze this relationship.

Descriptive research/method. This method entails systematically describing a situation or area of interest factually and accurately. Descriptive research can include public opinion surveys, fact-finding surveys, status studies, observation studies, literature surveys, anecdotal records, test score analyses, and normative data (see Isaac and Michael 1985).

Gathering teacher perceptions through interviews or self-report questionnaires to determine the effectiveness of the mentoring process is an example of the descriptive method (See Figure 9.1).

Figure 9.1 **Design for Descriptive Method**

$T \rightarrow O$ T = treatment (e.g., clinical supervision)
O = data gathered to determine teaching performance

Note that the letter "T" is the treatment and the letter "O" is the observation measure of the teaching performance. In other textbooks the letter "T" stands for testing and the letter "X" stands for treatment — so don't confuse the symbols. This "one-shot," most commonly used method or research design is non-experimental, but can help practitioners search for clues to the success or lack thereof in professional programming. However, because no random sampling occurs in this method, it cannot be used to determine whether a treatment had an effect.

Causal-comparative/correlational method. An example of the causal-comparative method is research that applies clinical supervision/mentoring strategies to a select group of teachers and no supervision to another select group of teachers. The researcher compares the teaching performances of the two groups to determine whether teacher behaviors or styles differ (see Figure 9.2).

Figure 9.2 **Design for Causal-Comparative Method**

$$G_1 \rightarrow T \rightarrow O$$

$$G_2 \longrightarrow O$$

G_1 = Group 1
T = treatment
O = measurement of impact
G_2 = Group 2
O = measurement for impact

While this method is similar to the correlation method and may show relationships, it is not always suitable for determining causality. However, because it is often impossible to carefully select groups and to control all of the variables in a school situation, the causal-comparative method can be used to gather useful data. Caution must be exercised in interpreting the data though because some factors other than the treatment may have caused the observed differences in performance. If the treatment group has a higher performance score than the control group, it could mean that the treatment caused the difference, or it might be that the groups were different to start with given that no random assignment was used to determine either group.

Experimental method. The experimental method is required to infer causality. This design involves random selection of subjects, precise measures of teacher behaviors, systematic and consistent applications and experimenter control of the treatment, and accurate measures of research findings (see Figure 9.3).

Figure 9.3 **Design for Experimental Method**

$$R_1 O_1 \rightarrow T \rightarrow O_2$$

$$R_2 O_3 \longrightarrow O_4$$

R_1 = random selection of experimental group
O_1 = pretest of teaching performance
T = treatment
O_2 = post-test of teaching performance

R_2 = random selection of control group
O_3 = pretest of teaching performance
O_4 = post-test of teaching performance

143

Using this method to assess the effectiveness of mentoring, researchers can request administrators trained in mentoring techniques to provide precise, well-controlled mentoring for one randomly selected group of teachers and no mentoring to another randomly selected group of teachers. Because the mentoring is an independent variable, any difference in the trained teachers' performance can be attributed to the mentoring.

The true experimental design is considered the most powerful research method because it provides adequate controls for all sources of internal validity (see later section on internal and external validity). If the treatment group has higher teaching performance scores on a post-test, it is very probable that the treatment caused the difference.

Constructivist/naturalistic method. This method, more commonly referred to as naturalistic inquiry, is growing in popularity as a descriptive research method. Proponents of this strategy believe that the typical "rationalistic paradigm" employed in educational research is inadequate to find the answers to complex educational problems. Naturalistic investigators do not attempt to form generalizations that will hold in all times and all places, but to form working hypotheses that can be transferred from one context to another depending on the degree of "fit" between the contexts (Guba and Lincoln 1981).

The traditional rationalistic procedure is the most accepted research procedure in education and is preferred by editorial boards reviewing papers submitted for blind review for scholarly journals. The newer qualitative/naturalistic paradigm has been a prime tool for scholars in history, anthropology, and political science for many years (Miles and Huberman 1994). By using naturalistic methodologies, researchers can observe many realities that interact and effect the entire organization. Erlandson and colleagues (1993, p. 12) write in *Doing Naturalistic Inquiry* that "the new paradigm (naturalistic) also assumes that there is not a single objective reality but multiple realities of which the researcher must be aware. Extended research leads to a rich awareness of divergent realities rather than to convergence on a single reality." Naturalistic researchers believe, for example, that each school must be examined with the same individual attention that a good doctor gives to each patient.

Naturalistic studies use observation by the researcher as the primary tool and express findings in qualitative terms. They do use numerical measures (i.e., test scores, teacher performance scores, school climate ratings), but other types of descriptions are stressed (Best and Kahn 1989). These descriptions, commonly referred to as "thick descriptions," contain data from a wide variety of sources, including interviews; classroom observations; faculty staff meeting procedures; teacher, student, and administrator portfolios; staff evaluation procedures; parent involvement records; test scores; and school climate ratings. Best and Kahn (1989) agree that both the quantitative/rationalistic and qualitative/naturalistic methods are vital for good educational research. "Both types of research are valid and useful. They are not mutually exclusive. It is possible for a single investigation to include both methods" (Best and Kahn 1989, p. 90).

Whether researchers choose the quantitative or qualitative method or a combination of the two,

Combining Qualitative and Quantitative Research Data

Shaw (1990) used qualitative and quantitative research methods in his study "The Organizational Cultures and Principals' Leadership Behaviors in Three Academically Dissimilar Middle Schools." Quantitative data were gathered by administering the School Culture Survey and the Leader Behavior Description Questionnaire-XII to teachers, parents, and students at three schools selected based on similar demographics and other characteristics. Shaw also spent five days in each of the schools observing; interviewing; gathering memos, teaching materials, and curriculum guides; analyzing standardized test results and teacher-made test scores; spending time in classrooms, and teachers' lounges; and meeting with student and parent groups.

Next, Shaw labeled the schools either "high achieving" or "low achieving" based on scores from tests administered to 7th graders in reading, writing, and mathematics. By corroborating the quantitative and qualitative data and using triangulation, Shaw discovered that "the culture and principal's leadership behaviors in the lower achieving school focused on maintaining the instructional program according to tradition, on a lecture-based instructional mode, and on self-preservation. The culture and leadership behaviors of the principal in the high-achieving school focused on meeting the individual needs of students and teachers alike; on the creation and maintenance of a warm, caring, and supportive teaching/learning environment; and on doing whatever was necessary to achieve success" (p. iv).

they must always be aware of internal and external validity factors in order to obtain research findings for solving educational problems.

Internal Validity

For research to have internal validity, experimental controls must allow the researcher to conclude that differences occurred as a result of the experimental treatment. The "Eight Demons" that can wreck internal validity are (Popham 1993, Tuckman 1979, Campbell and Stanley 1963):

(1) History. When a treatment extends over a period of time, it is possible that other events or experiences may have had equal or greater influence on the subjects' behaviors than the original treatment. Thus, time can cause a treatment to fade as the primary influence on a subject.

(2) Maturation. While an instructional treatment is in progress, natural growth processes occur in the learners (biological, psychological, or sociological) that can be more influential than the treatment.

(3) Testing. Subjects who take the same test twice as in a pretest/post-test design, can perform differently in the post-test as a result of being sensitized by the pretest. This is especially possible when the timeline between the pretest and post-test is short.

(4) Instrumentation. If a test is changed during an evaluation study, any apparent changes in subjects' performance might be more directly related to the change in the test than the actual treatment itself. For example, in a large county-wide Chapter 1 program, two different national reading tests designed to measure different reading skill areas were given as a pretest and post-test. Not surprisingly, little or no significance in differences were found in the children's reading performance.

(5) Instability. All measures used in evaluation processes are less than perfectly objective and reliable.

(6) Selection. In all evaluation studies where the performance of two or more groups are being analyzed, the effect of the treatment can be contaminated if subjects for different groups are selected differently.

(7) Mortality. If two or more groups are selected for an evaluation study and subjects drop out of one of the groups, the results of the study may be misleading.

(8) Statistical regression. When student subjects are selected for an evaluation study because of their extremely high or very low scores on a standardized test, their performance on a subsequent test will tend to "regress" toward the mean of a distribution because of the statistical unreliability of the test used.

External Validity

The term "external validity" refers to the representativeness of the findings of a study (Borg and Gall 1983). If the results of a study have both internal and external validity then the findings can be generalized to other groups of subjects in the population. Generalizations can never be made from the naturalistic/qualitative method, but are a requirement for quality research in quantitative/rationalistic studies. The two true experimental designs and one quasi-experimental design that follow help control for internal and external validity. [Refer to Borg and Gall (1983) or Tuckman (1979) for more information on more complex factorial and ex-post facto designs.]

True experimental designs. Two true experimental designs are the post-test-only control group design and the pretest/post-test control group design. The post-test-only control group design is considered the strongest true design (Tuckman 1979). It can be diagrammed as shown below where "T" designates a treatment and a blank space designates a control. An "O" is an observation or measurement and each "O" is numbered (i.e., O_1, O_2, O_3, etc.). The letter "R" designates that the subjects are selected through the use of a table of random numbers.

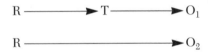

This design uses two groups (samples) randomly selected from the population. One group receives the treatment; the other group does not. Random selection of the groups carefully controls for selection and mortality weaknesses, and treating only one group controls for history and maturation. No pretest is given to either group. This controls for interactions between testing and treatments and for sample testing effects.

Sample Post-Test-Only Control Group Design

Dr. Bill Johnson of Accountability City Schools decides to test the impact of his new principal professional development program. He randomly selects 20 of his elementary principals and asks 10 of them to participate in extensive training on four of the skill areas/standards in this book. The other 10 principals receive no training. Post-test scores significantly favor the treatment group. Thus, he concludes that the training made a positive difference.

Another useful true experimental design is the pretest/post-test control group design. A diagram of the design is:

One of the two randomly selected groups receives the treatment (T) while the other group, the control group, does not. This design includes a pretest for both groups. Although this design controls for many of the same weaknesses as the post-test only design, there is no built-in control for the pretest/post-test connection. Subjects who become "testwise" and remember the items on the pretest contaminate the scores on the post-test, which may weaken internal validity. Under most circumstances, the post-test only design should be used to cover these problems, however, pretest data are necessary when researchers are interested in measuring the change produced by a treatment.

Quasi-experimental designs. Quasi-experimental designs are not completely true experimental designs because they do not involve control groups

Sample Pretest/Post-Test Control Group Design

Dr. Johnson wants to validate the results he found using the post-test-only control group design. He randomly selects 20 more elementary principals — 10 are placed in the experimental group and 10 in the control group. He then adds a pretest on the four administrative skill areas covered by the professional development training. One group is given training in the skills and the other is not. Dr. Johnson then compares the post-test scores to determine whether the training had an effect.

and control for only some of the sources of internal validity. In the quasi-experimental approach, a series of observations are collected over equal periods of time (Borg and Gall 1983). In the real world of education, especially public schools, these designs are often the most applicable because administrators and teachers are leery of researchers looking for "good" and "bad" effects caused by some educational experiment with children and teachers (Campbell and Stanley 1963). Quasi-experimental designs allow researchers freedom to conduct research without the stigma caused by placing students in a control group that receives no treatment.

This design includes experimental controls and can be used with minimal of classtime interference. The basic quasi-experimental design is a follows:

$$O_1 — O_2 — O_3 — O_4 — (T) — O_5 — O_6 — O_7 — O_8$$

Sample Quasi-Experimental Design

Dr. Johnson now wants to determine whether the administrative performance of his 15 central-office administrators will improve as a result of a week-long retreat in which five of the skills/standards in this book are stressed. He gathers relevant performance data on all 15 administrators during the four months before and after the retreat, and finds that 12 of the administrators' performances gradually improved each month after the retreat. He concludes that the training is probably causing the change in administrator performance.

This design provides a post hoc tool to evaluate educational interventions for which no comparison-group contrasts were preplanned. For example, suppose a school district initiated a special extra-curricular club program designed to make students' attitudes toward school more positive. If the school officials didn't decide on the importance of an evaluation until several months after the club had been in operation, then an after-the-fact, quasi-experimental strategy is the only way to gather such information(Popham 1993, p. 225). However, the best results are obtained by gathering data prior to and after the treatment when using this method.

This design is very useful for evaluating alternative school programs by collecting data on attendance; teacher, student, and parent attitudes; and grade point averages. Data are collected at equal time intervals on each student in the program beginning one year prior to the program and for one year after the program is underway. This method has also proven useful in evaluating the effects of Chapter 1 programs on student achievement in math and reading (Hoyle 1975, Hoyle and Stalcup 1982).

Selecting the Proper Data-Gathering, Analysis, and Interpretation Methods

Data-gathering strategies and processes must be carefully selected. Some problems are best handled by surveys, some by case studies or naturalistic inquiry, and some by documentary research. Many research tools exist; the test of a true professional is the proper selection of the right tool for the job.

Survey Research

Surveys are widely used and can be successful for determining educational trends, perceptions, and attitudes, and comparing present and past conditions to forecast future events. Montgomery (1995) used the survey technique to determine what a growing suburban community wanted its children and youth to learn in math, science, language arts, and social studies in the 21st century. The results of his comprehensive study has set the course for curriculum policy for the coming five years.

James McNamara (1997) of Texas A&M University offers an excellent model for conducting survey research. His article "Parental View on the Biggest Problems Facing Public Schools: National Versus Local Findings" is based on survey research that asked four specific questions:(1) What were the 1996 Annual Gallup Poll of Public Education national findings on the "biggest problems" question? (2) What were local school district findings on this same question? (3) What differences exist in the findings of these two surveys? (4) What specific advantages and key insights accrue to a local school district that asks the "biggest problem" question in its own survey of adults residing in the community?

McNamara and his staff trained 22 parents to conduct telephone interviews using a valid 68-question questionnaire. A single chart essay was used for each question. The findings were helpful in informing district policymakers during the development of the district plan for the 1997-98 through 2001-02 school years. [For a comprehensive, readable book on survey research see *Surveys and Experiments in Education Research*, McNamara (1994).]

Smith, McNamara, and Barona (1986) offer a 12-step process for conducting successful survey research, which is shown in Figure 9.4.

The interview method, especially face-to-face

Figure 9.4 12 Steps To Good Survey Results

STEPS	KEY ELEMENTS AND ROLES
1. Selecting a Collaborator	• District finds third party expert(s) knowledgeable about school systems and education
2. Establishing a Contract	• District and expert(s) clarifies scope of work and respective roles
	• District gives expert(s) control of data; district keeps control of interpretation
3. Specifying Information Requirements	• District specifies requirements
	• Expert(s) clarifies and provides technical assistance
4. Choosing a Sample	• District chooses target group(s)
	• Expert(s) clarifies and provides technical assistance
5. Writing the Questions	• Expert(s) writes/adapts/adopts questions
	• District responds/evaluates/approves
6. Generating the Data- Collection Procedures	• Expert(s) develops plan
	• District responds/evaluates/approves
7. Collecting the Data	• Expert(s) and district collaborate
8. Analyzing the Data	• Expert(s) produces descriptive, as opposed to prescriptive, results
9. Writing the Report	• Expert(s) prepares descriptive results in chart essay report
10. Presenting the Report	• Expert(s) presents report to district; District presents report to constituents
11. Elaborating the Implications	• District interprets report, integrates with other data, and develops implications for planning
12. Acting on the Implications	• District develops plan

Printed with permission of R. Smith, J. McNamara, and A. Barona.

interviewing, is preferred over mailed questionnaires because it allows interviewers to asks interviewees to clarify their answers. ". . . [A] skilled interviewer can often follow up responses of the interviewee in a manner obviously not possible with written questionnaires" (Popham 1993).

All interviews must be carefully planned. The best results from local telephone opinion interviews come when community members are well informed about the issues and expect to be contacted. Confidential information can usually be gathered if interviewers present requests honestly and intelligibly. Popham (1993, p. 101), however, also points out that "the difficulty with gathering data via interviews is that the procedure is much more expensive than questionnaire administration. The personnel costs for interviewers, in person or by telephone, not to mention the training requirements, represent the chief expense of this approach."

Three important rules relate to the interview method (Best and Kahn 1989, p. 202):

- The preparation of the interview guide and the conduct of the interview must be carefully planned. Interviewers must have a clear conception of just what information they need and they must clearly outline the sequence of the questions that will systematically bring out the desired responses.
- The relationship between the interviewer and the interviewee must be developed to ensure accurate responses. Interviewees must be assured that their responses are confidential. Whether the responses are gathered by notetaking or taperecorded, the exact wording should be retained. Interviewers should always ask interviewees' permission before using a taperecorder.
- The interviewer should be carefully trained in developing rapport, asking probing questions, and preparing for the interview.

Skillful interviews can lead subjects to reveal key information that they would not reveal on a written questionnaire. John Goodlad (1984) and his associates used observations, questionnaires, and interviews to produce *A Place Called School*. They formulated questions about schools and used them in questionnaires and interviews and used modified classroom observation techniques. After field testing the tools and processes, the survey methods were used to compile a large body of data about 38 schools from 8,624 parents, 1,350 teachers, and 17,163 students. Goodlad (1984) asserts that "one

cannot generalize to all schools from their sample. But certainly the 'thick descriptions' compiled from several different perspectives raise many questions about schooling and about other schools." This overall research effort, which relied heavily on interviews, is an example of the naturalistic/qualitative method.

More on Questionnaires

Carefully constructed questionnaires validated through frequent use can help gather information in a relatively short time period. As stated, a weakness of questionnaires is their impersonality and frequent poor return percentages. The likelihood of a high return rate is increased when stakeholders are involved in the development of the questionnaire based on their personal concerns. Montgomery (1995), who reported a 39 percent return equally distributed across all sub-populations of a 12-page long questionnaire, concludes that this relatively high mail-out return was a result of extensive community involvement in developing the questionnaire.

Construction of a good questionnaire is complicated. However, when properly constructed, distributed, and analyzed, questionnaires can provide vital information while letting stakeholders within and outside the school system know that their input is valued.

Using Basic Descriptive and Inferential Statistics

School leaders in most cases are not statisticians, but they must be able to interpret and even conduct research to make policy and program decisions based on what is best for the schools and the students. They also must have an understanding of statistical concepts and methods to benefit from research literature. *Understanding Education Statistics* (Bracey 1997, p.2) warns educators that ". . . you need to be a wise, shrewd consumer of statistics. . . . When there is something rotten in the state of Denmark, you need to be able to sniff it out by understanding the statistics."

Statistics: A Few Basic Terms

Statistics. The collection, organization, and analysis of data. Statistics is also the science of reaching sound conclusions from incomplete data.

Descriptive statistics. Statistics applied to describe and summarize data (e.g., surveys of voter attitudes or personnel needs assessments).

Population. Any group of individuals with one or more characteristics in common that are of interest to the researcher, (e.g., all public school teachers, or all 3rd graders in a school).

Sample. Any segment or part of a population that represents the entire population or universe. A sample must be carefully selected using a table of random numbers to be an accurate representation of the population.

Random sample. A sample in which every subject/person in the population has an equal chance of selection. This type of sample is used to predict the performance of a group, not an individual. For example, a pure random sample of all 3rd grader' math scores should represent all 3rd grade math scores in the school district.

Mean. The arithmetic average of scores, derived by adding all scores and dividing by the number of scores. Mean accurately measures group scores if there are no extreme scores at the high and low ends.

Median. The score above and below which one-half of the scores fall.

Mode. The score that appears most often in an array of scores.

Range. The difference between the highest and lowest scores minus one.

Quartiles. Scores divided in quarters.

Percentiles. Scores divided into 100 parts. A student who is in the 82nd percentile on a test scored lower than 18 percent of students taking the test and higher than 81 percent.

Variance. The sum of the squared deviations from the mean divided by the number in the sample. The higher the "hump" or curve the lower the variance.

Standard deviation. The average spread of the scores around the mean (i.e., the square root of the variance).

Statistical difference between groups. The determination of difference between two or more groups. The test of significant difference between the mean scores of two groups on a science test could be determined by a t-test.

Null hypothesis/level of significance. A null hypothesis takes the position that there is no significant difference between two or more groups. The rejection or acceptance of a null hypothesis is based upon some predetermined level of significance. The .05 level of significance is the most common standard for rejec-

tion of the null hypothesis. This .05 level suggests a .95 percent probability that the difference was due to the experimental treatment rather than a sampling error.

Degrees of freedom. The number of subjects in a study minus one. The more people in a study the stronger the results can be. The number of degrees of freedom in a distribution is the number of observations independent of each other. Larger numbers reduce the probability of extreme scores slanting the findings (Best and Kahn 1989).

Statistical and practical significance. Statistical significance is determined by calculating the probability that a given event could have occurred by chance. Practical significance is a judgment call based on a specified level of statistical significance, number of subjects in the study, and the importance and political implications for the results. For example, a researcher may find a .05 level of significance between the scores of students as a result of using two different reading programs. Even though the results are statistically significant, the school leader must ask if the study was carefully controlled in terms of selection of the two groups, the teaching process, and the type of test used, and also which of method the teachers believe will work better over the long haul. No matter how statistically significant the findings, if the teachers prefer one method over another, they will most likely continue to use it.

Using Statistics To Improve Schooling

Within practical constraints, this section of chapter 9 identifies and briefly describes data analysis procedures that are of basic importance to school leaders. For the computational mechanics of plugging numbers into formulas, refer to a standard statistics text. Many excellent standard and programmed statistics texts are available (See Turney and Robb 1973, Morris 1978, Isaac and Michael 1985).

School leaders can and should use basic concepts of descriptive and inferential statistics in their decision making about school programs and personnel. The following outline identifies some of the key statistical concepts that all school leaders should know in order to make informed decisions to improve the lives of children and youth.

Descriptive Statistics (statistics used to describe and summarize data)

    A. Measures of Central Tendency.
        1. **Mode:** the score occurring most frequently
        2. **Median:** the midpoint of a distribution

3. **Mean:** the average of the scores
   a. The statistical formula for mean

$$\overline{X} = \frac{\sum x}{N}$$

X = the mean of the distribution

x = the raw score

N = the number of raw scores

Σ = "the sum of"

Comparing Mode, Median, and Mean

Raw Scores	
x	4
4	8
8	8 The Mode is 8.
8	10
10	16
16	20
20	

Mode is the value occurring most frequently in a distribution.

Median is the midpoint of the distribution. (Half of frequencies are below the median, half are above. In this example, the median is halfway between the two center values of 8 and 10.) The median is an appropriate average to use when there are unusually high or low numbers.

$$10 + 8 = 18$$
$$18 \div 2 = 9$$

The median is 9.

Mean is the average of the scores

$$4 + 8 + 8 + 10 + 16 + 20 = 66$$
$$66 \div 6 = 11$$

The mean is 11.

Example of where scores fall on a graph

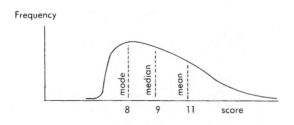

Frequency

mode median mean

8   9   11   score

B. **Measures of Variability.**

1. **Range:** the difference between the highest and lowest score +1. Using the raw scores above: $20 - 4 = 16 + 1 = 17$

2. **Variance:** refers to the distribution of scores around the mean. Mean scores become less representative of group scores as the variance increases.
   a. The statistical formula for variance:

$$S^2 = \frac{\sum x^2}{N}$$

S^2 = the variance of the sample

x = $X - x$ the difference between the raw score and the mean

N = the number of raw scores

Σ = "the sum of"

3. **Standard Deviation:** the square root of the variance. Standard deviation is the most commonly used measure a variability. It shows whether most of the scores cluster closely around the mean or are spread out along the scale. The larger the standard deviation, the more spread out the scores. Standard deviation is also useful for comparing groups and provides the basis for standardizing test scores by computing stanines and scale scores (Borg and Gall 1983).
   a. The statistical formula for standard deviation

$$S = \sqrt{\frac{\sum x^2}{N}}$$

S = the standard deviation of the sample

x = the difference between the raw score and the mean

N = the number of scores

Remember: Standard deviation is the square root of variance.

The Measure of Variability

Techniques in the measure of variability are the most important statistical skills needed by school leaders. Mean scores, for example, are frequently used to measure the achievement level of all students in a given school district, school, or grade level. It is unwise to make policy or initiate or change programs based on means scores because they can give an inaccurate picture by hiding the range and distribution of individual scores.

C. **Measures of Relationships** (expressed as correlational coefficients).

   1. **Correlation coefficients** indicate the degree and direction of relationship variables.

     a. A correlation coefficient of + 1.00 (or –1.00) indicates the variables are highly related.

     b. A correlation coefficient of .00 indicates no relationship.

Examples of Correlation

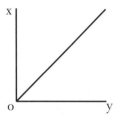

+1.00=perfect correlation

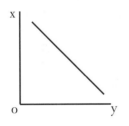

-1.00=perfect correlation

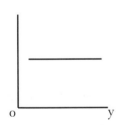

0 = no correlation at all

Thus, when high scores on one variable, administrator performance for example, are associated with high scores on a second variable, such as hours of inservice training, the variables are positively correlated. The same is true if both scores are low.When high scores on one variable are associated with low scores on a second variable, the variables are negatively correlated. However, some variables show no tendency to vary or change together. In this case, there is no correlation between the variables.

Again, the amount of relationship or correlation is not causation. Improved administrator performance may not be caused by the amount of inservice training, but an accumulation of correlational evidence can help build a credible case for causality between two variables.

D. **Measures of Dispersion** (or measures of relative position). These express how well an individual has performed compared to all other individuals in the sample.

   1. **Percentile rank** indicates the percentage of scores that fall below a given score.

     a. If a score of 70 corresponds to a percentile rank of 82, the 82nd percentile, this means 82 percent of the scores in the distribution are lower than 70.

     b. The median of a set of scores corresponds to the 50th percentile.

The following illustration indicates that students who have a rank of 82 did better than 82 percent of the students and not as well as 18 percent.

**Student in
82nd Percentile**

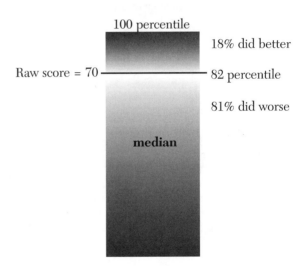

Sample divided into
100 equal parts

Characteristics of the Normal Curve

• Fifty percent of the scores are above the mean and 50 percent are below the mean.
• The mean, median, and mode are the same.
• Most scores are near the mean.
• A score occurs fewer times the farther it is from the mean.
• A normal distribution is symmetrical and unimodal.
• Ninety-nine percent of scores tend to be plus or minus 3 standard deviations from the mean.
• Over 95 percent of scores lie within 2 standard deviations (plus and minus) from the mean.

151

Examples of Normal Distribution

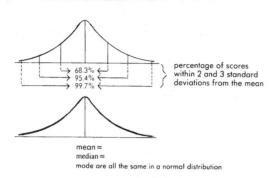

percentage of scores
within 2 and 3 standard
deviations from the mean

mean =
median =
mode are all the same in a normal distribution

For a normal distribution, the shape of the curve depends on the size of the variance or standard deviation. A small variance, S^2, results in a "higher hump," a large variance gives a flatter curve.

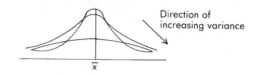

Direction of
increasing variance

$\overline{x}$

Skewed Distribution. A distribution is negatively skewed if the extreme scores are at the upper end of the distribution. A distribution is positively skewed if the extreme scores are at the lower end of the distribution. Skewed distributions sometimes indicate that a test is too easy, too difficult, or inappropriate for a particular group.

Examples of Normal Distribution

If the distribution of scores is skewed (where all the scores are at one end or the other), the curve will not be symmetrical and the three measures — mean, median, and mode — will not be equal

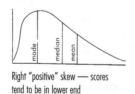

Left "negative" skew — scores
tend to be in higher end

Right "positive" skew — scores
tend to be in lower end

Inferential Statistics

Definition: Statistics used to determine the likelihood that the results of a sample, or samples, are the same results that would have been found for the entire population.

The T Test. Statistical procedure used to determine if statistically significant differences exist between the means of two samples; that is, differences not likely to be due to chance.

T Test Examples
Example 1:
Suppose we randomly assign students to two groups to compare the effectiveness of two methods of teaching reading. The groups are placed in different instructional situations for a semester. After the semester is over, the groups are tested in reading and their mean scores are determined. If the two groups have different achievement scores, we need a way to determine whether the differences that appear between the two groups are merely a result of chance factors or can be attributed to the different teaching styles. The t-test is an appropriate statistical tool to test the difference.

First, we must reject the null hypothesis; that is, *the difference between the means is a function of chance alone.* If the difference between the means is unlikely to be a function of chance alone, the null hypothesis is rejected.

Next, we must establish confidence intervals or probable limits within which the population mean falls.

A 95 percent confidence interval corresponds to .05 probability level that differences are due to chance.

Statistical formula:

$$\overline{X} \pm 1.96 = SE_{\overline{X}}$$

$$SE_{\overline{X}} = \text{Standard error of mean} = \frac{S}{\sqrt{\overline{X}}}$$

Ninety-percent confidence interval corresponds to 0.10 probability level of chance occurrence.

Statistical formula:

$$\overline{X} \pm 2.58 \, SE_{\overline{X}}$$

Note: with a sample size of 500 or more, see Table of T in a statistics book.

Now, run the **t** test:

$$t^* = \sqrt{\frac{\overline{X_1} - \overline{X_2}}{\frac{S_1^2}{n_1} + \frac{S_2^2}{n_2}}}$$

° Where t = the value by which the statistical significance will be judged.

$\overline{X_1}$ = mean of group 1

$\overline{X_2}$ = mean of group 2

S_1^2 = variance of group 1

S_2^2 = variance of group 1

n_1 = number of subjects in group 1
n_2 = number of subjects in group 2

If the obtained value is less than the tabled value, then the null hypothesis held true and any differences in data can be attributed to chance alone. If the obtained value of **t** equals or exceeds the tabled value, the null hypothesis is rejected, and we must attribute the differences to something other than chance (Popham 1993, Isaac and Michael 1985).

Example 2:

Two classes of 25 students each obtained the following results on the final examination in statistics:

Class 1: $\overline{X_1} = 85$ $S_1^2 = 400.15$

Class 1: $\overline{X_2} = 79$ $S_2^2 = 989.85$

Test the hypothesis that the two classes do not differ in average performance on the exam, that is $C_1 = C_2$.

Solution: $t^* = \sqrt{\frac{\overline{X_1} - \overline{X_2}}{\frac{S_1^2}{n_1} + \frac{S_2^2}{n_2}}}$

$$t = \frac{6}{7.46} = .805$$

Thus:

3.95 = obtained value
2.01 = book value at 0.05 with 49 degrees of freedom

° Fail to reject the null hypothesis and conclude that the two classes do not differ significantly in their performance.

ANOVA — Analysis of Variance. A statistical procedure designed to analyze the differences between the means of two or more samples. ANOVA analyzes the variations in groups and yields an F value that is interpreted like the T value. In this procedure, a different form of the treatment is applied to each of the groups, then the values of the treatment groups are compared. The use of ANOVA tells us whether any statistically significant mean differences exist between two or more groups. According to Popham (1993, p. 272-273):

At the conclusion of an ANOVA, the single resulting F value merely tells us whether there are any significant differences between two or more means in the groups under analysis. . . . If the resulting F value were significant, the researcher would follow up with some type of post hoc analysis that would isolate which groups were significantly different.

ANOVA is a very important test that can be used in a wide variety of research problems to find out which groups were actually affected by treatments or experiences. For example, by using the ANOVA, a researcher interested in the perceptions of teachers about their principal's decision-making skills could divide the teachers into five grade level groups, administer a questionnaire, and determine which groups were the most positive or negative about the principal's abilities. More detailed explanations and step-by-step procedures for applying ANOVA can be found in the statistics textbooks listed earlier in this chapter.

Computer Program Statistical Package for the Social Sciences (SPSS)

The most popular computer statistical package for non-statisticians is the SPSS-Windows version. The package is readily available in most larger

153

school districts, universities, and regional research laboratories. Practicing school leaders and graduate students completing dissertations can save time and energy by turning to this handy SPSS package. Figure 9.5 includes a sample of SPSS procedures accomplished by computer.

Figure 9.5 SPSS Procedures for Statistical Analyses

Procedure	SPSS Procedure Name
Mean	CONDESCRIPTIVE OR FREQUENCIES OR BREAKDOWN
Standard Deviation . . .	FREQUENCIES OR BREAKDOWN
T-Test for . . . . Unmatched Groups	T-TEST (GROUPS)
Chi-Square	CROSSTABS
Analysis of Variance . .	ANOVA
Factor Analysis	FACTOR

School leaders need a strong working knowledge of these basic statistical concepts and tools to conduct and interpret research to communicate to staff and the community the latest information that will build better school programs. The endless search for school improvement must be driven by good judgment grounded with sound statistical knowledge.

Using Research-Based Models and Standards for Educational Program Evaluation

Evaluation and school improvement go together like peanut butter and jelly. Popham (1993, p.7) writes that "The heart of the definition [of evaluation] involves an appraisal of quality or, in other words, a determination of worth." During the past 20 years several evaluation tools and strategies have been available to assist school leaders in program evaluation efforts. It is impossible to review all of these models or attempt to compare the merits of each one, but this section describes a few that practicing school leaders have found most helpful.

One excellent source that describe the importance of rigorous evaluation procedures is *The Program Evaluation Standards: How to Assess Evaluations of Educational Programs*, 2nd Edition (1994), published by The Joint Committee on Standards for Educational Evaluation. According to the committee, sound evaluations of education programs, projects, and materials in a variety of settings should use rigorous standards that include four basic attributes.

(1) Utility. Utility standards are intended to ensure that an evaluation serves the information needs of intended users.

(2) Feasibility. Feasibility standards are intended to ensure that an evaluation will be realistic, prudent, diplomatic, and frugal.

(3) Propriety. Propriety standards are intended to ensure that an evaluation will be conducted legally, ethically, and with due regard for the welfare of those involved in the evaluation, as well as those affected by its results.

(4) Accuracy. Accuracy standards are intended to ensure that an evaluation will reveal and convey technically adequate information about features that determine the worth or merit of the program being evaluated. (For a complete description of these attributes, see The Joint Committee on Standards for Educational Evaluation 1994).

The preface of *The Program Evaluation Standards* addresses the following concerns about the proper application of the standards. "The Standards are an effort to provide guidance to effective evaluation. The Standards alone cannot guarantee or ensure the quality of any evaluation. Sound evaluation will require the exercise of professional judgment in order to adequately apply the Standards to a particular evaluation setting" (p. xviii).

Evaluation Models

The two best known and most widely used evaluation models are the goal-attainment and the CIPP models.

Goal-attainment model. This model is usually associated with the work of the late Ralph W. Tyler. Tyler (1942) taught that the careful formulation of clear educational goals translated into measurable, behavioral objectives is vital to measuring the effectiveness of student performance. He believed that "If you can't write it down, you can't teach it" and advocated measuring student achievement to determine the degree to which previously established goals were achieved.

The goal-attainment model includes helpful steps for school leaders and state and national accrediting agencies. Metfessel and Michael's (1967, pp. 931-943) adaption of the model includes the following eight steps:

(1) Involve members of the total community.
(2) Construct broad goals and specific objectives.
(3) Translate specific objectives into communicable forms that facilitate learning.
(4) Develop measurement instrumentation.
(5) Carry out periodic measurements.
(6) Analyze measurement data.
(7) Interpret analyzed data.
(8) Formulate recommendations for program changes or modify the goals and objectives.

This model has been widely used by communitywide committees engaged in setting curriculum goals and objectives and in creating multiple-year plans for curriculum improvement and instructional design. Several other hybrids of the goal-attainment model have been designed, but the Metfessel-Michael model is preferred by the majority of practicing school leaders.

The CIPP model. This program evaluation model, used to facilitate educational decision making, was developed by evaluation experts Daniel Stufflebeam of Western Michigan University and Egon Guba, Professor Emeritus at Indiana University. The CIPP model captures the true essence of systematic program evaluation by assisting school leaders in delineating, obtaining, and providing useful information for judging decision alternatives (Stufflebeam et al. 1971).

The term CIPP represents four types of evaluation — Context, Input, Process, and Product. Gredler (1985, p. 49) sums up the CIPP model by saying, ". . . it delineates four different types of evaluation. Context evaluation addresses goals and objectives. Input evaluation assesses potential alternatives and analyzes their fit with the client's particular circumstances. Process evaluation documents and assesses implementation. And product evaluation assesses program effects."

Figure 9.6 provides an overview of the basic steps of the CIPP model.

The CIPP model and variations of it have been widely used for over 30 years to evaluate programs in education as well as physical therapy and federal government agencies (Worthen and Sanders 1987, Hoyle 1978a). Medical professionals and other have also found the CIPP model to be a very useful guide in conducting needs assessments, developing mission and goal statements, and estab-

lishing systematic processes to evaluate program progress.

• • •

School leaders must continue to upgrade their program evaluation skills to give concrete evidence to the public of the success of our school systems. This concrete evidence can be produced by combining testing information, other research and evaluation methods, and, above all, good judgment. The late Paul Salmon, former executive director of AASA, said it best: "School improvement councils, self-studies, visits by external evaluation teams, and examinations of whether existing programs are meeting real needs all contribute to the evolving science, or art, of effective evaluation" (see Lazarus 1982, p. 2).

Figure 9.6 **The CIPP Model**

Context Evaluation	Determination of unmet needs, that is, the discrepancies between the current status of the program and where it needs to be in the future (planning decisions)
Input Evaluation	Determinations of the most urgent program improvement needs and the amount of human, financial, and time resources (structuring decisions)
Process Evaluation	Selecting or developing measurement tools or strategies to determine the differences between program goals and assessment data through formative evaluation procedures (implementing decisions)
Product Evaluation	A summative evaluation to assess program outcomes (recycling decisions)

Stufflebeam et al. 1971

155

Engaging in Planning and Futuring

A key function for the school district, and thus a key responsibility of school leaders, is to anticipate and manage change through careful planning. Educational planning involves deciding how to improve teaching and learning in the most efficient manner. This process is vital to meeting the megachallenges described in Appendix A and the mini-challenges faced in each school system, building, or classroom everyday. The purpose of this section is to introduce the most useful planning and futures methods for school leadership and operations.

To effectively manage change, school leaders must:

(1) Delineate specific objectives and processes to bring about positive change based on the shared district and campus vision, mission, and goal statements;

(2) Anticipate the problems to be encountered and the necessary resources needed to accomplish the specified objectives.

(3) Create programs to accomplish each objective and processes to manage implementation;

(4) Gain the acceptance of the entire administrative team and other key advisory teams involved in or affected by the change(s);

(5) Establish an effective communications network to manage disagreement and agreements during the change process; and

(6) Provide resources to empower key people to get the job done.

The National Policy Board for Educational Administration calls the process of school planning "organizational oversight" (Erlandson, Stark, and Ward 1996), and uses the following verbs to describe the planning and implementation processes:

- *Planning and scheduling* the process of using one's own and others' work so that resources are used appropriately, and short- and long-term priorities and goals are met;
- *Scheduling* flows of activities;
- *Establishing* procedures to regulate activities;
- *Monitoring* projects to meet deadlines; and
- *Empowering* the process in appropriate places.

In the 1990s, planning changed in nature, scope, and purpose. School leaders have grown to appreciate the old saying, "Plans are sometimes useless, but the planning process is indispensable."

Noone can predict the future with complete accuracy or solve all problems, but using a proper planning process can reduce the number of surprises and help people to "re-vision," that is, to adjust to rapid change and stay on target. Thus, optimizing staff and student performance rather than accurately hitting the original target is the mark of a good planning process.

The most important point to remember about the planning process is that "people plan the plan — the plan does not plan the people." The literature is filled with intricate planning strategies and planning consultants travel the nation. However, school leaders can apply the most sophisticated or popular planning models and be miserable planners unless key colleagues and other customers are involved, trusted, and recognized for their expertise and contributions.

When conducting strategic planning, a school leader must ask the following questions.

- Is the plan realistic in my district or school?
- Will the staff and community understand the planning process or is it too complicated with too much confusing detail?
- Will the administrative and teaching staff support the plan and commit committee and individual time to implementing and assessing each step in the plan?
- Am I, the plan initiator, committed enough to the plan to give the energy and time required to sell the plan and encourage others?
- Are adequate resources available that can be dedicated to supporting the plan over the long haul?

Answering "no" to any of these questions is a sign that the planning process will not yield positive results. No one plan, no matter how attractive it may be in a book or a promotional brochure, can be superimposed on a district or school. The plan must be clear, simple, motivational, and measurable. School leaders are well advised to take the best ideas from this book and others written by Cook (1995), Carlson and Awkerman (1991), and Kauffman, Watters, and Herman (1996) and create the best alternative for their own district or school. No one is a better judge of planning needs than those who must implement the plan.

Planning and Futuring Models

The following five planning/futuring models are helpful to school leaders: The Nominal Group Technique (NGT) and its cousin the Cooperative

Planning: How To Do It

1. Establish a planning team that includes professional and support staff; parents and students; the superintendent and one member of the board; and 10 community leaders, including a member of the media.

2. Develop a plan for planning
   - Share the district vision, mission, and goal statements.
   - Indicate the specific target of the planning — curriculum, facilities, a bond issue, and so on.
   - Conduct a needs assessment if one has not been done recently.
   - Determine the greatest needs and prioritize them.
   - Establish a timeline for action.
   - Establish benchmarks and milestones for formative assessment.
   - Determine who is responsible for each step of the plan.
   - Allocate resources by placing a cost factor on each step of the plan.
   - Create a monitoring and reporting system to keep all customers informed.

(AASA, *Planning for Tomorrow's Schools*, 1984)

(Also see the strategic plan model in Chapter 1, which involves the steps listed above.)

Processing Model (CPM); the KIVA Model; the GANTT Model; the Futuring Method; and the Delphi Technique.

Nominal Group Technique (NGT). NGT is a good planning/futuring method that helps group members to view themselves as critical to the planning or problem-solving process (Delbecq and Vande Ven 1975, Hoyle 1978b). NGT uses a structured group of six to eight people to solve a problem or create ideas about future conditions.

NGT consists of four steps:

Step 1: Silent generation of ideas. The question under consideration is clearly communicated by the group facilitator and written down by all members. The group is then asked to write down as many change ideas or statements as come to mind in a five-minute period.

Step 2. Round Robin recording of ideas. Each group member is invited to share one idea at a time, which is written on a flipchart or blackboard. No discussion or judgment takes place. Each participant gives an idea or passes until all ideas have been recorded.

Step 3. Each idea is discussed and clarified in the order in which it was presented and recorded. Again, no judgment about any item is made during this step.

Step 4. Each group member rank orders a specific number (3-5) of items as the most important. Each person places an item number (the number listed on the flipchart) on the top right-hand corner of a 3X5 card and a ranking number on the upper left-hand corner. The votes are counted and discussion is encouraged to clarify and help finalize the three most critical changes needed. (Delbecq and Vande Ven 1975)

The NGT process ensures the individual involvement of each group member and promotes individual creativity and autonomy while encouraging group consensus.

Jim Sweeney and others have adapted the NGT to cut the time it takes for the four steps by changing the voting process. In Sweeney's Cooperative Processing, the group is asked to "clear out" items after step three. As the facilitator calls out each item number, group members display an open palm (elbow on the table with hand visible to all group members) for items they wish to leave in for final voting. A closed fist indicates a desire to eliminate the item from further consideration. The majority rules on the vote for each item. The final step requires each participant to vote (elbow on table) using five fingers for the top choice, and four or less for each other item. Five points can be given only one time by each member while the other numbers can be used over and over. Even though total consensus is rarely achieved, NGT and Cooperative Processing ensure each person equal opportunity to provide input and key ideas for problem solving or goal setting (Sweeney 1992, personal communication).

The KIVA model. The KIVA model (Cunningham 1987) works well in helping large group of people use their perspectives of past, present, and future events in the planning process. The model is a rendition of the planning process used by the Pueblo tribal leaders in the Southwest in which tribal leaders actually sat in a three-tiered circular setting to make decisions for the tribe. KIVA involves the following steps.

Step 1. Divide group members into three equal-sized groups and label group 1 as "past experts," group 2 as "present experts," and group 3, "future experts."

Step 2. Seat group 1, past experts, in chairs arranged in a circle and ask them to present a history of the problem being worked on and record each idea on a flipchart. After 20 minutes, tape the "past" information on the wall so it is visible to all group members. Note that only past experts are allowed to talk in Step 2; the present and future experts observe from behind the circle of chairs.

Step 3. Ask group 2, present experts, to give the current events affecting the plan using the process in step 2.

Step 4. Next group 3, future experts, give possible, probable, and likely events that will affect or be initiated by the plan using the process in step 2.

Step 5. The groups move into one big circle and discuss the past, present, and future events and their implications, problems, and strong points.

Step 6. KIVA leader should attempt to reach consensus on the most important needs that the school or district should address.

Step 7. The most important needs become the priorities upon which the planning process begins.

Gantt Chart. The Gantt Chart provides an orderly method for graphically displaying the steps in a planning project. Figure 9.7 is an example Gantt Chart for initiating and evaluating a new curriculum program. The task to be completed and the individuals assigned the responsibility are listed down the left side of the chart. Each activity is listed with a corresponding timeline and sequence.

The last step in the construction of a Gantt Chart is progress posting. Progress is posted at regular intervals so that activities getting off schedule can be identified and corrective action can be taken (Cunningham 1982).

PERT/CPM—Program Review Technique/Critical Path Method. PERT/CPM is a more complicated version of the Gantt Chart, which includes the duration of the project, the interrelationships among the activities, and time factors called "slack time" and "critical path." This technique can be helpful in the preparation of the operating budget or in planning school facilities.

A PERT network is a flow diagram consisting of the activities and events that must be accomplished to reach the program objectives (See Figure 9.8). It shows the logical and planned sequence of

---

Figure 9.7 **The Gantt Chart**

Activity and person(s) responsible	Jan,	Feb.	March	April	May
1. Conduct needs assessment	1——28				
2. Identify and prioritize needs		1——15			
3. Select evaluation teams		2/16————3/4			
4. Develop news releases	1/1———————————————————————————5/29				
5. Design program strategies			3/5—3/7		
6. Conduct inservice for staff			3/7————4/3		
7. Initiate program				4/3————5/7	
8. Monitor program impact				4/5————5/15	
9. Conduct final evaluation					5/15–5/18
10. Prepare final report					5/19–5/25

Figure 9.8 **Sample Project Using PERT**

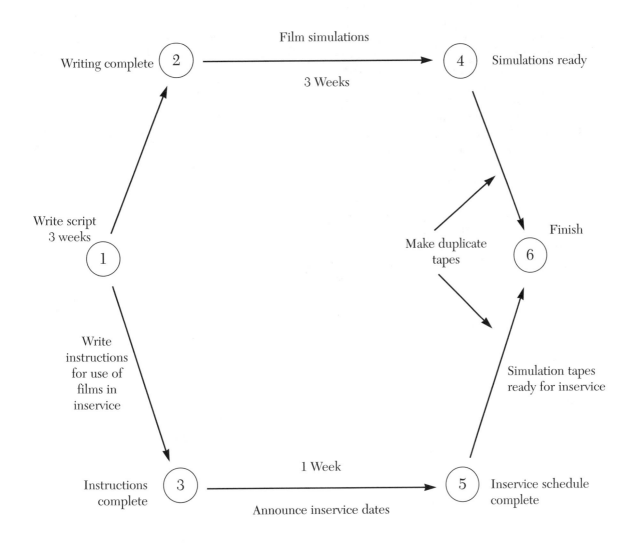

accomplishments and the interdependence and interrelationships between those accomplishments. A PERT network begins with the end in mind, which is represented by a circle and assigned a number. Activities that involve the expenditure of resources and lead to the accomplishment of an event are indicated by a straight line connecting two events. The sequence of activities required for project completion is written in numerical order.

Beginning with the final event, the project leader works backward to other events that must precede it (Cunningham 1982, Granger 1971). Figure 9.8 shows the steps used by an inservice coordinator to produce a videotape of simulated problems for principals.

The PERT chart shows six steps that go from generation of the original idea to final distribution of the video to principals. (We have, of course, simplified the steps for the purposes of this discussion). If a delay occurs in one of the steps — for example, if it takes longer than two weeks to film the simulations — the inservice coordinator can check the PERT chart to see how the delay will change the overall schedule.

Notice that the PERT chart diagram lists the time required for each step. The inservice coordinator has estimated the least possible amount of time needed for completion of the specific activities and events whose completion is critical to the entire project, which is called the Critical Path. This method of estimating project completion time is known as the Critical Path Method (CPM) (Granger 1971).

159

Futures Methods

Preparing leaders to anticipate and plan for the future has become a primary theme for university administrator preparation programs. Futuring is a creative approach to planning that investigates the interactions among economic, social, technological, and educational developments to create alternative scenarios for the future. Interest in futuring has created a new species of intellectuals — professional futurists. Based on careful trend analyses, futurists design multiple forecasts, which are valuable tools for decision makers.

The education division of the World Future Society (WFS)has complied a wide variety of materials and books related to the visioning/planning field that are useful for education planning. Over 400 colleges and universities offer courses in future studies and public schools have added futures components to social studies, science, English, and career education curricula. The use of futures methods is widespread in gifted and talented programs throughout the world. Educational Planning/Futurism, a graduate class at Texas A&M University, has been taught for over 20 years and attracts students from agriculture, architecture, business, liberal arts, and education. This course encourages students to think broadly by looking beyond the boundaries of the possible to the improbable — even the impossible.

The skills for visioning should be part of school leaders' leadership arsenal for transforming America's schools. Daniel Duke (1987, p. 33) writes that effective school leaders "possess and are able to articulate a vision of effective schooling, and they allocate their time in ways that increase the likelihood of realizing that vision." School leaders can use various techniques to develop a vision of the future for effective schools, and can enable others to share in the process. The following are the steps of an effective visioning exercise to help staff and community members think about and plan for high-quality future schools (Hoyle 1995).

Step 1. Select 25 community and school leaders for a one-day workshop and a consultant who can present ideas on future trends and the power of team planning.

Step 2. At the workshop, after the futures consultant speaks, divide the participants into groups of 5.

Step 3. Ask participants to close their eyes, relax, and project themselves to the year 2010.

Step 4. Tell participants that their school district has been selected as one of the three top in the United States, and ask each person to write down three or four reasons their district could have won national recognition.

Step 5. Conduct a mock interview by asking one person in each group to share with the entire group their three or four reasons for the honor.

Step 6. Record the responses on a flipchart.

Step 7. Organize futures taskforces around the major reasons the group listed and begin work to make the visions happen.

Intuition and school leadership. School leaders must make many decisions in a hurry with only partial information. When school leaders use mixed scanning (see Chapter 1) and intuition, most of these decisions are sound. Rowen (1987, pp. 11-12) defines intuition as "knowledge gained without rational thought. . . . New ideas [that] spring from a mind that organizes experiences, facts, and relationships to discern a path that has not been taken before. . . . [I]ntuition compresses years of learning and experience into an instantaneous flash" (p. 12).

Intuitive leadership is much more than gut-level decision making; it is based on the ways a person uses both hemispheres of the brain to process information and make decisions. New decision sciences are stressing intuition, "fuzzy logic," and "boundarylessness of thought" for making decisions. Jack Welch, CEO of General Electric, pushes frequent creative thought sessions that stress intuitive thinking for his employees.

Brain research, however, reveals that the U.S. education system is basically left brained; that is, students are taught linear, logical thinking, mathematical and analytical reasoning, and to be deductive in drawing conclusions. They are taught to learn systematically, and taught not to be out of step with the rest of the class. After Walt Disney's death, the Walt Disney Corporation hit troubled times because too many logical, left-brained people were making key decisions. Once directed to use the integrative whole-brain approach to intuitive management, the corporation gained new momentum (Agor 1988).

Scenarios. A scenario is a description of a series of future events and the outcome they produce. The late Herman Kahn turned scenario writing into an art form. His amazing ability to combine hundreds of social, demographic, technological, and political trends into alternative scenarios helped nations rebuild after WWII and guided international corporations to economic advantage (see Kahn et al. 1976).

Scenario writers describe future events and eventual outcomes by placing themselves in the future, describing the changes that they see, and reflecting on how and when these changes occurred. Scenarios have proven very helpful in the educational planning process (Dede and Allen 1981, Hoyle 1995).

The Delphi Technique. The Delphi Technique takes its name from the ancient city in Greece, where, more than 500 years before Christ, a woman oracle sat in the temple of Apollo and prophesied the future for kings and warriors about matters of war, marriage, wealth, and power. The Delphi Technique was initiated in the early 1950s as an Air Force-sponsored RAND Corporation study (Gorden and Helmer 1964). The technique involves a series of questionnaires that ask a panel of experts to share information or predictions on a topic. The first questionnaire asks them for general ideas or information. For example, a Delphi panel might respond to the question "What are five or six major factors that university planners will face in the next 15 years."

The second questionnaire consists of statements developed from the answers given during the first round. Panelists are asked to respond to forced-choice, Likert-type items.

The third questionnaire provides panelists with group averages from their second round, usually in the form of a mean, mode, medium, or interquartile range. Panelists are asked to reconsider their second-round responses based on the collective data and to either individually consider changing their responses to move closer to the group norm or state a reason they feel that a minority position is in order. A fourth questionnaire provides each participant with new consensus data and a summary of minority opinions and requests a final revision of responses (Cunningham 1982).

• • •

Skills in educational planning and related futures methods are vital for school leaders coping with the complexities of the future and planning for and making decisions about effective school programs. However, school leaders need staff and community support to be effective planners; the techniques of planning are the second consideration. School leaders peering into the next century must

One of the most useful evaluation instruments are available to school leaders is the Program Evaluation Kit developed at the Center for the Study of Evaluation at the University of California at Los Angeles(Morris 1978). The kit contains six booklets of instruments and methods evaluators can use to measure program implementation and impact

envision a learning community that maximizes the potential of all children and select the best planning techniques to build that future.

Selection, Administration, and Interpretation of Evaluation Instruments

Standardized tests. Successful 21st century school leaders must be able to interpret standardized test scores for staff and the public while working to select and administer a testing program that fits the local school situation. Standardized testing continues to dominate the practice of program evaluation even though several excellent forms of alternative student evaluation strategies have emerged in the 1990s. According to Mitchell Lazarus (1982, p.1), "There is a growing body of professional opinion to the effect that standardized testing, while usually the fastest, cheapest way to evaluate, is sometimes not the best way." Because of this, many states have added a test for graduation or some form of performance assessment for accountability purposes. The states, however, have not given up traditional standardized tests. School leaders trying to persuade the public to consider alternative forms of student assessment, including portfolios and performance demonstrations, often have little success. The public tends to like standardized tests, which yield numbers parents, realtors, and the business community can easily use to compare students and schools.

The Texas Assessment of Academic Skills (TAAS) is a good example of a state-mandated, standardized test. School administrators, staff, and community members celebrate their school being rated as "exemplary" or "recognized," and live in fear of them being labeled "probationary" or "low-performing." While state leaders believe the TAAS is the best available measure of school and student performance, the search continues to develop other, perhaps less feared, measures that are helpful for improving student and teacher performance.

Reporting test results. It is important to remember that school performance results can have a positive or negative effect on a community. In either case, school leaders are wise to be proactive about sharing results and outlining the steps a district plans to take toward improvement when test results are poor.

All staff should be informed about the nature of the testing program, what the tests are supposed to show and not show, and how the results are going to be used to improve student performance. Efforts should also be made to inform the media, parents, and other interested community members. This can be done through newsletters, news releases, individual visits, press conferences, and speeches to civic clubs and the chamber of commerce. Skills in selecting, analyzing, interpreting, and reporting the results from evaluation instruments are a critical part of a school leader's arsenal and help school leaders remain the guiding force for school change and improvement.

Conclusion

School leaders must be skilled at the interdependent skills of interpreting and conducting research, evaluating programs, and planning for the future. Preparation programs have stressed these skills in recent years but, for many reasons, busy school administrators are too often forced to focus on "quick fix" information. The public, however, is asking for hard data about the product and payoff of public education. Therefore, it is critical that school leaders master the skills covered in this chapter if America's school leaders are to win greater support for our schools.

Use the following Skill Accomplishment Checklist to assess your skill levels on each topic of the important topics discussed in this chapter

Skill Accomplish Checklist for Chapter 9

Skills	Readings and Activities for Skill Mastery
Use various research designs and methods.	**Readings:** Borg and Gall (1983), Popham (1993), Erlandson et al. (1993) **Activities:** 1. Using information from this chapter and the readings, conduct an assessment of the research designs and methods of gathering, analyzing, and interpreting data in your school/district.
Select the proper data-gathering analysis, and interpretation methods	**Readings:** McNamara (1994), Montgomery (1995), Isaac and Michael (1985) **Activities:** 1. Conduct a community survey using the suggestions in the chapter for designing, distributing, gathering, analyzing, and interpreting data. 2. Conduct a needs assessment among math teachers about the value of inservice programs; analyze, interpret, and report the findings to the teachers.
Use basic descriptive and inferential statistics.	**Readings:** Bracey (1997), Borg and Gall (1993), Isaac and Michael (1985) **Activities:** 1. Select a set of students' scores on an algebra test and compute the mean, median, mode, standard deviation, and range. 2. Randomly select algebra students from two similar classes and conduct a t-test on exam scores.
Demonstrate the use of qualitative research methods (e.g., constructivist, naturalistic techniques).	**Readings:** Erlandson et al. (1993), Miles and Huberman (1994), Guba and Lincoln (1989) **Activities:** 1. Using the readings listed above, develop a 5-6 page paper outlining the major differences between the constructivistic and rationalistic research methodologies. 2. After a careful study of the constructivistic method, observe a middle school for three days and write a paper for a state or national conference.

Skill Accomplish Checklist for Chapter 9—continued

Skills	Readings and Activities for Skill Mastery
Use research-based models and standards for evaluating educational programs.	**Readings:** Gredler (1996), Popham (1993), Worthen and Sanders (1988) **Activities:** 1. Write a paper comparing the goal-attainment and CIPP models. 2. Apply the CIPP model to evaluating the career education program in your school or district.
Engage in strategic planning and futuring.	**Readings:** Carlson and Awkerman (1991); Cook (1995); Erlandson, Stark, and Ward (1996); Hoyle (1995) **Activities:** 1. Re-read the planning sections in Chapters 1 and 9 of this book and compare the key planning components covered in them and the readings listed above. Look for the differences between planning and visioning. 2. Compare the strategic plans of two school districts or schools and select the better plan. Defend your selection in a 10-page paper. 3. Develop a Gantt Chart to detail a curriculum review process for a district or school.

Resources

Achilles, C. M. (October 1997). "Small Classes, Big Possibilities." *The School Administrator* 9, 54: 6-15.

Agor, W. H. (1988). "Don't Scoff at Intuitive Hunches." *The School Administrator* 7, 4: 19-22.

American Association of School Administrators. (1984). *Planning for Tomorrow's Schools.* Arlington, Va.: Author.

Anderson, J.(June 18, 1997). "Getting Better by Design." *Education Week* 48.

Ary, D., L. Jacobs, and A. Razavich. (1996). *Introduction to Research in Education.* (5th ed.) New York: Harcourt Brace College Publications.

Best, J.W., and J.V. Kahn. (1989). *Research in Education.* (6th ed.) Englewood Cliffs, N.J.: Prentice Hall.

Borg, W., and M. Gall. (1983). *Education Research: An Introduction.* (4th ed.) New York: Longman.

Bracey, G.W. (1997). *Understanding Educational Statistics: It's Easier and More Important Than You Think.* Arlington, Va.: Education Research Service and the American Association of School Administrators.

Campbell, D., and D.T. Stanley. (1963). "Experimental and Quasi-Experimental Designs for Research and Teaching." In *Handbook for Research and Teaching,* edited by N.L. Gage. Chicago, ll.: Rand-McNally.

Carlson, R.V., and G. Awkerman, eds. (1991). *Educational Planning: Concepts, Strategies, and Practices.* New York: Longman.

Cook, B. (1995). *Strategic Planning for America's Schools.* Arlington, Va.: American Association of School Administrators.

Cunningham, L. (1978). *"From Visions to Development: A Resources Center-Based Community Education Systems Model."* San Jose: San Jose State University.

Cunningham, W. (1982). *Systematic Planning for Educational Change.* Palo Alto, Calif.: Mayfield Publishing Co.

Dede, C., and D. Allen. (January 1981). "Education in the 21st Century: Scenarios as a Tool for Strategies Planning." *Phi Delta Kappan.*

Delbecq, A.L., and A. Vande Ven. (1975). *Group Techniques for Program Planning.* Glenview, Ill.: Scott Foresman and Co.

Duke, D.L. (1987). *School Leadership and Instructional Improvement*. New York: Random House.

Eisner, E. (1998). *The Enlightened Eye: Qualitative Inquiry and the Enhancement of Educational Practice*. Columbus, Ohio: Merrill (An Imprint of Prentice Hall).

Erlandson, D., E. Harris, B. Skipper, and S. Allen. (1993). *Doing Naturalistic Inquiry*. New York: Sage Publications.

Erlandson, D., P.L. Stark, and S.W. Ward. (1996). *Organizational Oversight: Planning and Scheduling for Effectiveness*. Larchmont, N.Y.: Eye on Education.

Goodlad, J. (1984). *A Place Called School*. New York: McGraw-Hill.

Gorden, T.J., and O. Helmer. (1964). *Report of Long-Range Forecasting Study*. RAND Corporation.

Granger, R.L. (1971). *Educational Leadership*. Scranton, Pa.: Intext Pub. Co.

Gredler, M.E. (1985). *Program Evaluation*. Englewood Cliffs, N.J: Prentice Hall.

Guba, E., and Y. Lincoln. (1981). *Effective Evaluation*. San Francisco: Jossey-Bass.

Hoyle, J. (1995). *Leadership and Futuring: Making Vision Happens*. Thousand Oaks, Calif.: Corwin Press.

Hoyle, J. (1990). "Texas Universities and Public Schools: Unification for Our Future." In *Educating Texans for the Information Age*, edited by V. Williams, N. Estes, and V. Bergin. Austin, Texas: College of Communication, The University of Texas at Austin.

Hoyle, J. (1978a, Sept.-Oct.). "Evaluation and Corrective Therapy." *American Corrective Therapy Journal* 22, 5: 141-144.

Hoyle, J. (1978b, Winter). "Teacher Versus Administrator: A Growing Crisis." *Planning and Changing* 9,4: 302-210.

Hoyle, J. (September 1975). "Evaluating an Alternative High School Program." *NASSP Spotlight*.

Hoyle, J., and R. Stalcup. (1982). "A Report on of the Evaluation of Dougherty County's Chapter 1 Program in Mathematics and Reading." Albany, Ga.: Chapter 1 Program.

Isaac, S., and W.B. Michael. (1985). *Handbook in Research and Evaluation*. (2nd Ed.) San Diego, Calif.: Edits Publisher.

The Joint Committee on Standards for Program Evaluation, J.R. Sanders, Chair. (1994). *The Program Evaluation Standards: How to Assess Evaluations for Educational Programs*. (2nd Ed.) Thousand Oaks, Calif.: Sage Publications.

Kahaner, L. (1996). *Competitive Intelligence*. New York: Simon & Schuster.

Kahn, H., et al. (1976). *The Next 2000 Years*. New York: Morrow and Co.

Kauffman, R., B. Watters, and J. Herman. (1996). *Educational Planning: Strategical, Technical, and Operational*. Lancaster, Pa.: Technomic Pub. Co., Inc.

Kerlinger, F. (1986). *Foundations of Behavioral Research*. (3rd Ed.) New York: Holt, Rinehart, and Winston.

Lazarus, M. (1982). *Evaluating Educational Programs*. Arlington, Va.: American Association of School Administrators.

McNamara, J. (1994). *Surveys and Experiments in Education Research*. Lancaster, Pa: Technomic Pub. Co., Inc.

McNamara, J. (1997). "Parental Views on the Biggest Problems Facing Public Schools: National Verses Local Findings." *International Journal of Educational Reform* 6,3: 377-389.

Metfessel, N.S., and W.B. Michael. (1967). "A Paradigm Involving Multiple Criterion Measures for the Evaluation of the Effectiveness of School Programs." *Educational and Psychological Measurement* 27: 931-943.

Miles, M., and A. Huberman. (1994). *Qualitative Data Analysis*. Thousand Oaks, Calif.: Sage Publications.

Montgomery, R. (1995). "Collaborative Planning for the 21st Century: A Suburban School District Envisions the Educated Child." Unpublished doctoral dissertation. College Station, Texas: Texas A&M University.

Morris, L.L. (1978a). *How to Calculate Statistics*. Beverly Hills: Sage Publications.

Morris, L.L. (Ed.) (1978b). *Program Evaluation Kit*. Beverly Hills: Sage Publications.

Olson, L. (January 1997). "Keeping Tabs on Quality." *Quality Counts. Education Week* Supplement. *Vol. XVI*.

Popham, J. (1993). *Educational Evaluation*. (3rd Ed.) Boston: Allyn and Bacon.

Rothstein, R. (1997). *What Do We Know about Declining (Or Rising) Student Achievement?* Arlington, Va.: Educational Research Service and the American Association of School Administrators.

Rowen, R. (1987). *Intuitive Management*. New York: Berkley Books.

Shaw, P. (1990). "The Organizational Cultures and Principals' Leadership Behaviors in Three Academically Dissimilar Middle Schools." Unpublished Doctoral Dissertation. College Station, Texas: Texas A&M University.

Smith, R.C., J.F. McNamara, and A. Barona. (1986). "Getting 'Good' Results from Survey Research: The SISD Experience." *Public Administration Quarterly* 10, 2: 233-248.

Stufflebeam, D., W. Foley, W. Gephart, E. Guba, R. Hammond, H. Merriman, and M. Provus. (1971). *Educational Evaluation and Decision Making*. Itasca, Ill.: F.E. Peacock Publishers.

Tuckman, B. (1979). *Conducting Educational Research*. (2nd Ed.) New York: Harcourt Brace, Javanovich, Inc.

Turney, B.L., and G.P. Robb. (1973). *Statistical Methods for Behavioral Science: With Feedback Exercises*. Beverly Hills, Calif.: Sage Publications.

Tyler, R. (1942). "General Statement of Evaluation." *Journal of Educational Research* 33: 492-501.

Worthen, R.R., and J.R. Sanders. (1987). *Educational Evaluation*. New York: Longman.

chapter 10

Values and Ethics of Leadership

America is in an ethics crisis. In a *USA Today* cover story, Del Jones (1997, pp. 1A-2A) reports that ". . . 48 percent of U.S. workers admit to taking unethical or illegal actions in the past year. . . . Workers say it's getting worse. Fifty-seven percent say they feel more pressure to be unethical than 5 year ago and 40 percent say it has gotten worse over the last year." At the same time, 78 percent of students admit that they have cheated and have difficulty distinguishing right from wrong (Stratton 1995).

Admonitions for high moral and ethical standards of behavior are easy to understand but more difficult to adhere to in contemporary society. Accused of unethical practices, school districts, universities, and the corporate world are looking for moral guidance. This renewed interest in ethics has led our colleges and universities to offer 11,000 courses in applied ethics (McBee 1985). Recent journal articles and books on values-based leadership and ethics fill bookstores and libraries, while ethics consultants travel the nation speaking on the subject.

Most school leaders are taught a code of ethics in their preparation programs. They sign professional employment contracts that require a vow of ethical conduct. But time and the urgency of completing paperwork or reports can make it tempting to cut corners and "forget" to tell the complete story. We hear of principals favoring one teacher over another in class and duty assignments, or administrators using categorical dollars for unauthorized programs in order to benefit students. Even though the vast majority of school leaders have never intentionally committed unethical behavior or condoned it for anyone else, the news is full of stories about school personnel who lose their direction and make immoral or unethical "mistakes" that ruin their careers and damage the professional image of all educators.

Amitai Etzioni (1996) in his book, *The New Golden Rule*, provides good advice for decision makers who face ethical dilemmas in school settings. He writes,

> A person should hold on to the values he or she finds most compelling, seeking to be joined by the community but steadfast even if others initially or ultimately do not approve. The community provides one with a normative foundation, a starting point, culture and tradition, fellowship, and a place for moral dialog, but is not the ultimate moral arbitrator. The members are. This is the ultimate reason that the communitarian paradigm entails a profound commitment to moral order that is basically voluntary, and to a social order that is well balanced with socially secured autonomy — the new golden rule. (p. 257)

James O'Toole (1995) supports Etzioni: "The ultimate disrespect of individuals is to attempt to impose one's will on them without regard for what they want or need and without consulting them. . . . Thus treating people with respect is what moral leadership is about, and nothing could be harder" (p.12). The difficult leadership process of consensus building through community involvement is a never-ending process, but anything less is inadequate for moral leadership.

Stephen Covey (1991) compares a sense of ethical consistency with "true north principles." According to Covey, "Correct principles are like compasses; they are always pointing the way. And if we know how to read them, we won't get lost, confused, or fooled by conflicting voices and values" (p. 19). Kidder (1996) found that communities seeking to determine their core values tend to converge on the same basic moral principles. "No matter how diverse the group, some versions of five core values emerge: honesty, fairness, compassion, respect, and responsibility" (p. 44). Thus, most of us have a moral compass that points to true north.

Superintendents and principals are handed the public trust and granted immense power to make decisions that affect many people. A paternalistic attitude toward the community can lead school officials to a breach of ethics that can wreck a career and damage the image of a district or school for years to come. Therefore, the authors have attempted to select the most important issues and topics surrounding the values and ethics of leadership that challenge practicing school leaders and the professors who prepare them. This chapter details the skills successful 21st century school leaders must possess to:

- Demonstrate ethical and personal integrity;
- Model accepted moral and ethical standards in all interactions;
- Promote democracy through public education;
- Exhibit multicultural and ethnic understanding and sensitivity; and
- Implement a strategy to promote respect for diversity.

Demonstrating Ethical and Personal Integrity

Charlemagne was a just and moral king who selected honest leaders for his governors. He was the first king in recorded history who personally listened to the problems of farm laborers and peasants, and he created schools for children of the poor as well as of the noble and rich. Charlemagne chose to rule using a set of moral beliefs to guide his behavior and the behavior of those under his command.

Albert Schweitzer was a surgeon, author, and compassionate servant to the natives of equatorial Africa. He chose service to others over riches and power to make the world a better place for thousands of poor and powerless people. For his lifetime of service to others, he was awarded the Nobel Prize for Peace.

St. Francis of Assisi, St. Augustine, Ghandi, and Mother Teresa are among the recognized moral leaders, but as you read this chapter you will certainly be able to list individuals you know personally who have lived the moral life and modeled integrity. Your parent(s), teacher, coach, minister, professor, brother, sister, or friend may come to mind as your model of integrity and moral leadership. These individuals in the words of O'Toole (1995), "know who they are." People with integrity do not spend their days scheming to rule the world or to capture its wealth. Emerson said it best: "See how the mass of men worry themselves into nameless graves, while here and there a great unselfish soul forgets himself into immortality" (Barton 1952, p. 95).

So what is ethics? Briggs (1959) writes that ethics is the objective study of morals. Pojman (1990, p. 3) notes that "ethics is concerned with values — not what is, but what ought to be." Regardless of the definition given, we know the essential importance of ethics in school leadership.

Weldon Beckner (1997), a professor of educational administration at Baylor University, teaches a course on professional ethics to future administrators. He calls for a much better-defined, content-based approach to teaching ethics to educational leaders rather than continued reliance on a set of ethics adapted from the business world. Beckner sees the education world as one with a unique set of ethical dilemmas caused by situations for which no easy solutions exist because each decision is based on more than cold facts. Beckner (1997, p. 3) says it this way:

Concepts of fairness, equality, human rights, and justice intervene. Any experienced educational leader can give many examples, such as the following:

(1) A student is an extreme discipline problem in the classroom. Should the student be punished in some way and left in the classroom, where additional disruptions will probably occur, to the loss of educational opportunity and possible physical harm to the other students, or should the student be expelled from school, in which case the student will probably get into more serious trouble on the streets and lose opportunities to receive needed education?

(2) Should students be placed in classrooms with certain teachers on the basis of what is best for most students or according to the desires of their politically powerful parents?

(3) Should a mediocre teacher who happens to be a very nice person and related to the city mayor be employed over a more competent one?

(4) How much "academic freedom" is appropriate for a health education teacher, who also happens to be politically powerful, who tends to venture into subject matter deemed inappropriate by local religious leaders?

(5) When is it ethical to ask for a release from an employment contract in order to accept a new and better position?

These examples fall into the categories of purely moral dilemmas (1,5) and moral vs. political dilemmas (2,3,4). Examples like these underline the need for improved instruction in the ethics of leadership. The historical, theoretical, and applied content of ethics must be included in the learning experience of all school administrators. Stronger preparation in the scholarship and practice of ethics is a first step in preparing future school leaders to make good ethical decisions based on intelligent thought and best moral judgment.

Michael P. Thomas (1992, p.47), who teaches future administrators at the University of Texas at Austin, believes that administrator preparation programs should be held to high ethical standards, which should address at least two issues: "the selection of people who on some basis it might be predicted have the potential for high-level performance in the administration of America's schools, and the character of the programs themselves and the resources available for their prosecution." He urges the National Policy Board for Educational Administration to work toward the development of ethical principles for the administration of educational organizations. Thomas goes on to suggest four professional [ethical] standards that should be key to administrators in schools:

(1) A keen sense of distributive justice, especially as it comes to bear in discussions of equity and access to educational opportunity.

(2) A commitment to acting on the belief that all individuals are ends and should never be used as means to an end; a belief that is consistent with the traditions of individualized education and objectives of helping each child reach his or her potential.

(3) A willingness to act on the basis of justice and fairness.

(4) A commitment to informing decisions with the knowledge of the best available research and the traditions of thought about issues related to those decisions. (p. 48)

Addressing the need for professors of educational administration to display strong moral and ethical leadership, Lesley H. Browder (1997, p. 33) of Hofstra University, asserts that:

There is the added expectation that, in the act of practicing what one professes, one will be embracing a vocational calling as a service ideal. A moral leader is concerned with acting responsibly on his or her held ideals and values and is motivated by ethical principles to help others . . . .

Robert Heslep (1997) of the University of Georgia believes that ethics must not be taught merely as a set of standards but should be included in each course and learning activity. He believes that "all participants in educational leadership logically are moral agents and therefore are logically subject to the Principles of Moral Value, Moral Rights, and Moral Duty" (p. 9).

Clearly, if school leaders are to do the right thing, they need much improved preparation and role models who will help them understand the insights and actions related to ethical decision making.

Modeling Accepted Moral and Ethical Standards in all Interactions

Mary Anne Raywid (1994) takes a convincing position on the importance of the ethical dimensions of administrative behavior by writing, "As administrators think and act, these behaviors have moral bearings, whether the actors intend them or not, indeed, as we have seen, even the decision not to intend them, that is, to exclude moral considerations from one's thinking is in itself a decision of profound moral bearing" (p. 539). Raywid advocates the following criteria for assessing ethical behavior.

- The integrity of one's dealings with others.
- One's commitment to operating according to the rules of the game.
- One's willingness to respect and honor the rights of all to freedom and growth opportunities.
- One's willingness to treat people as subjects rather than objects, as agents rather than pawns, as ends rather than means.
- One's commitment to exploring arrangements and possibilities employing a no harm principle — and to finding alternatives to doing injury.

Uchida, Cetron, and McKenzie (1996) asked a distinguished panel of 55 national leaders to list the most important behaviors for America's children and youth. Not surprisingly, "understanding and practicing honesty, integrity, and the golden rule" ranked highest. According to their report, "Treating others as we would like to be treated, personal and organizational integrity and basic honesty came up time after time, in nearly every section of this study" (p.20).

The charge for school leaders is clear — model accepted moral and ethical behavior. The importance of moral leadership is being raised in

169

each set of standards developed by professional administrator organizations. While AASA, NASSP, and NAESP, for example, have developed sets of "ethical standards," little formal attention has been given to the standards until the last five or six years. But when 78 percent of students admit that they have cheated and have lost their boundaries of right and wrong (Stratton 1995), it is time to pay serious attention to the ethical dimensions of leadership in schools. AASA has led the way with its 1993 publication *Professional Standards for the Superintendency* (Hoyle et al., 1993). AASA's Standard 8, "Values and Ethics of Leadership," was influenced by the earlier AASA *Statement of Ethics* (1981), which states that an ethical leader:

- Makes the well-being of students the fundamental value of all decision making and actions;
- Fulfills professional responsibilities with honesty and integrity;
- Supports the principle of due process and protects the civil and human rights of all individuals;
- Obeys local, state, and national laws and does not knowingly join or support organizations that advocate, directly or indirectly, the overthrow of the government;
- Implements the governing board of education's policies and administrative rules and regulations;
- Pursues appropriate measures to correct those laws, policies, and regulations that are not consistent with sound educational goals;
- Avoids using positions for personal gain through political, social, religious, economic, or other influences;
- Accepts academic degrees or professional certification only from duly accredited institutions;
- Maintains the standards and seeks to improve the effectiveness of the profession through research and continuing professional development; and
- Honors all contracts with fulfillment, release, or dissolution mutually agreed upon by all parties to the contract.

Lynn Beck (1996, pp. 8-11) stresses the vital importance of ethical leadership for school leaders by writing:

> We must wrestle with what it means to be moral leaders of school systems, individuals who embody justice and caring and demonstrate a genuine concern for the development of others and their communities. . . . At least four characteristics of our

professional lives compel us to take seriously the challenges at hand. . . . (1) The situations that challenge our moral reasoning are complex. (2) The stakes are high in situations that challenge our moral reasoning. (3) The impact of our moral decisions and actions is enormous. (4) Institutions that traditionally guided our moral reasoning are crumbling.

Thus, doing the right thing may be difficult and take more time, but anything less is wrong. According to Hope (1997, p. 7), "Truth and openness is believing in the people you work with and for. It is being able to honestly discuss problems with a superior even if it is critical of the superior. This open communication will be the source of strength for the organization."

Case Study: Sex Education and Ethical Leadership

Marvin Montgomery was elated. He had just received word that he had been named superintendent of a 70,000-student suburban school district near America's third largest city. The district had a good reputation in terms of student academic performance and had a strong tax base. The district had grown from 30,000 to 70,000 students in 15 years. Most students were from upper-income families of professionals who commuted to jobs in the city. The power structure in the community was controlled principally by "the old guard" who easily won election to the city council and school board. The power base was being threatened by the "new" neighbors who were thrusting themselves into community and school matters.

Montgomery had a smooth first year. Test scores remained high and one high school football team reached the state quarter finals. Then the hammer fell. In October, Montgomery received a two-page letter from a parent about two female health teachers in two of the high schools who assigned a book for students to read that included detailed information about sexual orientation and other sensitive issues. The letter also implied that the two health teachers appeared to be lesbians. The letter ended with a request for a conference with the writer and five other parents in two days.
What would you do? What is ethical leadership in this situation?

Promoting Democracy Through Public Education

Moral school leaders stress the importance of the democratic process and attempt to apply democratic principals in restructuring their schools for the 21st century. According to Slater and Crow (1996) there are major differences between what is said about democratic schooling and the reality. They tell us that,

Promoting and sustaining democracy in America has always been acknowledged as one of the most important goals of public schooling, but the rhetoric has not always lived up to the reality. Witness the recent school reform movement. Democracy was not the major question in *A Nation at Risk* (NCEE 1983). Economic competitiveness was. And while democracy has been a theme in school restructuring it has by no means been the dominant one. (p. 3)

While democracy is stressed in reform efforts (e.g., site-based decision making, which calls for greater staff and community involvement in decisions affecting the schools), the process is not without serious problems. Democracy can be a "messy" and time-consuming process. Some school districts claim that the site-based movement has made little difference in decision making and student performance. Other districts rave about better decisions about curriculum, personnel, and budgeting through the process of shared decision making. But as Slater and Crow have found, ". . . even in the most optimistic cases, conflict and instability are not uncommon" (p. 3).Slater and Crow continue: "Democracy is the rule by the many, but when many are involved in decision making, the diversity of opinions and points of view increases. The potential for miscommunication, disagreement, conflict, and confusion grows" (p. 5).

John Kenneth Galbraith (1996, p. 71) stresses the importance of education to a democratic society this way: " Education not only makes democracy possible; it also makes it essential. Education not only brings into existence a population with an understanding of the public tasks; it also creates their demand to be heard." Well-educated people will not stand in "silent subjugation" and allow a dictator to determine their fate.

The Bureaucratic Legacy in Schools

Short and Greer (1997) address the slow and painful change from the traditional hierarchy of decision making to open democracy. "Schools have been entrenched as bureaucratic organizations, offering teachers and students little say . . . . This type of organizational structure impedes the development of a professional organization. . . ." (p. 69)

School leaders in the past have been socialized to "take charge" of their school district or school and call the shots for all personnel. This take-charge model also has a firm grip on the minds of many school board members who perceive the need to hire a tough decision maker who can "come in here and bring some order to this district." Superintendents and personnel administrators prepare job descriptions for high school principals that list "instructional leader" as the highest priority, but actually hire individuals who can keep order and good discipline in the building. School board members express their desire for a decentralized school district with site-based decision making, but tell the superintendent to "keep reasonable control of what goes on at each campus." This problem of calling for democratic schools and empowerment of staff while also calling for controls to stifle individual initiative is common. This doublespeak is the primary reason that site-based decision making has not lived up to its promise in districts across America and it creates ethical shortfalls in school leadership.

To shed light on this problem and to suggest strategies to promote a more democratic approach to school leadership, Clark and Meloy (1989, p. 291-292) offer five propositions:

(1) Schools must be built on the assumption of the consent of the governed.

(2) Schools must be built on shared authority and responsibility, not delegation of authority and responsibility.

(3) The staff of a school must trade assignments and work in multiple groups to remain in touch with the schools as a whole.

(4) Formal rewards to the staff — salary, tenure, forms of promotion — should be under the control of the staff of the school as a whole.

(5) The goals of the school must be formulated and agreed to through group consensus. The professional staff is responsible for negotiating the acceptability of the goals to the school community.

School leaders must be sensitive to the differences between the schools' application of democracy versus society's application. In school, individual student's freedoms are somewhat limited. The rules for behavior are much more stringent than students find in most homes or at the mall. Teachers in restrictive school environments feel less freedom than they find on the "outside" as community leaders in civic, church, or political organizations. This organizational artifact of control within the walls of the school must be recognized and ameliorated by enlightened school leaders.

Democracy and the School Board

Democracy can sometimes create curves and bumps in the road to freedom of thought and action for individuals in roles of leadership. While Americans rely on elected and appointed officials to represent them in running our government and schools, voters can go to the polls and voice their discontent about these same officials. However, when a small minority of the voters go to the polls and elect "their" school board members, the democratic process can be in jeopardy. The frequent lack of interest in school affairs by the voters opens the doors for special interest groups to elect their representative to the school board. These groups' special interests might be honorable or destructive to democratic schooling. School superintendents live in fear of school board elections that lead to an undemocratic agenda. When board members are elected to press a religious or political agenda that is narrow and exclusive, school superintendents either hunker down and wait for the storm to pass, resign and look elsewhere, or stay and fight for a democratic process that places the students first.

But how does one remain ethical when the school board approves an item that is not sound policy for students? First, the superintendent must know board policy and state and federal law and be prepared to lead the board to decisions that will benefit the school district, its citizens, and, above all, each student. Next, if the board fails to approve a program, budget, or personnel recommendation made by the superintendent, he or she must act in an ethical manner and work with the board to reach the best solution for the district. Barber (1992) tells us why we must continue the pursuit of democracy in our school:

> Public education is education for citizenship. In aristocratic nations, in elitist regimes, in technocratic societies, it may appear as a luxury. In such places, educa-

tion is the private apprenticeship in the professions, the credentialing of elites, and perhaps the scholarly training of a few for lives of solitary intellect. But in democracies, education is the indispensable concomitant of citizenship. (p. 15)

It is, therefore, the responsibility of all school leaders and those who prepare them to embrace the tenets of democratic leadership, which will promote the ideals of freedom and teach all students the responsibilities of citizenship. Nothing else will do. Thomas Jefferson reminds us that: "If a nation expects to be ignorant and free, in a state of civilization, it expects what never was nor ever will be."

Democracy and Site-Based Teams. Given that the role of the superintendent in the district and the principal in each school is to model and promote democratic leadership that ensures open and honest debate on the best procedures and policies for school operation, principals can find themselves in a "catch 22" situation when site-based teams decide to implement a program, project, or activity that the

Case Study: Selecting an Assistant Principal

Amanda Lopez, a middle school principal, prides herself on being an ethical, democratic leader. She believes that she empowers her teachers to make the best instructional decisions for their students, gives them autonomy, and treats them as professionals. The school improvement team (SIT) has been functioning for three years and their efforts have led to greater staff harmony and improved student performance. Lopez is a member of the SIT, but also has final say regarding recommendations by SIT in matters pertaining to curriculum, personnel, and budget.

Recently, SIT was charged with interviewing three finalists for a new position of assistant principal. The committee presented their first choice, who was a young white male with six years experience as a 5th grade teacher. Lopez, however, ignored their recommendations and selected the committee's third choice, who was a Hispanic male with four years of high school coaching and teaching experience.

Did Lopez show ethical leadership by her choice? What would you have done?

principal views as not being in the best interest of the school. If the program or project is within board policy and the law, the principal is best advised to support the team decision but should feel free to voice any sound reservations. If, on the other hand, the team decision is detrimental to any staff member or student, then the principal is ethically obligated to fight the team decision with good data and rationale. After all, "To lead [in a democracy] is to influence others to achieve mutually agreed upon and socially valued goals that help an organization to stretch to a higher level. . . . Leading does not mean moving people through time in a status quo environment. That's management. Or bossing. Or something else." (Patterson 1997, p.5). (See Chapter 2 for a more complete discussion about school governance and democratic leadership.)

Exhibiting Multicultural and Ethnic Understanding and Sensitivity

Being sensitive to the feelings of others, especially those who are different, is perhaps the most important skill or understanding a school leader can possess. Webster's *Ninth Collegiate Dictionary* offers two related interpersonal definitions of "sensitivity." One is "the capacity of being easily hurt"; the other is "awareness of the needs and emotions of others." Erika Sanders caught the true essence of what it means to be sensitive during President Clinton's 1997 national town meeting on race in Akron, Ohio. Sanders, a Tallmadge High School senior, proclaimed, "The nation needs to become more sensitive to race issues. It's one thing for me to be outraged when something happens within the black community, but I need to be sensitive to the Hispanic community, to the Jewish community. The more sensitive you are, the more productive you can be" (McMahan 1997). School leaders find themselves coping with how to treat others with sensitivity during the rush of each school day. The NPBEA (1993) defines sensitivity as "perceiving the needs and concerns of others; dealing tactfully with others; working with others in emotionally stressful situations or in conflict; managing conflict; obtaining feedback; recognizing multicultural differences; and relating to people of varying backgrounds."

How can school leaders who often face public pressures created by insensitive parents, teachers, extremist groups, central-office administrators, state departments, or school boards manage to be sensitive to the problems of others around them?

And how do superintendents, principals, and other school administrators increase their interpersonal sensitivity to cultural and ethnic differences?

Diversity and multiculturalism is no longer news to school personnel. By the year 2005, in practically all urban areas and in several states, the minority will be the majority and the number of minority students will continue to increase. These demographic changes have strengthened interests in the cultural and ethnic roots for Americans. While many of us celebrate these differences and find joy in learning more about the historical roots of all Americans, some people close their eyes and hearts to difference. As a result, inequality remains a reality in some communities. School leaders who find themselves in communities that proclaim racial and cultural equality, but fail to back their claims with equal support for all school children and youth must take the ethical high ground and lead the way to equal opportunity in the name of legal and moral justice.

School leaders struggle with creating educational programs that respect all cultures and lifestyles without losing the focus of a common unity of purpose. Lieberman (1993, p. 165) writes, "Proposals for a curriculum that will emphasize what the American people share in common instead of their differences are an understandable reaction to increasing heterogeneity. The problem is that a certain level of unity is required to achieve agreement on what students should be unified over." While hundreds of multicultural education programs across America are carefully planned, other programs are little more than window dressing. People who oppose multicultural education take the self-righteous approach that they treat every person the same and, therefore, question why it is necessary to teach black, Hispanic, or Native American culture and history if we are all Americans. School leaders who face this narrow-minded view of multiculturalism must continue to strengthen curriculum and instructional programs that respect differences but bring unity of purpose. Such a curriculum will help ensure a life of achievement for all students, regardless of ethnicity.

The most successful multicultural education programs/curricula are those that educators integrate into the total school environment. To guide this effort, school leaders must promote the inclusion of multicultural programming in the schools. Professors who prepare future school administrators, inservice programmers, and professional associations need to offer learning opportunities about

173

multicultural differences among school children and youth. School leaders must continue learning about the differences among the people in their districts and the students they serve. This knowledge makes it possible to use the strengths of those differences to bring the school together as one family in a community of respect for the unique gifts that each student, teacher, and parent brings to the school (Hoyle and Crenshaw 1997).

Lachman and Taylor (1995, p.26) observe that "Many school districts have developed successful, comprehensive programs in which student achievement has improved, intergroup relations are more positive, and community and family involvement have increased." This has proven to be true in Somerville, Texas, where elementary principal Richard Skuza (1997) worked with others to create a Parent Center. Skuza worked for two years to interest parents, primarily those from low-income, multiracial neighborhoods, in becoming part of the school family. Attempts at back-to-school or family nights met with little success. A few parents would silently slip into the school, spend a few minutes in their child's classroom, and leave without talking to anyone.

Frustrated in his efforts to bring Hispanic, African-American, and Anglo parents together to help their children and to support multicultural education programs, Skuza created a new vision. After reading the literature on parent involvement, integrated school services, and multicultural programming, Skuza found funds and began working on his vision of a Parent Center. The center's success exceeded all expectations. Parents came to the center for fellowship, food, and educational opportunities, which included reading, skill development for parents, and multicultural projects and programs produced by the children. Within two years the center became "the place" for family gatherings. Skuza found several positive spin-offs from the center, including improved student attendance and student test performance. Skuza, like hundreds of other school leaders, was doing the right thing to create a learning community that promotes multicultural and ethnic tolerance and understanding.

Waldemar Rojas, superintendent of San Francisco's multicultural school system, is leading the community by involving professional staff and hundreds of volunteers to help raise the scholastic achievement of minority students. Rojas' multifaceted effort includes preschool for incoming kindergartners; three parent-resource centers in African-American, Hispanic, and Asian-American neighbor-

Case Study — Multicultural Sensitivity in the Principal's Office

Jack Burkhart had enjoyed nine years as principal of Wilson High School in a bedroom community of a major city in a southeastern state. His community was typical of many fast-growing areas that once consisted of farming and rural surroundings. Suburbanization was rapidly turning the community into strip shopping malls and new housing areas. The school population was changing from locals born in the county to "move-ins" from the East, West, deep South, Europe, India, and Asia. Old Wilson High was changing.

The new parents were creating intense pressure for more college prep math and science and more stress on higher ACT and SAT scores. While the school board patiently listened to the requests from these "Yankees and foreigners," they were slow to act. Since the board members were, with one exception, locals, they felt that the high school was doing a fine job in educating the students. One board member told a parent group: "We welcome your comments and suggestions about how to improve the schools, but remember we send over 70 percent of our kids to college now. We are proud of our high school faculty and Jack Burkhart."

A group of parents led by four upwardly mobile professionals new to the community made an appointment to visit Burkhart in his office. The group began telling him how weak his curriculum was and demanded that their kids be taken out of classes that were integrated with African-Americans and "unmotivated farm kids." The spokesperson for the group told Burkhart: "We believe that under the guise of cooperative learning and other education fads, you and the teaching staff have dumbed down the curriculum to the point that our kids will not be competitive to enter the best universities on the east and west coasts. We want to know what you are going to do about our concerns?"

What steps should Jack take? What is the ethical thing to do?

hoods; tutoring centers; handbooks for parents to help their children in reading, math, and science; and having churches dedicate one Sunday each month to education. The children and youth in San Francisco are feeling success as a result of this communitywide effort. Reading and math scores have risen steadily in the 62,000-student district where more than 50 percent of the students are eligible for free lunches and one-third do not speak fluent English.

Rojas strongly believes that the schools of San Francisco can make major strides in student achievement if the entire community joins to help, explaining that "People for too long have thought schools were the only ones responsible for educating children, and that 180 days a year was the answer. We can't be the only player." This communitarian approach to moral leadership is not only improving test scores, it also an example of a school leader doing the right thing for all of the children and youth of San Francisco (Reinhard 1997).

Case Study — Who Are Your Gifted Students?

Elaine Sanders was a star elementary school principal. She was past president of her state principals association and had been runner-up in the state Principal-of-the Year competition. Her school was rated exemplary according to test results and class attendance. She hand picked her faculty when they opened the new school three years ago and the PTO was extremely active and supportive of all programs. The PTO, the superintendent, and the community were especially proud of the school's award-winning gifted-and-talented program, which included 120 students.

During Sanders' third year, five African-American and three Hispanic parents made an appointment to speak with her about the gifted-and-talented program. The parents wanted to know why only 19 minority children — 10 of whom were Asian American — were in the gifted-and-talented classes, given that 20 percent (116 of 580) of the student body were African-Americans or Hispanics.

What would be your response to the parents of these children? Is there an ethical dilemma here? What steps should Sanders take to correct this situation?

Implementing a Strategy To Promote Respect for Diversity

Religious Differences

Religious differences in America cause serious schisms in school communities. The issues of displaying religious scenes and symbols, organized school prayer, Bible study, and teaching or not teaching religion continue to occupy the time of school administrators and school boards. Over 80 percent of Americans claim to believe in a supreme being, while only 20 percent actually practice their religion by attending church, synagogue, mosque, or temple on a regular basis. But whether people regularly practice their religious beliefs has little bearing on their feelings about religion and the schools. Every one has an opinion. These opinions have led to prohibiting Christmas decorations that include religious messages or symbols and greatly restricting traditional Halloween celebrations, costumes, and decorations.

When a group feels that it is under religious attack or that its rights are being denied, the entire community can become embroiled in heated and lengthy controversy with school authorities. For example, some believe that their children's schools should begin the day with a prayer, while others object to their children praying. Despite the First Amendment's guarantee of freedom to practice one's religion and the right to avoid the practice of religion, emotions are tapped when religious practices occur in schools. According to Meyers and Meyers (1995, p. 320),

> It is the clash of basic American values that prompts most, if not all, court cases about religious freedoms in schools. . . . All of this has direct implications for teachers' and school administrators' decisions and actions in at least two ways: (1) teachers and administrators must know and follow the Constitution and the law in what they do, and (2) they must decide what to do when the application of court decisions to the specific situations they face is not clear. . . . We suggest the following: (1) Know the applicable court ruling and the law; (2) make sure you understand the issues being disputed and the beliefs behind the positions being advocated by both sides; and

175

(3) respond to the specific situation carefully and rationally and in a way that avoids serious confrontations, angry words, and hurt feelings.

In recent years, parents and religious groups have pressured the courts and school leaders to include certain religious teachings in the school curriculum. These efforts have led to release time for religious instruction during the school day. The courts have ruled that this practice is acceptable as long as the instruction in not held on school property and does not use public moneys.

Another strategy designed to teach religion in school is known as the child benefit theory. The theory is based on the fact that public funds may be given to students attending private schools for religious instruction. These funds are intended to benefit the child and not promote a religious belief. Meyers and Meyers (1995, p. 326) claim that

> Probably the decision that set the clearest guidelines regarding the use of public funds for private, religious education was *Lemon v. Kurtzman* (1971), which listed three questions that need to be addressed in such cases: (1) Does the function for which funds are being spent have a secular purpose? (2) Does the primary effect of the function either advance or inhibit religion? (3) Does funding the function excessively entangle government and religion? These three questions have become known as the Lemon test.

Clearly, the issues surrounding religion in schools are not going away. The issues and emotions will resurface and will continue to create litigation, court rulings and problems for school leaders trying to do the right thing. Graduate preparation programs must teach prospective administrators both the basic tenets of world religions and what is legal with regard to religion in the schools.

Diversity

Terms and concepts such as "mainstreaming," "inclusion," "multiculturalism," "multilingualism," and "diversity" have become important issues to all school leaders. To provide moral leadership means treating all children and youth with respect and providing them with equal opportunity to benefit academically and socially as members of the school family.

Principals and superintendents must be the models of virtue in language and deed on issues of gender, race, and the special needs of students, faculty, staff, and community members. To claim that one is sensitive to these issues, but make decisions that disregard the needs and feelings of others is a breach of ethical conduct. Boschee and colleagues (1997) support this view, noting that a school leader is:

> [T]he role model for educational leadership in your school or district. As a result of your guiding example and informed leadership, you and your faculty will have the opportunity to develop the best and most effective programs serving all your students. (p.xiv)

Conclusion

To be a virtuous school leader when much of society lacks virtue is a challenge of huge proportions. News headlines tell about corporate leaders accepting illegal bribes and political leaders accepting illegal campaign funds. Watergate, Tailhook, and Whitewater make us wonder where ethical behavior among America's leaders is gone. Likewise, when we hear about a superintendent, central-office, or building administrator being charged for a violation of professional ethics or being indicted for a major crime, we are saddened and wonder why. Why do individuals lose their moral centers and commit unethical acts that ruin their careers and damage the image of their organizations and professions? Must a need for power and its manifestations always push individuals to act in self-centered ways that cause them to lose a sense of right and wrong? Absolutely not.

Ethical behavior is taught by parents, teachers, coaches, church leaders, and school administrators by the words they use and the deeds they do. The formal study and teaching of ethics is taught in our universities, corporate board rooms, the military, and other organizations. The overwhelming majority of all individuals are moral agents of correctness who model ethical practices for others. To prepare ethical school leaders requires programs that include problem-based curricula that stress moral behavior. These programs must underline what it means to be ethical and to provide moral leadership.

School leaders must have a passion for a communitarian sharing of power and a commitment to honesty and integrity. Schools can no longer tolerate administrators who keep a "hidden agenda" about programs, personnel, and budget. Ethical behavior means that administrators and teachers become moral agents for each other and for students. The values and ethics of leadership must be lived by all educators if all students are to be helped to become the best that they can be.

Use the following Skill Accomplishment Checklist to asses you skill level on each of the important topics discussed in this chapter.

Skill Assessment Checklist for Chapter 10

Skills	Readings and Activities for Skill Mastery
Demonstrate ethical and personal integrity.	**Readings:** Covey (1991), Etzioni (1996), Pojman (1990), *The School Administrator* (October 1996) **Activities:** 1. Interview a respected minister, teacher, military officer, and high school senior about how they maintain their integrity and remain ethical. 2. Write a five-page essay about a time when you could have compromised your integrity but decided to do the right thing.
Model accepted moral and ethical standards in all interactions.	**Readings:** Maxey (1991), Kidder (1996), Raywid (1994) **Activities:** 1. Review the five ethical dilemmas presented by Beckner in this chapter and conduct group discussions about solutions. 2. Re-read the "Sex Education and Ethical Leadership" case study. Ask each group member to write a one-page action plan to share and discuss.
Promote democracy though public education.	**Readings:** Barber (1992), Galbraith (1996), Maxey (1991), Short and Greer (1997), Slater and Crow (1996),) **Activities:** 1. Discuss the democratic and undemocratic programs and behaviors in your district or school. 2. Review the case study "Selecting an Assistant Principal. " Was Amanda Lopez ethical? Write a 10-page paper to defend your position.
Exhibit multicultural and ethnic understanding and sensitivity.	**Readings:** Bennett (1995), Hoyle and Crenshaw (1997), Lachman and Taylor (1995) **Activities:** 1. Prepare a 20-min. speech about multicultural education for an audience that is 35 percent Anglo, 35 percent African American, 15 percent Hispanic, and 15 percent Asian American. 2. Evaluate your district curriculum as to its multicultural components. 3. Investigate the number of ethnic groups in your district and their cultural customs and holidays.
Implement a strategy to promote respect for diversity.	**Readings:** Boschee, et al. (1997); Corrigan (1997); Etzioni (1996); Lachman and Taylor (1995); Meyers and Meyers (1995), pp. 319-330; Spring (1991), pp. 233-236 **Activities:** 1. Develop a research paper on the topic of religious diversity in America. 2. Prepare a 20-min. presentation on the most controversial issues related to religion and the schools. 3. Define and discuss inclusion, diversity, gender equity, and special populations.

Resources

American Association of School Administrators. (1981). *The American Association of School Administrators Code of Ethics*. Arlington, Va.: author.

American Association of School Administrators. (October 1996). *The School Administrator*, 9 (54). Theme Issue.

Barber, B. (1992). *An Aristocracy of Everyone*. New York: Ballentine Books.

Barton, B. (1952). *The Man Nobody Knows*. New York: Collier Books, Macmillan Pub. Co.

Beck, L. (October 1996). "Why Ethics? Thoughts on the Moral Challenge Facing Educational Leaders." *The School Administrator* 9, 54: 8-11.

Beckner, W. (1997, August). "Doing the Right Thing: Ethics Foundations for Educational Leaders." Paper presented at the annual meeting of the National Council of Professors of Educational Administration in Vail, Colo.

Bennett, C. (1995). *Multicultural Education: Theory and Practice*. (2nd ed.) Boston, Mass.: Allyn & Bacon.

Blackwood, R., and A. Herman, eds. (1975). *Problems in Philosophy West and East*. Englewood Cliffs, N.J.: Prentice-Hall.

Boschee, F., B. Beyer, J. Engleking, and M. Boschee. (1997). *Special and Compensation Programs: The Administrator's Role*. Lancaster, Pa.: Technomic Pub. Co., Inc.

Briggs, M. (1959). *Handbook of Philosophy*. New York: Philosophical Library.

Browder, L. (August 1997). "Tomorrow's Service Ideal: A Vocational Calling or Token Obligation?" Paper presented at the annual meeting of the National Council of Professors of Educational Administration in Vail, Colo.

Clark, D., and J. Meloy. (1989). "Renouncing Bureaucracy: A Democratic Structure for Leadership in Schools. In *Schooling for Tomorrow: Directing Reform to Issues that Count*, edited by T. Sergiovanni and J. Moore. Boston, Mass.: Allyn & Bacon.

Corrigan, D. (1997). "The Role of the University in Community Building." *The Education Forum* 62: 14-24.

Covey, S. (1991). *Principle-Centered Leadership*. New York: Summit Books.

Etzioni, A. (1996). *The New Golden Rule*. New York: Basis Books.

Foster, W. (1986). *Paradigms and Promises: New Approaches to Educational Administration*. Buffalo, N.Y.: Prometheus Books.

Fulghum, R. (1988). *All I Really Need to Know I Learned in Kindergarten*. New York: Villard Books.

Galbraith, J. (1996). *The Good Society*. Boston, Mass.: Houghton Mifflin Co.

Heslep, R. (1997, August). "Ethics in Educational Leadership." Paper presented at the annual meeting of the National Council of Professors of Educational Administration in Vail, Colo.

Hope, M. (April 16, 1997). "The Importance of Ethics in School Leadership." Paper presented at Texas A&M University.

Hoyle, J., et al. (1993). *Professional Standards for the Superintendency*. Arlington, Va.: American Association of School Administrators.

Hoyle, J., and H. Crenshaw. (1997). *Interpersonal Sensitivity: The School Leadership Library*. Larchmont, N.Y.: Eye on Education.

Jones, D. (April 4-6, 1997). "48% of Workers Admit to Unethical or Illegal Acts." *USA Today*.

Kidder, R. (1996). "Do Values Top Your Agenda?" *The School Administrator* 9, 54: 44.

Kouzes, J., and B. Posner. (1987). *The Leadership Challenge*. San Francisco, Calif.: Jossey-Bass.

Lachman, L., and L. Taylor. (1995). *Schools for All*. Albany, N.Y.: Delmar Publishers.

Lieberman, M. (1993). *Public Education: An Autopsy*. Cambridge, Mass.: Harvard University Press.

Maxey, S. (1991). *Educational Leadership: A Critical Pragmatic Perspective*. New York: Bergin and Garvey.

McBee, S. (December 9, 1985). "The State of American Values." *U.S. News and World Report*.

McMahan, K. (December 5, 1997). "Ohio Students Eloquence Speaks Volumes About Race Issues in U.S." *The Houston Chronicle*

Meyers, C., and L. Meyers. (1995). *The Professional Educator*. Albany, N.Y.: Wadsworth Publ. Co.

National Commission of Excellence in Education. (1983). *A Nation at Risk: The Imperative for Educational Reform*. Washington, D.C.: U.S. Government Printing Office.

National Policy Board for Educational Administration. (1993). *Interpersonal Sensitivity*. Fairfax, Va.: author.

OToole, J. (1995). *Leading Change*. New York: Ballentine Books.

Patterson, J. (1997). *Coming Clean About Organizational Change*. Arlington, Va.: The American Association of School Administrators.

Pojman, L. (1990). *Ethics: Discovering Right and Wrong*. Belmont, Calif.: Wadsworth Publ. Co.

Raywid, M. (1994). "Some Moral Dimensions of Administrative Theory and Practice." In *The UCEA Document Base*, edited by W. Hoy. New York: McGraw-Hill.

Reinhard, B. (November 26,1997). "S. F. Schools Launch Campaign To Help Minority Students." *Education Week*.

Short, P., and J. Greer. (1997). *Leadership in Empowered Schools*. Upper Saddle River, N.J.: Merrill.

Skuza, R. (1997). "The Impact of an Elementary Parent Center on Parent Involvement and Student Classroom Performance as Perceived by Parents and Professional Staff in Somerville, Texas." Unpublished dissertation. Texas A&M University, College Station, Texas.

Slater, R., and C. Crow. (1996). *Educating Democracy: The Role of Systematic Leadership*. Fairfax, Va.: National Policy Board for Educational Administration.

Spring, J. (1991). *American Education: An Introduction to Social and Political Aspects*. (5th ed.). New York: Longman.

Stratton, J. (1995). *How Students Have Changed*. Arlington, Va.: The American Association of School Administrators.

Thomas, M. (1992). "Strengthening Professionalism: The Ethical Dimensions. In *School Leadership: A Blueprint for Change*, edited by S. Thomson. Newbury Park, Calif.: Corwin Press.

Uchida, D., M. Cetron, and F. McKenzie. (1996). *Preparing Students for the 21st Century*. Arlington, Va.: The American Association of School Administrators.

appendix A | *Teaching the Standards*

Acquiring the skills to be a successful school leader requires time and effort. After years of education, training, and on-the-job seasoning, some educators move to the forefront as a result of their experiences, while others become lost in the ever-changing environment that characterizes education today. The authors believe that this textbook will help enable more men and women to move forward as skilled, ethical, and accomplished leaders. The 10 chapters in this book are based on the knowledge base, skills, and standards that have emerged in the discipline and professional practice of educational administration over the past century.

Standards developed by AASA, NAESP, NASSP, NCATE, NPBEA, ASCD, CCSSO and various other education organizations and universities and state departments of education are the benchmarks that measure the criteria for successful performance in the complicated world of school leadership. Mastery of every skill related to each standard may not be possible, but school leaders and the professors who prepare them should strive to master the structural components of each area and to "sharpen their saws" throughout their careers.

So which teaching and learning strategies hold the greatest promise for producing the successful school leaders for the new millennium? Universities involved in administrator preparation are in the process of updating curricula, which include the standards and skills in this text. The authors have attempted to assist curriculum developers by combining all sets of standards and skills to facilitate the cross-referencing of course objectives. (A review of current standards reveals an 80-90 percent overlap between indicators.) Though academic preparation programs should not be limited to the standards/skills included in this text, the knowledge base undergirding them is the accumulation of research and wisdom about educational administration as an academic discipline and professional practice.

What then is an ideal model for teaching and preparing the "best and brightest" school leaders for

the 21st century? The following is our attempt to combine the best practices found in the most respected university programs in the United States and Canada to present a preparation program that ensures that students master the key skills and knowledge needed to meet the standards in this text.

The Ideal Leadership Preparation Model

The Ideal Leadership Preparation model is a combination of the best preparation practices, which involve the knowledge base and clinical or field-base experiences. It is based on ideas drawn from traditional programs, which are campus-bound and require a one-year or two consecutive-semester residency for students, and from the recent Professional Studies Model (PSM) designed for full-time administrators and others who wish to pursue the doctorate. Though the Ideal model is primarily directed at the doctorate, most of the ideas can be applied to Master's and Specialist degree programs.

Rationale for the Ideal Leadership Preparation Model

While we believe that full-time study on a university campus is a very valuable learning experience, it is no longer a viable option for many potential and practicing school administrators who desire to pursue a graduate degree and licensure. Administrator preparation is part of the "hyperinformation age" and must undergo major changes if schools are to be led by outstanding professionals. Students in educational administration, especially those with families, can no longer count on recovering the financial loss of one year's salary and loans while in full-time study. Therefore, program planners have turned to various forms of the PSM, which allows students to fulfill the residency requirement without giving up their jobs. Upper-level university administrators, while reluctant to drop traditional residency requirements, have relented to alternative professional degree models in order to enroll students.

Since 1990 numerous PSMs have been developed, including those at The University of Colorado-Denver, Indiana State University, Texas A&M University, Duquesne University, Harvard University, Baylor University, University of Texas-Arlington, The College of William & Mary, and Vanderbilt University.

The PSM centers on a cohort of students who are practicing or aspiring administrators selected by a committee consisting of both university faculty and practicing school administrators. The students undergo a one-year program to earn a Master's or Specialist degree and a three- to four-year program for the Ed.D. or Ph.D. Efforts are made to teach knowledge "domains" rather than traditional courses that follow no sequence. The faculty consist of both university and clinical faculty (i.e., superintendents and principals) who plan and teach together. Classes are conducted over "extended weekends," intensive summer sessions running for two to four weeks, or for five hours one night per week. Program planners attempt to connect the in-class content with the real world of practice and the final product is usually action research, often a combination of qualitative and quantitative methodologies, focused on local school evaluation needs.

The cohort is together for all class and most clinical sessions, but members usually conduct independent research projects. Some of the programs require students to undergo comprehensive written and oral exams while others employ a portfolio performance evaluation of each student. Some students are encouraged to share databases and complete co-dissertations. Student evaluations of their programs are generally positive with comments about the strong bonding among cohort members and the value of team learning. The students praise the faculty for their willingness to commute to their homesite and their ease of communication with distance learning via satellite TV, e-mail, faxes, the web, and video conferencing.

The Duquesne IDPEL Model. Duquesne University's Interdisciplinary Doctoral Program for Educational Leaders (IDPEL), which began in 1993, includes most of the elements described in the Ideal Model (Henderson 1995). The knowledge and skill areas in the Duquesne program are similar to the standards and skills in this text because their program is centered on *The Professional Standards*

for the Superintendency. A cohort of 30 is selected every three years into a program of 60 semester hours of study. Daytime classes are held two weekdays each month and on occasional Saturdays during the school year. Summer sessions lasting nine non-consecutive days each are conducted during the three years of cohort study.

Professional problem-solving teams, study groups, continuous networking, and benchmarking and feedback on each participant's progress are features of the program. Instructional delivery modes include Duquesne faculty lectures, expert practitioner seminars, nationally renowned resource persons, study guides, simulations, case studies for problem-based learning, position papers, video analyses, computer networking, and field studies. Each cohort member selects a campus faculty advisor as well as a field mentor-practitioner and becomes part of a scholarly community of practitioners and university faculty.

For more information on the Duquesne program, contact James E. Henderson, Director, IDPEL, Duquesne University, School of Education, 410B Canevin Hall, Pittsburgh, PA 15228-0502.

For complete descriptions of successful Professional Studies Models, see Guzman, S., and R. Muth, "Revolution, and Collaboration: Creating New Programs and Paradigms in Doctoral Studies for Educational Leaders," a paper presented in August 1997 at the Annual Conference of the National Council for Professors of Educational Administration in Vail, Colorado. Also see Bratlien, M., S. Genzer, J. Hoyle, and A. Oates. (January 1992). "The Professional Studies Doctorate: Leaders for Learning." *Journal of School Leadership* 2, 75-89.

For a description of a Masters degree PSM program, contact Elaine L. Wilmore, Director of Educational Leadership, The University of Texas at Arlington, Box 19227 Arlington, Texas 76019-0227.

For a description of a Specialist degree or PSM degree, contact Connie L. Fulmer, Associate Chair, Dept. of Leadership and Policy Studies, Northern Illinois University Dekalb, IL 60155.

The Ideal Program Design Steps

The Ideal Program is a model that can be adapted for use in a variety of graduate school settings. The following steps and components are offered to assist faculty teams in examining current programs or in planning new ones:

Step 1: Mapping the standards. A three-person team of campus and clinical faculty should take the necessary time to cross reference and map the standards and related skills in this book and other specific skills found among the "bullets" in the ISLLC listing, NPBEA's 21 Domains, and NCATE's *Curriculum Guide* criteria with program course requirements. This mapping can be done by lining up the nine standards/skills in this book with the course requirements in the program (See Figure A1 on page 184). After the mapping is complete, the faculty must determine instructional areas that need enhancing within the faculty and identify faculty in other departments or divisions with the expertise needed. Caution should be taken to identify individuals who support the PSM and are sensitive to the needs of very busy adult learners. The authors have found that some of the busiest students become the high performers who produce scholarly dissertations. Experience has shown that carefully selected professors are honored to be invited to teach in the program and become active committee members.

Step 2: Selecting a cohort of students. Select a cohort of 15-30 students who have the talent, interest, and character for a career in public school administration. The selection process should be a joint effort among public school superintendents, principals, state department leaders, and the university. Each applicant should present a portfolio consisting of academic records, past achievements, and future plans. Also, the selection committee should review GRE or other exam scores, a writing sample, and letters of reference from former employers, and conduct an intensive interview of each student. If an assessment center is accessible and affordable, its use can be valuable to corroborate other selection data.

Step 3: Beginning portfolios. Once cohort members have been chosen, assign a mentor to each student. Mentors will administer a pre-assessment of each cohort member's skill level on each of the nine standards and then guide the student in preparing a portfolio that should include a curriculum map of the standard/skill areas and projects completed to demonstrate mastery of each stan-

dard. The projects should include research papers, evidence of actual school improvement efforts in the student's district or school, and targeted personal professional development activities. The mentor and student should keep a record of each successful step and work together to find alternative learning strategies to seek mastery of each standard/skill.

Duquesne faculty developed a practica checklist, which provides a framework for the student and mentor to gauge the student's progress in demonstrating mastery of the identified skill indicators. Each semester the mentor and student confer regarding the student's progress. The student presents evidence (written/graphic evidence is preferred) to the mentor of each skill indicator mastered. Once the mentor is convinced of the student's conceptual and practical mastery of a skill, the mentor initials the dates and area of completion. The following are helpful tips for ensuring the success of the Ideal Model.

- Develop an umbrella delivery system for each standard area by carefully fusing the course content with related field or clinical learnings. The program must not be limited to skill mastery, it must be an intellectually challenging set of learning experiences that requires students to think beyond the skill base to the why, the what, and the how of school leadership and problem solving. Emphases on problem-based learning activities facilitate the fusing of theory to practice. This delivery system will ensure that the program is not a set of mechanical management skills that mark some state certification requirements, but one that challenges the multiple phases of intelligence (Gardner 1994).
- Take advantage of new delivery technologies (i.e., distance learning, satellite TV, e-mail, video conferencing, the web, and the fax). The web, along with chat windows, e-mail, fax, and electronic white boards give professors and students ample opportunity for dialog and information exchange.

After each semester the campus and clinical professors should conduct a comprehensive performance assessment using the Skill Accomplishment Checklist at the end of each chapter of this text to determine cohort members' mastery level on each of the nine standards/skill areas. This information will provide each student and instructor valuable prescriptive data. Also, each student should keep a reflective journal as part of his/her portfolio throughout the program to record events, ideas, and knowledge acquired during the journey toward the doctorate. The entries in the journal are a valuable artifact for the learner and a record for others who follow.

Problem-based learning. Each learning activity should be tied to a variety of problem-based learning opportunities. The use of actual district or school problems or case studies from the literature will lift the course content to higher meaning and relevance for the learner (Bridges and Hallinger 1993). When designing problem-based learning units, remember that:

(1) The starting point of the learning is a problem.

(2) The problem should be one that students are apt to face in the future.
(3) Subject matter is organized around the problem rather than the discipline.
(4) The student has the major responsibility for learning and instruction.
(5) Small groups are preferred to individual study.

Research. During the first year of the program, each student should be encouraged to begin a research agenda by identifying an area of research interest. By identifying a research problem early, students can become more focused on literature

---

Figure A.1 **Mapping The Standards/Skills/Indicators with Courses**

Standard and Related Skills/Indicators	University Courses
Standard One: Provide Visionary Leadership (Chapter One)	
Skill— Create and effectively communicate a district or school vision.	EDAD 621, Educational Planning/Futurism EDAD 622, Total Quality Management of Ed
Skill—Establish priorities in the context of the community culture and student and staff needs.	EDAD 641 Community Ed. EDAD 639, Foundations of EDAD EDAD 618, Multicultural Ed. EDAD 689, Interagency Collaboration
Skill—Conduct district and school climate assessments.	EDAD 620, Program Evaluation EDCI 607, Supervision
Skill—Assess student achievement data.	EDAD 620, Program Evaluation EPSY 622, Tests and Measurements
Skill—Develop a strategic plan for the district or school.	EDAD 621, Educ. Planning/Futurism EDAD 622, Total Quality Management of Ed EDAD 615, The Superintendency
Skill—Empower others to reach high levels of performance.	EDAD 604 & 605, Elem & Sec. Principalship EDAD 653, The Nature & Prob. of Administrative Behavior
Skill—Align financial, human, and material resources with the vision, mission, and goals of the district.	EDAD 622, Total Quality Management of Ed Systems EDAD, 608 School Finance EDAD, 651 Business Principles

Note-The same mapping strategy should be followed for each of the other eight standards and related ISLLC, NPBEA, and NCATE indicators and skills. The majority of the courses that address the skills will be those in educational administration, curriculum, educational psychology, and foundations. However, courses in anthropology, political science, management, and systems analysis, among others, can help strengthen the knowledge and skill base. This mapping process will assist program planners and each professor in determining where the major overlaps occur and spotting the gaps in the delivery system. In each skill area a blend of classroom content and field experience is the key to student progress toward mastery. The mentor and the student must work closely and continually to align the student's learning experiences with the standards and related skills.

reviews and research methodologies. At this point, the mentor's role is to familiarize students with a wide range of related literature and research studies that will lead the student into the challenging and exciting world of scholarly inquiry.

Group membership. The cohort should be strongly encouraged to become active members of their state and national administrator associations and to attend and present programs at conferences and conventions. Active membership in these organizations provides students with learning opportunities and gives them visibility for professional opportunities.

Interpersonal and presentation skills. Each cohort member should be provided opportunities to give formal speeches, conduct group meetings, practice conflict-resolution skills, serve as the Master-of-Ceremonies for banquets, practice proper introductions of dignitaries and other people, learn listening skills, participate in fitness and proper nutrition programs, and be provided advice on proper dress for various occasions. Each student should be videotaped while practicing some of these skills and critiqued by faculty and other cohort members.

Creating a fulfilling student experience. Throughout the three- or four- year time frame, each faculty member must strive to model democratic leadership and to contribute to the scholarly community. Every effort must be made to help each student "capture the true spirit" of the university even though they spend very little time mixing with the regular student body or being part of traditional campus life. These "part-time" graduate students can become the strongest supporters of the university when they take their places as leading superintendents, central-office administrators, principals, and leaders in community colleges and universities.

Example of Instructional Delivery for Standard 1: Visionary Leadership

Standard 1 includes a wide-ranging knowledge base with key skill indicators. In order to facilitate student learning of the intricacies of this standard, a member of the campus faculty must be responsible for coordinating its delivery. A faculty member with expertise in visioning, planning, and continuous improvement, paired with a clinical faculty member with skills in conducting climate assessments and site-based team building can best team teach the standard and its related skills/indicators.

Course Rationale

The concepts and ideas presented in this class/seminar are predicated on the belief that school leaders must be persons who have a passion for what they do and can express their passion in visions that capture the imagination of and energize others. Cohort members will share intriguing concepts from the fields of leadership, futurism, strategic planning, quality improvement, school culture, climate and student assessment, and program evaluation. At the completion of this seminar, each learner will have gained new leadership and futuring talents that help them take school planning, community visioning, and team building to higher levels for all children and youth in their schools and districts.

Assignments

1. Readings. Learners are asked to read all or parts of one or two selected books before each of the two-day sessions.

2. Vision Statements. Prior to the first two-day session, each member of the cohort will develop a personal vision statement. Each student will also bring his/her district or school vision statement to the seminar.

3. Personal Scenario. Each learner will write a one-page (250-word) personal scenario to be presented to the cohort at the end of the first two-day seminar.

4. Strategic Plans. Each learner will share her/his district/school strategic plan for critique and discussion during the second two-day seminar, and the revised plan will then be presented during the third two-day session for critique and evaluation by cohort members and faculty.

5. Student Performance Data. Each learner will present the district or selected school climate and student test achievement/performance profiles to the cohort. Learners will discuss the strategies of data display, disaggregation, and instructional goal setting based on the data available.

6. Model Learning Community for the Year 2013. Three-person teams will design and present an ideal learning community for the year 2013. This creative exercise is a major product of the six-ses-

sion seminar. Prizes will be given based on creativity, feasibility, presentation, teamwork, and interrelatedness.

Cohort Evaluation

1. Vision statement presentations	15%
2. Scenario presentations	15%
3. Strategic plan presentations and alterations	15%
4. Climate and student assessment presentations	15%
5. Model learning community team presentation	20%
6. Portfolio accumulation and quality	20%

Class Activities

The professors and students will present research findings and best practice on each of the skills/indicators through lectures, problem-based learning projects, visioning exercises, discussions, debates, videos, and simulations.

The cohort will make presentations and participate in strategic planning analysis teams and model learning community teams. The focus of the instruction will be on real-world educational issues and the challenging ideas from the literature of education, business, futuring, planning, decision making, climate assessment, student assessment, quality improvement, and leadership. The cohort and faculty will utilize e-mail, computer conferencing, faxes, and satellite TV to facilitate communication and add value to the learning experiences.

Readings

See suggested readings in the bibliography and Skill Accomplishment Checklist at the end of Chapter 1 of *Skills for Successful 21st Century School Leaders*.

Sources

Bridges, E., and P. Hallinger. (1993). "Problem-Based Learning in Medical and Managerial Education. In *Cognitive Perspectives on Educational Leadership*, edited by P. Hallinger, K. Leithwood, and J. Murphy. New York: Teachers College Press.

Gardner, H. (1994). *Frames of Mind: The Theory of Multiple Intelligences*. New York: Basic Books.

Henderson, J. (Spring 1995). "Translating Theory into Practice: Preparing Educational Leaders with Mentoring and Practice Experience." *The AASA Professor 17*, 4:1-4.

Hoy, W. (1994). *The UCEA Document Base*. New York: McGraw-Hill.

Hoyle, J. (Fall/Winter 1991). "Educational Administration Has a Knowledge Base." *Record in Educational Administration* 12,1: 21-27.

McCleary, L. (1992). "The Knowledge Base for School Leaders." In *School Leadership: A Blueprint for Change*, edited by S.D. Thomas. Newbury Park, Calif.: Corwin Press.

Wildman, L., B. Blair, A. Cuellar, R. Daugherty, C. Fischer, K. Lane, J. Parker, S. Swartz, A. Townley, and W. Zachmier. (1993). In *NCPEA: In a New Voice. The First Yearbook of the National Council of Professors of Educational Administration*, edited by J. Hoyle and D. Estes. Lancaster, Pa.: Technomic Pub. Co., Inc.

appendix B Future Trends and the School Leader

Futurists and demographers have presented detailed lists of the many demographic, social, economic, technological, and educational trends that school leaders face. School leaders must study these trends and anticipate their impact on America's social, technological, and economic structure in order to engage in long-term thinking and effective strategic planning. Indeed, successful school leaders understand and anticipate future developments and lead others to think globally and act locally to build learning communities for the present and the future.

What the Experts Say

Here are facts and experts' projections concerning the trends that will affect the work of 21st century education leaders. The following is drawn from the works of Harold Hodgkinson (1988), Marvin Cetron (1997), Ed Cornish (1995, 1996, 1997), David Wallechinsky (1997), and other sources listed at the end of this appendix. The trends presented are demographic, social and economic, technological, and educational.

Demographic Trends

- The current population in the United States is 265 million and will increase to 314 million by 2020.
- The current world population is 5 billion and will double by 2050.
- 51.7 million children entered school in 1996-97. Over 75 percent of these children have baby boom era parents.
- 54.6 million students will be attending public and private schools in 2006.
- 6,000 new schools will be needed by 2006.
- 190,000 new teachers must be hired by 2007.
- Over 40 percent of all public school students are minorities; one in three of the total population will be minority by 2005.

- States such as Texas, Florida, Alabama, Delaware, Maryland, Oregon, and Washington will see a 10 percent increase in their student populations.

Social and Economic Trends

- Cases of child abuse and neglect tripled between 1980 and 1997.
- Since 1960, delinquency rates for young people ages 13 to 17 have increased by 130 percent. The rate will increase another 50 percent by 2010.
- Fifteen percent of all children entering school in 1997 were either physically or mentally challenged, and over 10 percent were living with emotional handicaps.
- The United States leads the world in the number of millionaires, billionaires, gold reserves, and total imports and exports.
- Only 55.3 percent of U.S. 2-year olds received immunizations for preventable childhood diseases in 1995.
- Twenty-four percent of all children live below the poverty level.
- The teen birth rate in the United States in twice that of any other Western nation; most of these babies are born into poverty and will have health and learning difficulties.
- The United States has the most Nobel Prize winners in every category except literature.
- The size of the U.S. armed forces is now second only to China.
- The United States is the biggest producer of computers, electricity, cigarettes, pharmaceuticals, corn, soybeans, cheese, beer, tomatoes, and strawberries.
- The United States is the world's biggest consumer of cocaine and gin.
- The U.S. divorce rate is the highest of the world's major countries.
- The U.S. murder rate is second only to Russia's.
- The gap between the wealthiest and the poorest 10 percent of people is greater in the United States than in any country except Russia.

- Living standards will continue to rise, and the next 30 years will see an increase in the number of super rich people.
- The median income for a household of four in 1998 is approximately $36,000 — $42,550 for whites, $32,610 for blacks, and $31,620 for Hispanics.
- As many as 90 percent of the world's languages may disappear in the next century due to the ability of information technology to a create a global village.
- If current trends continue, U.S. women won't achieve parity with men in top management positions until the year 2270, or in Congress until 2500.
- Temporary workers may be a permanent hiring trend. The use of temps has increased 240 percent in the past decade.
- Of 147 million jobs in the United States in 2005, only 32 million (21%) will require a college degree.
- By the year 2005, over 50 billion will be spent in the United States for AIDS research and treatment. The average taxpayer will be paying $500 a year to care for AIDS patients in the year 2015.
- The U.S. economy, which has experienced unparalleled success in the late 1990s, will go into a slow decline by the year 2002 until the Pacific Rim countries recover from major economic downturns.

Technological Trends

- By 2006, artificial intelligence will be universally used by companies, universities, and government agencies to help assimilate data and solve problems.
- Computers tiny enough to fit in our pockets will run 50 times faster than today's supercomputers and have much more power.
- Kitchens will feature smart toasters and ovens. Recipes from a CD-ROM will time and prepare each course and adjust to individual taste requirements.
- Personal information is a hot commodity, and technologies will continue to make it easier for organizations to access it.
- While we are more connected to others via the web, e-mail and so on, we face losing our privacy and becoming more isolated and less civil as a society.
- Information technology (infotech) has freed people to work more at home and to live in rural and resort areas away from urban congestion.

- Infotech will greatly reduce the need for workers in practically all information-related jobs.
- Fewer middle managers will be needed as a result of wired organizations and employees will communicate directly with the CEO on ideas for improving operations.
- Smart cards to record medical data, shopping records, and personal schedules will be common by 2005.
- Electronic systems will permit and encourage citizens to have more say in local, state, and national government.
- Busses and cars driven by infrared cameras and computers will operate more safely than those driven today by humans.

Educational Trends

- Schooling will soon begin in the crib with interactive educational toys that stimulate early development of mental faculties.
- The number of home schoolers has grown from 10,000 to over 500,000 in the last 20 years.
- Universities and public school systems will unite to teach students from age three through postgraduate training.
- Telecommunications will allow almost all coursework to be shared with other school districts or colleges and universities in other states or nations.
- Businesses will increasingly be involved in schools and job training programs. The investment of corporations in employee education and re-training — now about 100 billion a year — will double by 2010.
- Institutions will increasingly apply the growing knowledge about the human brain, higher-order thinking, and learning to educational institutions.
- Instructional strategies will move from the lecture model to problem-based, team-driven project learning.
- Distance learning via satellite, computer conferencing, e-mail, and CD-ROM will improve learning techniques and reduce learning time by one-sixth.
- Most university and public libraries around the world will be on-line by 2008.
- Eighty percent of U.S. homes will have computers by 2007, compared to 35 percent today.
- Teachers will become "infoknowledge brokers" by 2009 and will receive higher salaries than today.
- Greater emphasis will be placed on educating students for high-skill/high-wage jobs rather than merely providing four-year college degrees.
- Community colleges will become much bigger

players in educating young people for the high-paying jobs in technical fields.

- School facilities will be constructed as modular, flexible structures to accommodate high-tech programming and for use as centers for collaborative community health and social activities.
- Local school boards will be restructured to better represent the needs of diverse publics. Board members will be elected to represent the special interests of all children and youth, and to respect the cultural differences of various ethnic, racial, and religious groups.

The School Leader's Role in a Changing Future

School leaders cannot ignore the dynamic trends that unfold each second before their eyes. They must be ready for the future they believe likely given the numerous interacting trends because they must shape our schools accordingly.

But how can school leaders alter the societal trends of soaring crime drug abuse, child abuse, teenage pregnancy, school dropout, and poverty rates? Faced with some of the gloomy forecasts for the beginning of the 21st century and beyond for schools, educational leaders at all levels must take the initiative and fight for equity for children. School leaders must share a common vision if we are to create great schools for the 21st century.

School leaders need to share a common vision of how high school graduates should look, act, and learn. They must establish a shared vision for 21st century schools — what they should be; what kinds of people will be needed to staff them; what knowledge and skills administrators and teachers must possess; what learning and teaching technologies are preferred; and what university, agency, corporation, and professional collaboration can produce and support them. To achieve a shared vision for the success of every child and youth, school leaders must ask parents, retirees, university faculties and students, business people, and other citizens to assist in the teaching, mentoring, and tutoring of our future leaders. School leaders must never end their quest for a cause beyond themselves; they must continue sharing their vision for the success and happiness of every student who passes through the school system.

School leaders can shape the future to ensure that 21st century students think globally and are aware that all social institutions, countries, corporations, and people are interconnected. These stu-dents will become the next futurists, and will be able to model humane, democratic, and creative thinking, doing, and being. So armed, they surely will be prepared to some day lead their local communities and the larger society to greater productivity; a healthier, cleaner environment; and greater world peace.

There is much intellectual excitement in designing the future based on imagery, but it takes a moral commitment, clear priorities, careful labor, and persistence to make the vision a reality.

Sources

Cetron, M., and O. Davies. (July-August 1997). "Get Ready for a Digital Future: Smart Toasters, Media Butlers, and More." *The Futurist 31*: 4.

Cetron, M., W. Rocha, and R. Luckins. (1988). "Into the 21st Century: Long-Term Trends Affecting the United States." *The Futurist 22,4*: 29-40.

Cornish, E. (January-February 1996). "The Cyber Future: 92 Ways Our Lives Will Change by the Year 2025." *The Futurist 30*, 1: 1-15.

Cornish, E. (November-December 1996). "Outlook '97: Recent Forecasts from *The Futurist* Magazine for 1997 and Beyond." *The Futurist 30*, 6: 1-7.

Cornish, E. (November-December 1997). Outlook '98: Recent Forecasts from *The Futurist* Magazine for 1998 and Beyond." *The Futurist 31*, 6: 1-7.

Hodgkinson, H. (1988). *All One System: Demographics of Education, Kindergarten Through Graduate School*. Washington, D.C.: The Institute for Educational Leadership.

Hoyle, J. (May 1982). "Urban Education 1999: Alternative Futures." *Education and Urban Society 13,3*: 357-380.

Russell, C. (1996). *The Mid-Youth Market: Baby Boomers in Their Peak Earning and Spending Years*. New Strategist Publications. (For a synopsis of key ideas, see "Demography" in the May-June 1996 Issue of *The Futurist* magazine.)

U.S. Bureau of the Census. (1996). *Statistical Abstract of the United States*. Washington, D.C.: United States Government Documents.

U.S. Department of Education. (1997). *The Social Context of Education*. 10. Washington, D.C.: National Center for Education Statistics.

Wallechinsky, D. (April 13, 1997). "Are We Still Number One?" *Parade Magazine*.

World Future Society. (May-June 1996). "World Trends and Forecasts." *The Futurist 30*, 3: 40-48.

World Future Society. (March-April 1997). "World Trends and Forecasts." *The Futurist 31*, 2: 59-67.

Index

About the Authors

Fenwick W. English

Fenwick English is vice chancellor of academic affairs at Indiana University-Purdue University Fort Wayne, Indiana. Formerly, he was a professor of educational administration at the Universities of Kentucky, Cincinnati, and Lehigh.

Dr. English has also served as a superintendent of schools in New York, has authored or co-authored 16 books, and has worked or consulted in 48 states and 10 countries. English received his B.S. and M.S. from the University of Southern California and his Ph.D. from Arizona State University.

John R. Hoyle

John Hoyle is a distinguished teacher, noted futurist, speaker, and writer, and currently professor of educational administration at Texas A&M University in College Station, Texas. Dr. Hoyle has had more than 90 articles, books chapters, and books published, including *Leadership and Futuring: Making Visions Happen,* published by Corwin Press.

Hoyle is past-president of the National Council of Professors of Educational Administration and a leader in the standards movement in the preparation of school leaders. He chaired the AASA national commission on Professional Standards for the Superintendency and authored the 1982 *Guidelines for the Preparation of School Administrators.* Hoyle has served as a public school teacher, administrator, and coach. Among his honors are two Distinguished Teaching Awards and the Golden Deeds for Education Award.

Betty E. Steffy

Betty Steffy is professor and dean of the School of Education at Indiana University–Purdue University Fort Wayne, and also serves as director of program evaluation for the Fort Wayne Community Schools.

Formerly, Dr. Steffy has served as deputy superintendent of instruction in the Kentucky Department of Education, as associate professor in educational administration at the University of Kentucky, and as a superintendent of schools in New Jersey. She has authored or co-authored six books. Steffy received her B.A., MAT, and Ed.D. from the University of Pittsburgh.